The Congested Districts Board of Ireland, 1891–1923

Cork Studies in History & Culture

1 Donncadh Ó Corráin (ed.), *James Hogan: revolutionary, historian and political scientist*

2 David Edwards, *The Ormond lordship in County Kilkenny, 1515–1642*

3 Mervyn O'Driscoll, *Ireland, Germany and the Nazis: politics and diplomacy, 1919–1935*

4 Gillian Doherty, *The Irish Ordnance Survey: history, culture and memory*

5 Ciara Breathnach, *The Congested Districts Board of Ireland, 1891–1923: poverty and development in the west of Ireland*

The Congested Districts Board of Ireland, 1891–1923

Poverty and Development in the West of Ireland

CIARA BREATHNACH

FOUR COURTS PRESS

Set in 10.5 pt on 13 pt Times for
FOUR COURTS PRESS LTD
7 Malpas Street, Dublin 8, Ireland
e-mail: info@four-courts-press.ie
http://www.four-courts-press.ie
and in North America by
FOUR COURTS PRESS
c/o ISBS, 920 N.E. 58th Avenue, Suite 300, Portland, OR 97213.

© Ciara Breathnach 2005

A catalogue record for this title
is available from the British Library.

ISBN 1–85182–919–9

All rights reserved. No part of this publication may be reproduced, stored in or introduced into a retrieval system, or transmitted, in any form or by any means (electronic, mechanical, photocopying, recording or otherwise), without the prior written permission of both the copyright owner and publisher of this book.

Printed in England
by Antony Rowe Ltd, Chippenham, Wilts.

Contents

LIST OF APPENDICES	6
ABBREVIATIONS	7
ACKNOWLEDGMENTS	9
LIST OF ILLUSTRATIONS	10
1 The foundation	11
2 Industries	47
3 Maritime industries	73
4 Agriculture under the CDB	109
5 Amalgamation and land purchase	137
CONCLUSION	170
APPENDICES	175
BIBLIOGRAPHY	185
INDEX	195

List of appendices

A	List of congested districts	175
B	List of baseline headings of inquiry	176
C	Course outline for domestic economy classes	178
D	CDB receipts and expenditure, 1892–1923	180
E	Letter of gratitude from Saorstát Éireann to CDB	182

Abbreviations

BL	British Library
BH	*Business History*
CSHS	*Comparative Studies in History and Society*
DA	*Donegal Annual*
DATI	Department of Agriculture and Technical Instruction
DORA	Defence of the Realm Acts
EHR	*Economic History Review*
EI	*Éire/Ireland*
ESR	*Economic and Social Review*
HJ	*Historical Journal*
IB	*Irish Builder*
IESH	*Irish Economic and Social History*
IAOS	Irish Agricultural Organisation Society
IH	*Irish Homestead*
IHS	*Irish Historical Studies*
IPP	Irish Parliamentary Party
JATI	*Journal of Agriculture and Technical Instruction*
JCHAS	*Journal of the Cork Historical and Archaeological Society*
JDHS	*Journal of the Donegal Historical Society*
JFH	*Journal of Family History*
JHG	*Journal of Historical Geography*
JSSISI	*Journal of the Statistical and Social Inquiry of Ireland*
JWHS	*Cathair na Mart: Journal of the Westport Historical Society*
NIR	*New Ireland Review*
NMHASJ	*North Mayo Historical and Archaeological Society Journal*
NS	Northern Scotland
PRIA	*Proceedings of the Royal Irish Academy*
PRONI	Public Records Office Northern Ireland
RCCI	Royal Commission on Congestion for Ireland
SBCIP	Society for Bettering the Condition of the Irish Poor
SH	*Studia Hibernica*
SHR	*Scottish Historical Review*
SHS	Swinford Historical Society
UF	*Ulster Folklife*
UIL	United Irish League

For my mother, Kathleen and i ndíl chuimhne m'athair

Acknowledgments

This study would not have been completed without the hard work, advice, support and encouragement of my PhD supervisor, Dr Laurence Geary. I am very grateful for his many indisputable corrections and comments. I am indebted to the staff of the Special Collections Library, UCC for their efforts on my behalf. I also wish to thank the staff of the National Library of Ireland, the National Photographic Archive, the Board of Trinity College Dublin, the Public Records Office of Northern Ireland, Queen's University Belfast, the British Library, the Library of the Society of Friends, London, the Archives of the Irish Sisters of Charity and the County librarians in Mayo, Donegal, Kerry and Sligo. I am very grateful to Michael Adams, Anthony Tierney and Martin Fanning of Four Courts Press for their help in shaping this book. I wish to acknowledge Kerry County Council for its partial funding of this work and to Údarás na Gaeltachta for providing a grant in aid of publication.

My particular thanks go to my dear friends June, Ruth, Sarah and Yvonne who have facilitated this work in every possible way. I am very grateful to my family for their consistent help and patience; my late Uncle Eamon deserves a special mention for his recollections of and discussions about the history of Irish farming. Thanks to my long-suffering siblings Bob and Ted, my sisters, Mary, Sinead, Caitriona and Deirdre (Mná na hÉireann) and to their children for the comic relief. Thanks to Kevin for his help and for putting up with me in general. Finally I wish to extend a sincere debt of gratitude to my mother, Kathleen, for her kindness and endless support.

Illustrations

Plate section between pages 96 and 97

1 Woman collecting fish, Tuke 4.
2 Women carrying baskets of seaweed, Tuke 42.
3 Members of the CDB receiving directions from a local woman, CDB 95.
4 View of unsanitary house in Monivea, Co. Galway, CDB 9.
5 New dwelling house in Monivea, Co. Galway, CDB 11.
6 Downings Pier, Co. Donegal, CDB 47.
7 Downings Pier, Co. Donegal, CDB 46.
8 Curing fish, Downings Pier, Co. Donegal, CDB 48.
9 Curing fish, Downings Pier, Co. Donegal, CDB 71.
10 Nurse visiting a family, Arranmore, Co. Donegal, CDB 55.

ACKNOWLEDGMENT

Photographs are reproduced courtesy of the National Library of Ireland.

MAPS

The Congested Districts of Ireland, 1891	183
The Congested Districts of Ireland, 1909	184

1

The foundation

The Congested Districts Board of Ireland was established in 1891 as a form of 'Constructive Unionism', a policy that aimed at 'pacifying' Irish agrarian unrest by a combination of coercive and conciliatory measures.[1] The board was designed to deal specifically with rural poverty in regions of the western counties of Donegal, Sligo, Mayo, Leitrim, Roscommon, Kerry and the west riding of Cork. This was a new departure in Conservative Party policy in that it pinpointed areas of exceptional distress. Prior to this money was allocated from the imperial exchequer to the relief of distress in Ireland under the terms of various acts. The establishment of the board marked a notable advance on quick-fix policies of outdoor relief because it posed long-term solutions to rural poverty. 'Congested' was a label applied to the western counties in 1882 in the first report of 'Mr Tuke's Fund'; these reports accounted for the process of assisting emigration from the west of Ireland to North America, assisted emigration being a traditional remedy for congestion or overpopulation, used to ameliorate conditions in the poorest parts of the west of Ireland (all the western counties came to be called 'congested districts').[2] The term 'congested' is misleading: not all of the areas in question were overpopulated. In fact, the density of population in the congested districts was only 89 persons per square mile, a much lower figure than the Irish average of 134.[3] In many respects, congestion was a euphemism for relative poverty stemming from an over-dependency on smallholdings (holdings in the congests were on average four acres).[4]

A complex structure of local administration dealt with poverty in the latter half of the nineteenth century. Ireland was divided into 130 poor law unions, whose officials dispensed aid through relief schemes. The poor law, enacted in 1833 and extended to Ireland in 1837, operated on a system akin to modern,

---

[1] See L.P. Curtis Jr., *Coercion and conciliation in Ireland: a study in Conservative Unionism* (1963). [2] Royal Commission on Congestion in Ireland (hereafter, RCCI), Appendix to First Report, 1906; evidence of W. Micks, p. 4. See G.P. Moran, *Sending out Ireland's poor: assisted emigration to North America in the nineteenth century* (2004). [3] T.W. Grimshaw, *Facts and figures about Ireland, part two* (1893), p. 14. [4] The words 'congests', 'western counties' and 'the west' denote the areas scheduled as congested in 1891.

means-tested social welfare benefits. Under it, the Board of Works took charge of outdoor relief, by providing seed, and by paying men to build roads and bridges. Boards of guardians dealt with indoor relief schemes solely, until the 1880 Relief of Distress Act. Under the terms of that act, guardians were enabled to administer outdoor relief with money borrowed from the Board of Works. Any board of guardians wishing to create employment in its union had to raise a deposit, a percentage of the total cost of the intended works, and this money could only come from poor rates. Guardians collected poor rates from landlords who owned over four acres; tenants of holdings under four acres paid a lower rate, called a 'county cess'.[5] Under the 1870 land act, tenants were entitled to deduct the county cess from their rents, so this expense was borne by the landlords. Because landlords paid the majority of local taxes they had a disproportionate amount of control over county management.[6] As tenants of smallholdings were more common in the western counties, less money was collected in rates there, poorer unions had fewer funds available for outdoor relief, and therefore infrastructural development was kept at a bare minimum.[7] Of a total expenditure of £850,252 on poor relief in Ireland in 1888, only £89,721 was allocated to Connacht, the poorest province. This figure included the salaries of poor law officers and teachers, of whom Connacht employed the least.[8] Numbers in receipt of relief money decreased in Connacht in the 1880s, but this does not indicate an improvement of circumstances; it is more probable that it reflects the paltry sum collected in rates and people's fear of the workhouse. Anecdotal evidence shows that people were slow to avail of indoor relief or the workhouse system because it meant having to surrender the land. As Christine Kineally notes, the workhouse system 'embodied a deterrent principle'; even the diet in workhouses was designed to be inferior to a typical labourer's diet (but for labourers in some parts of Mayo the workhouse diet was superior to their own).[9] To the western inhabitants, availing of indoor relief symbolized defeat, failure and death, despite the fact that the people indirectly paid for all the official relief measures, either through labour or in repayments.

In the second half of the nineteenth century, bad weather and backward agricultural practices produced potential famine conditions; government help, being confined to temporary relief, did not deal with the long-term ramifications of crop failures. Conditions in Ireland in the early 1880s were particu-

---

5 R. O'Shaughnessy, 'Local taxation in Ireland' (1882). **6** V. Crossman, *Local government in nineteenth century Ireland* (1994), p. 41. **7** H.D. Gribbon, 'Economic and social history, 1850–1921' (1996), pp 260–1. Indeed, the Mayo unions of Belmullet, Swinford and Newport were dissolved in 1882 because they did not collect enough money in rates. **8** Seventeenth Report on the Poor Law in Ireland [c.5769], HC 1889, xxxvi, Appendix D, p. 116. **9** C. Kineally, 'Administration of poor law in Mayo, 1838–1898' (1986). See also H. Burke, *The people and the poor law in nineteenth century Ireland* (1987).

larly grim, due to bad weather and three consecutive bad harvests from 1877 to 1879. Two assistant land commissioners, Professor Baldwin and Major Robertson, appointed by the government to visit the western coast in 1879, were so horrified with the level of destitution there that they made a special report on distress to the government; and a deputation of bishops went to Dublin Castle at that time to plead on behalf of the people for more public works.[10] Despite this, the government was not willing to take action. In practically all the congested districts, religious groups, of all denominations, played a silent role in alleviating poverty.[11] Charitable groups provided other forms of relief to western inhabitants on an unconditional basis, and many groups of philanthropists were at work during the latter half of the nineteenth century, including the Marlborough Relief Committee and the Mansion House Relief Committee. The first was organized by the duchess of Marlborough, who wrote letters to *The Times* appealing to English benevolence for aid 'to supplement the ordinary system of Poor Law relief'; her appeal led to the foundation of the Duchess of Marlborough Relief Committee.[12] Dwyer Grey, lord mayor of Dublin and proprietor of the *Freeman's Journal* established a similar entity, called the Mansion House Relief Committee, in 1879, which also used newspapers to raise awareness and gather funds. Availing themselves of the channels of local government to assess the situation and dispense aid, both committees gave relief in food, fuel and clothing, their purpose being to supplement, not replace, government initiatives.[13] The Marlborough committee found that Irish farming methods were so backward that the people thought nothing of eating seed potatoes in times of hardship, and that, although public works provided paid employment, cash was worth less in the poorer districts. Money earned was invariably money owed, usually to the local shopkeeper. In 1880, the Mansion House Committee reported that the people in Castlerea, Co. Galway, could only pay 15 per cent of the previous year's credit and still owed the shopkeepers £40,000.[14] Philanthropists (like Lady Burdett-Coutts of Baltimore, Co. Cork) were denounced for degrading the people with their 'almsgiving', but the intervention of charities, resident landlords and clergy was of paramount importance during times of shortage.[15] In many respects the government relied heavily on the benevolence of landlords and clergy to deal with short-term distress in their areas, and did not provide adequate help or compensation afterwards.

10 *The Times,* 16 December 1879, cited in Dublin Mansion House Relief Committee, *The Irish crisis of 1879–1880* (1880), p. 12. 11 M.C. Ní Ghiobúin, *Dugort, Achill Island, 1831–61* (2001), pp 1–9. 12 *The Times,* 16 December 1879, cited in Mansion House Relief Committee, *The Irish crisis,* p. 12. 13 G.P. Moran, 'Famine and the land war, relief and distress in Mayo, 1879–81' (1986). 14 Mansion House Relief Committee, *The Irish crisis,* p. 8. 15 J.A. Blake, *The sea fisheries of Ireland* (1868), pp 108–10. 16 R.J. Kelly, 'The congested districts' (1891), pp 495–6.

In a presentation to the Statistical and Social Inquiry Society of Ireland, in 1891, Richard J. Kelly identified high rents as the root cause of poverty.[16] But, contrary to popular belief, rents were not high in the congested districts: they were in line with the valuation per acre, and according to Grimshaw's 1891 analysis of rateable valuation this was low in the western counties. Judicial rents were based on the Griffith Valuation[17] and, as Barbara Solow highlights, by 1890 this was outdated so rents were lower than they should have been.[18] The national average valuation was 14*s*. per statute acre; counties Mayo, Donegal and Kerry had a valuation of 5*s*., Galway, Leitrim, Clare and Sligo had valuations of 6, 7, 8 and 9 shillings respectively.[19] But rent was an outlay of cash in a barely fluid economy. Irrespective of the general lack of liquidity, the west was commercialized to a large degree but retained certain elements of a backward economy; credit dealings and payment in kind were extensive. Aside from the sale of an animal, almost all of the cash generated in the west was earned off the farm (mainly through labouring), or was received in the form of remittances. Cash was used to pay off credit accounts with local merchants and to pay rents. Local government officials observed that the people were rarely out of the clutches of shopkeepers who were powerful, rich and feared in their localities.[20] The west was not serviced to the same degree as the east, particularly in transportation terms, and this made it possible for shopkeepers to maintain a retail monopoly. According to the 1891 census, the average number of persons per thousand of each county belonging to the commercial class was eighteen. Indeed, only seven counties (Londonderry, Down, Cork, Louth, Waterford, Antrim and Dublin) exceeded the national average. All the western counties had an average of less than ten. Mayo had a low of four per thousand.[21] By virtue of a trading monopoly, the shopkeepers exercised control over farm produce prices, and this ensured that the west retained a lifestyle isolated from modern market trends. Because cash flow was limited, the existence of what F.S.L. Lyons terms the 'shopocracy' relied on the ability to give credit for extended periods. This in turn depended heavily on the personal credit ratings shopkeepers had with respective suppliers.[22] In 1882–3, when shopkeepers in poor areas of Galway, Mayo and Donegal stopped giving credit, not only were the effects devastating for the people, levels of distress soared.[23] Shopkeepers

---

17 This was a survey of property ownership (1848–64) and was called after Richard Griffith, its director. **18** B. Solow, *The land question and the Irish economy, 1870–1900* (1971), pp 57–60. The valuation was determined by the value of five crops at outdated prices and did not make allowances for fluctuating prices. **19** Grimshaw, *Facts and figures*, p. 16. **20** L. Kennedy, 'Retail markets in rural Ireland at the end of the nineteenth century' (1978); L. Kennedy, 'Traders in the Irish rural economy, 1880–1914' (1979). **21** Grimshaw, *Facts and figures*, p. 18. **22** F.S.L. Lyons, *Culture and anarchy in Ireland, 1890–1939* (1979), pp 7–13. **23** Local Government Board for Ireland, Report regarding Distress, HC 1883, vol. lix.

took this drastic measure when there were huge outstanding debts or when they risked bankruptcy themselves. Losses were recovered by giving people less than the market value for farm produce, which shopkeepers then sold at an elevated profit. Their best customers were those who were deepest in debt. But, for the customer, being 'in the red' with the local shopkeeper not only curtailed consumption; it determined whether or not he or she could migrate: shopkeepers were usually ticket agents for rail and steam companies, and very often they advanced the cash necessary to buy tickets for the journey.[24]

Farming was subsidized through a variety of industries that varied regionally and in some households provided the only cash income. In the absence of mineral reserves and investment, industry remained cottage-based; knitting, hand-spinning and weaving were important to many households but had no reliable or official market. Moreover, the textile industry was in decline by the 1890s because of the widespread introduction of mass-produced, machine-spun goods. Outside of agricultural sales, money earned through 'seasonal migration' was an inestimable boon to the western economy and probably the most important source of cash income in the congested districts. The term 'seasonal migration' was used to describe the months when adults migrated for the harvest season to the extensively tilled regions of Great Britain. This custom was strongest in Mayo; it is estimated that in the late nineteenth century, 33.3 per thousand of all able-bodied persons migrated for a minimum of three harvest months a year.[25] As it hinged on good climatic conditions at home and abroad, seasonal migration was a volatile business; conditions were good in the early 1880s, but harsh weather in the mid and late 1880s meant that harvest yields were low, there was less demand for Irish migrant workers, and the resulting agricultural difficulties led to mass emigration that exceeded the high levels of the 1870s.[26] However, CDB reports highlight that for many families the cash earned through seasonal migration or hiring out children made tenant farming possible. Ann O'Dowd has shown how a migrant's absence spared resources at home, perhaps a weekly saving of 2*s*. 6*d*. per person in 1890.[27] Seasonal earnings provided cash for rents, and in this respect it perpetuated a hand-to-mouth, subsistence economy in the west.

Younger migrants tended to go *in aimsir* (directly translated as 'in time' or 'in service'). This was usually internal migration and it meant they were hired out as servants to merchants or farmers in more prosperous areas in Ireland: for instance, girls from North Kerry went to areas of Limerick. In Donegal, where the people were notably more industrious than in other western counties, chil-

---

24 A. O'Dowd, *Spalpeens, and tattie hookers* (1990), p. 249. **25** Grimshaw, *Facts and figures*, pp 17–18. **26** L.M. Cullen, *An economic history of Ireland since 1660* (1972), pp 150–1. **27** A. O'Dowd, 'Seasonal migration to the Lagan and Scotland' (1995).

dren between the age of 13 (school-leaving age) and 18 went to the 'Lagan', an area encompassing anywhere eastwards from Muckish Mountain in Donegal to Co. Antrim, and, according to MacGowan, 'it [hiring out] meant slavery, struggle, extortion and work from morning till night'.[28] For the youth of Donegal, time spent in the Lagan was seen as a prerequisite to seasonal migration (or going to Britain for three to six months of the year). Part of the money was saved from 'hiring out' to fund seasonal migration and earnings from the latter helped to provide the fare and a preparation for eventual permanent emigration. Traditionally, seasonal earnings provided a financial safety net for many, but reliance on them ensured that the people did not endeavour to better their condition through any means other than farming. Seasonal migration also nurtured poverty by leaving women, the very young (children usually left school to do farm work), and feeble, old people at home, to tend to the harvest. These crops were usually for home consumption, and any surplus was sold or exchanged for the cheaper alternative foods such as Indian meal (there were cases of very poor families that sold the entire crop to buy enough Indian meal to last the year). Because the people of the west chose to invest time and energy in short-term, cash ventures such as seasonal migration, they were not engaged in full-time employment on their own holdings and they continued to use primitive agricultural practices, planting the same crops year after year. Contemporary advances in agricultural science, indicated that if the people made a full-time commitment to farming, living conditions in the west could be improved by investing money in modern cultivation methods.[29]

Both census returns and the annual agricultural statistics indicate that the majority of the populace were engaged in farming and were unskilled. A more notable feature in the census is the general absence of a professional class in the west; medical needs, for example, were met by poorly and precariously financed dispensaries. The dispensary system was founded in 1815 and was altered in 1851; independent of this service, very few could afford to pay for medical services. Dispensaries were good distances apart and, as compared with urban areas, very few doctors or nurses lived in the congested districts.[30] Census returns indicate that the same was true of teachers. This can be partially explained by salary conditions: under the National School Teachers Act, 1875, national schoolteachers received a flat rate of pay, supplemented by an accountability system based on the results students achieved. Due to absenteeism, grades in the congested districts were low, so there was very little financial incentive for teachers to reside there. Teachers did not receive the results fees unless the

---

28 M. MacGowan, *The hard road to Klondike* (1969), pp 16–17. See also J. Bell 'Hiring fairs in Ulster' (1979). **29** Kelly, 'The congested districts', pp 495–6. **30** L.M. Geary, *Medicine and charity in Ireland* (2004); R.B. McDowell, *The Irish administration, 1801–1914* (1964) p. 166.

respective poor law union raised a rate equal to one-third of the results fees earned.[31] Most poor law unions were in arrears and some unions such as Glenties, Co. Donegal, refused to participate in the scheme, arguing that there were too many schools in proportion with valuation.[32] Education was the preserve of the wealthier classes, who could afford to do without child earnings. There was a general apathy or a disregard for education, and Akenson's examination of the census indicates that 22 per cent of Irish Catholics over the age of five were illiterate in 1891 and an even higher percentage pertained in the congested districts.[33] Grimshaw's analysis of illiteracy in the western counties shows a return as high as 33.9 percent for Galway, 32 for Mayo and 31 for Donegal.[34] It is worth noting that this represents people who could not read nor write; there was also a 'read-only' category.

Although life on the land was unprofitable, people were loath to leaving their holdings; so, without outside intervention and investment the uneducated masses had little opportunity to escape the poverty trap at home or abroad. Mechanisms of poor relief, official and unofficial, made no effort to make the poor economically independent. Without the abolition of outstanding debt and compensation for the local dealers, the cycle of poverty could not be broken. By 1890, the west needed remedial measures to stabilize the economy and bring it into some kind of convergence with the rest of the UK; but poverty and distress did not receive due consideration in Westminster because Irish politics revolved around the land question in the latter half of the nineteenth century. Politicians, Irish and British alike, failed to address the problem of Irish poverty as a separate issue from the land question, and these issues were inextricably linked in the congested districts. The succession of land-related laws from the 1850s on did little to satisfy agrarian discontent and less to cure economic ills, especially since they coincided with harsh weather and poor agricultural yields. Horace Plunkett, founder of the co-operative movement in Ireland and a member of the CDB, argued that foreign competition with Irish goods on the British market 'counterbalanced' all legal concessions received by tenants in the land acts.[35] For example, Irish agricultural produce depreciated from £72 million between 1866 and 1870 to £54 million in the four years between 1884 and 1888 due to increased British consumption of cheap grain, imported from Russia and North America.[36] Regardless of inopportune timing, in terms of coinciding with advances in world trade and laissez faire policies (whereby the government did

---

31 The use of rates to subsidize public initiatives was commonplace and will be discussed in later chapters. See Akenson, 'Pre-university education, 1890–1921' (1996), pp 532–3. **32** List of non-contributory unions under the 1875 National School Teachers Act HC (1876–7) lxiii, 657. **33** D.H. Akenson, *The Irish educational experiment* (1970), pp 376–7. **34** Grimshaw, *Facts and figures*, p. 21. **35** RCCI, Third report, 1907 evidence of Sir H. Plunkett, p. 233. See also R.A. Anderson, *With Plunkett in Ireland* (1935), p. 62. **36** Curtis, *Coercion and conciliation*, p. 336.

not intervene in economic affairs), the greatest flaw in the various land acts was the general manner in which they were devised, especially since levels of prosperity differed dramatically in Ireland from east to west and from region to region. The term 'tenant farmer' was used to describe both prosperous commercial farmers and tenants renting plots.[37] Politicians lobbying for change did not emphasize the difference between economic and uneconomic holdings, that is, those who could afford their rent from the sale of agricultural produce and those who could not; therefore, none of the land acts incorporated a distinction between these types of holdings.

Parliament was made well aware of the defects in land legislation, for example, Gladstone's liberal administration appointed the Bessborough Commission in the autumn of 1880 to investigate the condition of Irish agriculture and the economy; its findings led to the inclusion of an 'Assisted Emigration' clause in the 1881 act. While the 1881 land act was considered more favourable to tenant farmers, its terms required a lump sum from prospective buyers; since typical congested district residents rarely saved money, they were automatically excluded. On 29 September 1886 the Cowper Commission was appointed to conduct inquiries into the workings of the 1885 Ashbourne act, which was also inapplicable to the majority of the congested district residents. Both the Bessborough and Cowper commissions identified over-dependency on smallholdings of one to 15 acres, and the ratio between the population and the amount of cultivated land in the west, as being major contributory factors to economic stagnation.[38] The commissions recognized the need for legislation regarding uneconomic holdings and suggested that an assisted emigration and migration fund be set up as an alternative to the creation of a peasant proprietorship of poor land; they also recommended technical instruction classes for the inhabitants.[39] Although the commissions had political intentions, both acknowledged the increasing problem of rural Irish poverty and suggested a separate legislative response.[40]

High levels of poverty fuelled agrarian discontent, which political groups (the Land League in particular) harnessed to further political agendas to such an extent that land ownership became a metaphor for the larger issue of nationality. The Land League drew the bulk of its support from the poorer western areas initially, rather than from the more prosperous farming areas of Leinster. Through conducting mass meetings it rapidly gained momentum and led a substantial percentage of the western population to believe that tenant proprietorship would promote prosperity.[41] However, the harsh reality remained that land

---

37 P. Bull, *Land, politics and nationalism* (1996), p. 23. **38** Royal Commission on Land Law (Ireland) Act, Mr Knipes Report, [C.5015] HC 1887, xxvi, pp 976–1015, evidence of C. Townsend. **39** J.E. Pomfret, *The struggle for land in Ireland, 1800–1923* (1930), pp 245–51. **40** M. O'Callaghan, *British high politics and nationalist Ireland* (1994), p. 140. **41** Bull, *Land, politics and nationalism,* p. 81–95.

holdings in the west were too small and tenant proprietorship could not 'transform the rocks and bogs of Donegal to places "flowing with milk and honey" or make it possible for hundreds of people to obtain a decent living from land which was not sufficiently prolific to adequately provide for ten'.[42]

By the late 1870s the Irish land question had evolved into the question of home rule, but it continued to reflect agrarian values.[43] Legislative responses (land acts) remained the same until Herbert Gladstone 'flew the Hawarden kite', pledging his father's (William Gladstone, Liberal Party leader and current prime minister) commitment to home rule in 1885. Needless to add, this raised Irish nationalist morale, but it also caused a split in the Liberal Party, leading to the dissolution of parliament and a swift return of Conservative rule under Lord Salisbury. Salisbury appointed Sir Michael Hicks Beach to the position of Irish chief secretary on 25 July 1886, an office he held until March 1887, when Arthur James Balfour took over. Irish politicians were surprised that Salisbury should appoint his nephew to such a taxing position, commenting, 'We have killed Forster, blinded Beach, and smashed up Trevelyan, – what shall we do with this weakling.'[44] Balfour had received his baptism of fire in the area of agrarian unrest in his previous post in Scotland, which left him particularly intolerant of men of violence and acutely aware of the bad example the Irish agitation was setting for the English and Scottish poor.[45]

Kieran Flanagan calls the office of chief secretary 'the fulcrum of the Irish executive'; as such it was possibly the worst cabinet position because the responsibilities of the post exceeded its powers.[46] The chief secretary was technically head of the Irish administration; he was in direct control of the two Irish police forces (the Royal Irish Constabulary and the Dublin Metropolitan Police), the prisons, some legal offices and the permanent magistracy. In executive terms he was effectively an interior or justice minister answerable to the House of Commons for the policy and operation of all twenty-nine Irish departments, but his office was totally subordinate to the Treasury in London.[47] Eunan O'Halpin outlines the dangers in generalizing 'about where the power lay in the Irish administration' but is happy to quote Mayo MP John Dillon: querying 'how any one of a group of five, the lord lieutenant, chief secretary, attorney general, lord chancellor or under-secretary, could have dominated the Irish administration by dint of personality or ability … that even the strongest figures could not control the

---

[42] A. Bennett, *John Bull and his other island* (1889), p. 81. [43] A. O'Day, *Irish home rule, 1867–1921* (1998), p. 4. [44] B. Alderson, *Arthur James Balfour* (1903), pp 62–4, cited in Curtis, *Coercion and conciliation*, p. 176. [45] C.B. Shannon, *Arthur J. Balfour and Ireland, 1874–1922* (1988), p. 22. [46] K. Flanagan, 'Chief Secretary's Office, 1853–1914' (1984), p. 197. [47] N. Mansergh, *The unresolved question* (1991), p. 15. Mansergh highlights that the office of chief secretary was not officially part of the Act of Union until 1804; its precarious origins go some way towards explaining why the duties were so extensive.

whole apparatus.'[48] This point is true to a certain extent, but it is important to mention that Arthur Balfour emerged as a powerful public figure in Ireland and a very persuasive personality in Westminster. From the land war in 1879 to Balfour's appointment in 1887, nine different people occupied the position in quick succession; indeed, since the inception of the office in 1804, only two others held office as long as Balfour's stint from 1887 until 1891.[49]

Balfour believed that Irish politicians were opportunists who used poverty and agrarian agitation to incite the people to support nationalism. He pioneered the concept of Constructive Unionism by dealing with the causes of unrest, which, he believed, like Hicks Beach before him, were purely economic.[50] The Conservatives were clearly opposed to home rule, and the more militant nationalists were annoyed by slow, and in some cases, no progress. As a result a 'Plan of Campaign' was launched in October 1886. Devised by Tim Harrington, promoted through *United Ireland*, and led by John Dillon and William O'Brien, it was later claimed to be an unlawful and criminal conspiracy. Parnell disapproved of the Plan of Campaign but he had no control over it. Dillon, its driving force, had a few MPs on his side, but the Catholic clergy played an active role. The Plan was a device for collective bargaining on individual estates. When a landlord refused to lower rent demands, the tenants combined efforts and offered an average rate. If the offer was refused, then the tenants abstained from paying rents.[51] This aggressive and illegal policy (officially outlawed on 18 December 1886) was akin to schemes conducted during the land war from 1879 to 1882 and had the potential to cause serious damage. Crime rates rose during the land war, and to avert the possibility of agrarian unrest arising from the Plan, Balfour introduced the Criminal Law and Procedures Act in 1887 (more commonly known as a coercion act), a law that gave wider powers to local magistrates to deal with agrarian crime (suspects of agrarian crime could be tried without a jury and sentenced to six months' imprisonment).[52] Although the act was designed to prevent crime, it gave rise to very violent incidents, the most notorious being at Mitchelstown on 9 September 1887, when a crowd had gathered in the town for the trial of John Mandeville, a local gentleman, and William O'Brien on the charge of incitement to resist eviction. Brandishing sticks, the crowd became agitated, and the local constabulary fired, killing two and injuring twelve, one of whom died later.

48 E. O'Halpin, *The decline of the Union: British government in Ireland, 1892–1920* (1987), pp 7–8. **49** M.J. M'Carthy, *Mr Balfour's rule in Ireland* (1891), pp 72–3. **50** Ibid., p. 11. **51** For an in-depth analysis of the Plan see L.M. Geary, *The Plan of Campaign, 1886–91* (1986). **52** J.J. Clancy, *A year of 'Unionist' coercion* (1888), pp 118–44. Clancy, MP for North Dublin, argued that Balfour's administration was distinguished by meanness and cruelty and condemned it as a failure that incited hatred rather than fear. He asserted that Balfour found very little crime when he introduced his Coercion bill, 'so little that he declined to base his justification for the Bill on the statistics of crime'.

While his coercion policy received a lot of nationalist media coverage, it created a suitable 'parliamentary climate in which desperately needed programmes of land purchase and land development could not be easily jettisoned'.[53] Balfour's appointment as chief secretary was greeted with 'a scream of mocking laughter', but by the end of his term he had earned, because of Mitchelstown, the sinister nickname of 'Bloody Balfour'. His policies were both repressive and remedial but ran contrary to Gladstonian commitment to home rule.[54] O'Halpin points to the lack of financial discretion as one of the greatest drawbacks of the chief secretary's office, which meant he had to work by persuasion, not command.[55] Balfour managed to overcome a great obstacle by improving the poor relationship between the chief secretary's office and the Treasury in London. The fact that his uncle, Lord Salisbury, was prime minister helped, and this allowed him to concentrate on the crux of Irish problems. His first ameliorative measure was the introduction of the Light Railways Act 1889, which allowed for state aided construction of light railways in remote areas of Ireland, namely, in the west.[56]

Statistical evidence had for many years warranted the foundation of an independent body to deal specifically with poverty, but Balfour's period in office presented a more opportune time than his predecessors' for founding the CDB. Its foundation was a logical measure following his 1889 Light Railways Act. While Balfour believed in the rigid enforcement of the workhouse test and in the existing machinery of the poor law to deal with indoor relief, he was averse to using boards of guardians to distribute outdoor relief.[57] He commenced drafting the 1891 act during his autumn holiday in 1889; when it was introduced on 24 March 1890, it was defeated, primarily because it was very complex (the *Daily News* called it 'Balfour's puzzle'). At this time a special commission on Parnellism and Crime was ongoing. This was instigated by the Piggott forgeries, which linked Parnell to the Phoenix Park murders. The commission infuriated the Irish Party to such a degree that obstructionism reached its zenith and bills were 'dissected clause by clause'.[58]

To date, the instigating factors for the foundation of the CDB have not been fully explored and Balfour has probably been over-accredited. In fact, it was books and pamphlets, written by distinguished visitors, that heightened public awareness of Irish poverty and forced the government to deal with it.[59] The most notable example was Mr James Hack Tuke, an influential Quaker philanthropist and a highly respected and prolific writer on the subject of Irish distress,

---

53 Shannon, *Balfour and Ireland,* p. 44. **54** M'Carthy, *Mr Balfour's rule,* pp 37–8. **55** O'Halpin, *The decline of the Union*, pp 7–8. **56** For further basic information on this act see Gribbon, 'Economic and social history', pp 312–13. **57** BL Add. MS 49817 ff. 248–55. Balfour papers, Balfour to Tuke. **58** Curtis, *Coercion and conciliation,* pp 304–6. **59** Examples include the publication of A. Bennett, *John Bull and his other island* (1889).

who began his crusade in 1845, after his visit to the west with the current under-secretary, W.E. Forster (later chief secretary, 1880–2) and subsequently published a vivid account of his travels. Tuke consistently wrote letters to *The Times*, reiterating the need for separate legislation to deal with Irish poverty. Tuke's 'philanthropic canvassing'[60] culminated with the publication of his pamphlet *Irish Distress and Its Remedies* (1881), which described life along the western seaboard and suggested that Ireland be divided into two economic zones.[61] His study of Irish affairs and suggested remedies pertained to the west alone: 'Let me say, that I confine my remarks chiefly to the west of Ireland. With the East, I do not profess to deal; this distinction is extremely important.'[62] Believing that Irish distress was due to economic and not to political causes, he reiterated the need for separate land legislation for holders of uneconomic farms. His other suggested remedies included state-aided land purchase, the gradual establishment of peasant proprietorship, the construction of light railways in remote districts and state fostering of fishing and other local industries. Tuke was devoted to the relief of distress in the west, and his assisted emigration schemes in the 1880s were very successful.[63] Chief secretaries of both Liberal and Conservative ministries sought his advice on nearly all Irish questions, and most of his economic policies were adopted.[64] On Tuke's demise in 1896, Gerald Balfour, then chief secretary of Ireland, wrote to his widow on behalf of the board, stating how its work was 'but a continuation and extension of work with which Mr Tuke was identified for half a century'.[65] William Micks, first secretary of the CDB and longest serving member of staff, later praised Tuke, attributing 'to his pen and efforts much of the publicity as called the attention of Government to the condition of the west of Ireland and to the possibility of making improvements such as Mr Balfour provided in the Act of 1891'.[66]

Balfour employed Tuke's services in 1889, albeit in an unofficial capacity, to help him assess the situation in the west in order to devise a strategy. Because of past associations, he was accepted by the people of Donegal as a friend and could get truthful accounts; he also acquired information from the constabulary and local clergy. During this investigation, he spoke with Dr O'Donnell, Catholic bishop of Raphoe, who believed that there was no exceptional distress and certainly no famine but that the area did need an infusion of industry to reduce the

---

60 Term used by P. Bolger, 'The CDB and the co-operatives' (1995), p. 16. **61** Tuke wrote prolifically on the subject of Irish distress his first publication was; *A visit to Connacht in the autumn of 1847* (1848). In all he published about 15 pamphlets pertaining to Ireland. Some of his papers are held at the Library of the Society of Friends, London. **62** G.F. Trench, *Are the landlords worth preserving or, forty years management of an Irish estate?* (1881), p. 6. **63** For further information on assisted emigration see Moran, *Sending out Ireland's poor*. **64** *DNB*, lvii (1899), p. 299. **65** E. Fry, *James Hack Tuke, a memoir* (1899), p. 323. **66** W.L. Micks, *An account of ... the Congested Districts Board of Ireland* (1925), p. 16.

dependence on agriculture. The bishop expressed his opposition to adopting short-term relief measures because he believed that their long-term effects pauperized the people.[67] During his visit Tuke reported regularly and directly to Balfour on 2 May 1889 he wrote:

> Happily so far I am accepted as on my old ground of a private investigator and not as a Government Commissioner as the papers tried to put it. It would ruin my chance in many quarters of getting any knowledge. And as I honestly do not consider myself in any sense a Government Commissioner though honoured by my friend Mr Smith and yourself with a friendly intimation that you would be glad of my opinion of these districts, it is important that the position should be maintained. How you can make use of my services, when the inquiry is finished, is a question I should be glad of your opinion upon. Would *The Times* be the best medium?[68]

His accounts were written in letter format and, in liaison with Balfour, purposely placed in *The Times* (20, 27 May and 29 June, 1889) as propaganda to gain support for the pending land purchase bill. In a memo addressed to Balfour, dated 12 May 1889, Tuke expressed his anxiety about the necessity of reviewing the allocation system and believed that 'existing lines' of administration were incapable of dealing with congestion. To justify this claim he used the example of how relief money given in 1886 had been squandered. At that time Tuke was involved in the distribution of seed potatoes on Achill Island and along the coasts of Mayo and Galway when £36,000 was made available for outdoor relief and the distribution and management of seed was placed in the hands of local authorities. Tuke believed from his long acquaintance with the districts that no local board or authority was honest enough to handle funds fairly or refrain from sharing in the spoil. He had gone to London specifically to convince the chief secretary of the day, John Morley, to set up a group separate from the local authorities to carry out relief spending. Up to this, local authorities had spent relief funds ineffectually on short-term remedies that dealt with the consequences of distress, and had not used money in preventative measures. He contended that outdoor relief schemes provided only very short-term relief, had a subsequent demoralizing effect on the people, and were ultimately a waste of money. But Morley could not be swayed.

An inquest examining how the 1886 relief money was spent discovered that in the space of a few weeks over 98,000 persons were placed on outdoor relief in the six unions of Oughterard, Belmullet, Swinford, Clifden, Galway and Westport.[69] At the time that the grant was sanctioned, only 248 people had been

---

[67] BL Add. MS 49817 ff. 204–6. Balfour papers, Report written by Tuke, Letterkenny, 27 April 1889. [68] BL Add. MS 49817 ff. 220–1. Balfour papers, Tuke to Balfour. [69] See Report of Poor

receiving outdoor relief. In eight weeks the £20,000 grant from the Treasury, plus a sum of £16,000 raised by the unions was, according to Tuke, foolishly spent. The inquiry commissioners reported that in one district the number on the relief list exceeded the total population of the district; in another, 1,824 out of a population of 1,947 were on the list; and in a third everyone that applied was put on.

> Among those who thus obtained relief we find a Contractor to the Workhouse, a pensioner having £60 a year, Gombeen men and others having good balances at the Bank. Whilst well to do farmers owning flocks of sheep and herds of cattle (some of whom rented over 1000 acres of land) were equally relieved with the Con-acre man whose only stock might be a pig and a few head of poultry. Truly as Mr Morley says this portion of his relief measure met with 'a melancholy fate'. The money handed over to the Guardians 'was poured out with lavish profligacy on well-to-do and poor alike and tended directly to the pauperising and injury of the people'.[70]

Balfour was genuinely intent on solving the problem of congestion and he visited the west of Ireland in the autumn of 1890 to gather more evidence. He was accompanied by his sister Alice, Sir Joseph West-Ridgeway, the undersecretary, and George Wyndham. The journey lasted a fortnight and began in Connemara on Friday 25 October. The Dublin to Galway trip was made by train, but after that it was entirely by jaunting car and followed the proposed route for the light railways in Galway, Mayo and Donegal. Considering that the areas he travelled through were the venues of Land League mass meetings and strongholds of the Plan of Campaign, Balfour's safety was not a certainty. A certain degree of caution was exercised and their initial location was not common knowledge.[71]

According to Blanche Dugdale, Balfour's niece and biographer, 'Pressmen followed but no detectives, a sign of changed times since 1887.'[72] Dugdale is referring particularly to Balfour's coercion regime and implies that in spite of it there was little to suggest a feeling of animosity towards him in the west. Wyndham wrote to his wife daily about the trip, commenting that although the terrain was rough he did not fear being attacked.[73] The *Daily Express* covered the tour and commented that it was considered by most as a huge gesture of goodwill and concern, the people shouting 'Balfour the brave' when he passed. One observer commented that 'It was good to see Mr Balfour travelling with-

---

Relief Ireland Inquiry Commission, [c. 5043], HC 1887, xxxviii. **70** BL Add. MS 49817 ff. 230–1. Balfour papers, Tuke to Balfour. **71** Special Commissioner of the *Daily Express*. All of the articles were compiled and published as a book entitled *Mr Balfour's tours in Connemara and Donegal* (n.d.), p. 4. **72** B.E.C. Dugdale, *Arthur James Balfour*, 2 vols (1936), i, p. 176. **73** George Wyndham papers, PRONI, Ref. T.3221/1/136, Wyndham to his wife.

out an escort. He would see now for himself that he needed none in Mayo. The misfortune was that the governors of the country never before came to see for themselves, and to learn their (the residents) feelings.'[74] The *Freeman's Journal* protested that this account was false and said that Balfour was 'without doubt closely followed by a detective in plain clothes.'[75] It was also claimed that his cruel administration of the Coercion Act 'had rendered him unworthy of the confidence of any section or class of the people' and that its own accounts afforded the people of Great Britain the opportunity of seeing how untruthful the *Express* articles were. Public feeling about Balfour's visit was well documented by nationalist newspapers. The *Western People* on 15 November reported a speech by a Father Stephens at a nationalist meeting in Letterkenny:

> A few priests, whose anxiety for the safety of their starving flocks seems to have run away with their common sense, went out of their way to confer with Mr Balfour on the subject of impending famine. At Gweedore, which he entered in the clouds of night, the people were preparing to show their real feelings towards a man who trampled on them but on hearing an address embodying the sentiments of the Gweedorites was about being presented to him by Mr Dalton, their representative, Balfour to use a familiar phrase, 'ran away like a redshank' in the darkness of early morning. To Falcarragh, the centre of all his evil doings in Donegal, he gave a wide berth. I say then the reception accorded to Mr Balfour in some districts of Donegal is not a fair index of the feelings of the people towards him. The people of Donegal hate Balfourism with a deadly hatred, which no amount of bribes in the shape of light railways could prevent them from manifesting, had the opportunity been offered.[76]

The *Freeman's Journal* printed the same article and many others criticizing Balfour's tour and the favourable coverage given to it in the *Daily Express*.[77] The *Freeman* also maintained that the tour was well arranged and the preparations worked smoothly because the visit did not include stops in any place where the coercion regime prevailed.[78] The *Mayo Examiner* commended Balfour's efforts: 'This was the first visit of the chief secretary to the West, and to one so observant the many disadvantages of past neglect and misrule must be plainly visible in the face of the country. He appears determined to do what he means to do promptly, and that is precisely the most effective way.'[79] In Galway there was no hostility, despite threats reported in local newspapers that the nationalists had organized 'a fitting reception for the Chief Coercionist'; in fact, the contrary occurred: the people and local clergymen in each village greeted them.[80] The *Freeman* also contested the accounts that Balfour examined many fields,

---

74 *Mr Balfour's tours*, p. 6   **75** *Freeman's Journal*, 30 October 1890.   **76** *Western People*, 15 November 1890.   **77** Ibid., 31 October 1890.   **78** *Freeman's Journal*, 6 November 1891.   **79** *Mayo Examiner*, 1 November 1890.   **80** *Mr Balfour's tours*, p. 4.

saying that he entered only one. However, it did not apportion blame to the ordinary people who welcomed or co-operated with him:

> It is hard to blame the wretched people who see hunger staring them in the face, and who know not where to find food during the bitter winter for their wives and little ones, if they gather to cheer the Chief Secretary, who they are told comes as a ministering angel to relieve their distress. Drowning men catch at straws, and starving men will kiss the hand that feeds them. Naturally too, a few shopkeepers in every village are ready to fawn upon Mr Balfour. How is the gombeen man to obtain his principal and usurious interest unless public works enable his creditors to earn some money?[81]

Despite conflicting evidence in various newspapers about particulars of his visit, one incident was consistently reported. During his speech at Gweedore, Balfour was interupted by Mr Swift McNeill MP, who had come to speak with the chief secretary on behalf of his poor constituents (incidentally, McNeill remained opposed to Balfour's land bill for longer than any of his colleagues).[82] He highlighted the 'terrible barbarities' as the primary characteristic of Balfour's rule in Ireland and mentioned the tenants of the nearby Olphert estate as a prime example of contradictory policy: 'when you investigate the condition on the one hand, you are going to give the forces of the Crown the power to exterminate them on the other'. Ironically, McNeill provided Balfour the perfect opportunity to publicly reiterate that the sole purpose of his visit was to assess levels of economic distress in order to devise a more effective strategy in the forthcoming land act. Mr Sweeney, a local trader who had accompanied McNeill to the meeting and was owed £9,000 by the people of the area, stated how he did not expect to retrieve one third of the outstanding sum. He believed that 'it would be out of the power of the merchants to supply the people unless the people got some employment or the means of earning a living' and begged Balfour to disregard McNeill's outburst, stating that he did not speak on behalf of the people.[83] The *Freeman's Journal* criticized Sweeney as 'a poor creature who, with as much spirit as the oatmeal he sells his customers, having heard the chink of the Chief Secretary's sovereign, thought he saw them vanishing, gets up and tells Mr Balfour that something "practical" must be done for the district because he wants to collect his shop debts'.[84]

---

[81] *Freeman's Journal*, 6 November 1891. For other nationalist accounts see also the *Ballinrobe Chronicle*, the *Ballina Journal* and the *Mayo Examiner* on the dates in question. [82] During the final stages of the deliberations Balfour referred to his opposition specifically in relation to the CDB (Part Two of the bill): 'Gentlemen above the gangway accept this part of the Bill with pleasure, Gentlemen below the gangway have accepted it with gratitude. [Mr McNeill: No, No!] All excepting the Member for Donegal, who represents a county, though he does not even live in it'. Hansard, vol. 354–55, 9–30 June 1891, pp 487–8. [83] *Mr Balfour's tours*, pp 76–83. [84] *Freeman's*

However, the bickering media circus that surrounded Balfour's visit failed to capture what Wyndham wrote to his wife;

> And here we found at [Carraroe] a far greater depth of misery than any we have seen or I have ever imagined. It really made one sick to think of the extreme wretchedness of these people living on potatoes growing in mud and water between the rocks, their houses standing in morasses. For the first time, the people looked pinched and yellow and frightened. They all turned out, and gave Arthur shrill cheers. A most pathetic sight. You cannot conceive the poverty of this district. Hardly anyone can talk English. The majority have never seen a plough or harrow. There is no mill for twenty miles. They never eat meat, and are always on the brink of starvation. I do not trust we may be able to help them. The whole country is nothing but yellow, marshy grass growing between gray boulders, and yet the people are crowded into it like rabbits in a warren ... I can only think of the iniquity of the hundreds of thousands of pounds which the Parnellites have screwed out of the people and spent on war, with this kind of desolation standing to be redressed.[85]

Balfour displayed a more enlightened policy in relation to Ireland and his visit to the west set him apart from his predecessors. As a result of his visit he felt strongly about solving the problem of poverty and devised a system to deal with it by placing it on a separate forum from other political issues. To counteract anticipated opposition to the foundation of the CDB in the House of Commons, Tuke and William Micks, a local government inspector whom Balfour had met on his visit to Donegal, were officially deployed to assess the real circumstances of districts in Donegal, which were reputedly the worst off in Ireland. Truthful accounts of distress were difficult to acquire, as the people and their public representatives were notorious for exaggeration. During his investigations Micks stayed in Gweedore and, while there, was informed that Father McFadden was watching for some death in his parish that would give the appearance of poverty severe enough to make an allegation of death by starvation.[86] Micks wrote the following account to Under-secretary West Ridgeway:

> I may, as my report is unofficial, mention one of two incidents of my inspection. In one house the conversation gave me an opportunity of asking whether 'the Sergeant' (RIC) 'had been round lately'. The woman that I was speaking to laughed and said he was, and that she hid her cow when she heard he was on the way. This showed that my precaution was necessary. After I had left one house a man told me that he and his family had nothing to eat; I immediately went into the back and found in a room off the main room at least a ton and a half of potatoes. Another man made a similar statement to me about having nothing to eat and I found almost an entire bag of meal in his house.[87]

Journal, 6 November 1891. **85** George Wyndham papers, PRONI, ref. T.3221/1/143. Wyndham to his wife. **86** BL Add. MS 49817 ff. 169–73. Balfour papers, Micks to Balfour. **87** Ibid., ff.

He even travelled to Rannafast in The Rosses by boat to get to the townland undetected by the shopkeepers and told the people that the reason for his visit was to measure the quantity of seeds they received under the seed supply act. The reason, he explained, was to: 'see the people without any preparations on their part for the purposes of getting up the appearances of distress ... In order to get to the Townland unseen by the shopkeepers etc., I landed by boat and worked from the shore to the public road.'[88] Micks employed the services of a young man named O'Donnell who showed him shortcuts from house to house and told him how his brother, a shopkeeper in Donegal, wrote a series of letters to the *Derry Journal,* exaggerating distress in Rannafast. By doing so he attracted attention to the predicament of the residents; they subsequently received relief and in turn spent their relief tickets in his shop.[89] Micks made an unannounced house-to-house inspection of three other townlands between 11 and 13 March 1891 to list all the inhabitants and observe their circumstances.[90] His findings document the varying levels of wealth in the Rosses electoral division and show that people were always on the brink of starvation or distress. For example, the household of Biddy Breen was considered well off because she had a son going to Scotland, another going to the Lagan, and owned one cow. In contrast, Charles Breen and his wife were described as delicate but they had two cattle, a son going to Scotland and were not considered very well off. Denis Hurley was considered poor because he was old and his wife was of weak mind. James McCullagh was a lame man and, because of his disability he made very little money when he went to Scotland. He had two young children and was recommended to be included in the distress fund. Mary McFadden (Rhinamona) was an 'old maid' who earned money from knitting and seemed comfortable. Biddy Doogan of Rhinamona was described as a single woman who would 'pull along'.[91]

Micks' evaluation of the levels of poverty in Donegal seems very harsh, but his aim was to get truthful accounts and his survey can be weighed against contemporary classifications of poverty. Sociologists divide poverty into two types, relative and absolute. Peter Townend's 1979 definition of relative poverty is widely accepted as a situation when individuals 'lack the resources to obtain the type of diet ... living conditions and amenities which are customary ... in the societies to

178–80. Balfour papers, Micks to West Ridgeway. **88** Ibid. (this area is called Ranefast and Rannefarset in the records, today it is known as Rannafast). **89** BL Add. MS 49817 ff. 169–73. Balfour papers, Micks to Balfour. **90** Official returns indicated that there were 78 houses in the Rannafast district but in fact there were only 74, two families lived in some houses. He visited the homes of all 74 families and found that only five were in receipt of relief from the Irish Distress Fund. Besides recommending the inclusion of five more families in the relief fund he concluded that the remaining 64 families were in comfortable circumstances and that any allegations of distress among these families were dishonest. BL Add. MSS 49817 ff 178–9. **91** BL Add. MS 49817 ff. 174–7. Balfour papers, Micks to Balfour.

which they belong'.[92] Absolute poverty is defined as the minimum necessary for survival in any given area.[93] Absolute poverty can exist in any society, but in modern terms it is more prevalent in underdeveloped or third world countries. Poverty was the norm in the west of Ireland but it varied from relative to absolute, so distress of the severest kind was necessary to invoke a government response. Famine or starvation was not an issue in March 1891, but scarcity was a reality for many families. Evidence in the baseline samples shows definite cases of absolute poverty in the Rosses, but if Townsend's definition had been rigidly applied, then the entire district would have been judged to be in absolute poverty in relation to the rest of rural Ireland. The concept of absolute poverty was equal to ordinary circumstances in the congested districts, while relative poverty indicated extremely poor conditions. For example, in the district of Cloghaneely (Donegal) and Knockadaff (see table 1.2), returns were made for families in exceptionally impoverished circumstances as well as those in ordinary circumstances.

As a result of his visit to the west, Balfour realized the necessity of pushing his ameliorative legislation in the House of Commons. He had witnessed the penury of the resident population at first hand and realized how close the people were to periodic famine, and he vowed to address their problems and 'to meet in every way they could the distress which threatened'.[94] Balfour spent almost two years drafting the bill and (with the help of Tuke and Micks) had enough statistical evidence to substantiate the necessity for a new and separate board to deal specifically with poverty. He had to exercise extreme caution in devising the statutory definition of a congested district because the act was to include migration clauses. A previous measure of state-aided emigration had provided £100,000 under the 1882 Arrears of Rent Act, and despite the fact that this money was very carefully and humanely allocated (see reports of Mr Tuke's fund), Irish nationalists viewed that measure as a form of deportation and an unfair scheme to rid the country of long-term paupers, who were not equipped for life abroad.[95] With respect to how nationalists viewed the successful 1882 scheme, he decided that the fairest way to assess a district was to apply a test for congestion, and the test was the following mathematical equation: if the total valuation of an electoral division when divided by the resident population gave a sum of less than £1 10*s.*, the area was congested. The statutory definition, or, more specifically, section 36 of the act stipulated that for a district to receive aid from the board it had to be located within a congested county. A congested county was defined as one where more than 20 per cent of the population (except in the case of Co. Cork, which was divided into East and West Riding) lived in congested electoral divisions.[96]

---

92 P. Townsend, *Poverty in the United Kingdom* (1979), p. 31. **93** T. Callan and B. Nolan, *Poverty in the 1990s* (1996), pp 1–30. **94** *Mr Balfour's tours*, p. 8. **95** G. Moran, 'State-aided emigration from Ireland to Canada in the 1880s' (1994), p. 11.

Under these conditions, the counties of Donegal, Leitrim, Roscommon, Mayo, Galway, Kerry, and the West Riding of Cork were considered congested. The only scope for appeal was that for one year after the passing of the act, the lord lieutenant, following a recommendation from the board, was permitted to include other electoral divisions, provided they were in a congested county. This clause was inserted to accommodate the 1891 census returns, which were not complete until 1892. However, the provisions of the act, especially the inclusion of the 'twenty per cent' clause, meant that several needy areas failed the test for congestion. Balfour later defended the definition, stating that, while the test was 'rough and ready', it sufficed at the time, and 'if the Board was to be given the power of defining its own areas instead of carrying out the duties conferred upon it by Parliament it would spend most of its time arranging the areas.'[97]

Nationalist politicians voiced limited criticism of the congested districts portion of the act, stating that it was what the *Western People* called forced emigration, and the *Freeman's Journal* argued that it was 'akin to deportation.'[98] Relatively speaking, the second part of the act incorporating plans to found the CDB, met with relatively little informed criticism, except from Charles Gavan Duffy, who argued that the congested districts portion should not have been coupled with land purchase in the first place. This was put forward indirectly in a letter printed in the *Contemporary Review* (October 1890): 'I have refrained from speaking of the scheme in Mr Balfour's Bill for relieving congested districts and stimulating local industries because I believe it will be best dealt with on a separate occasion.'[99] Incidentally, Morley, Balfour's predecessor, was opposed to the introduction of the CDB clause in the 1891 act, arguing that the proposed money for relief in the 1890 land purchase bill would have the same 'melancholy fate' as the relief act of 1886.[1] But timing was on Balfour's side, as a result of the Parnellite split the Irish Parliamentary Party was silenced, and the 1891 Land Purchase (Ireland) Act sailed through the house without major deliberations; under its terms, the Congested Districts Board of Ireland was established.[2] Its foundation was a radical new departure. It presented long-term solutions to deal with the increasing problem of rural poverty.

First efforts and the baseline reports

From its establishment, 5 August 1891, the board was to continue in existence for twenty years and after that at the discretion of parliament. Balfour believed

---

96 CDB, First annual report, 1892, p. 1. **97** RCCI, Appendix to fourth report, 1907. Evidence of Arthur Balfour, p. 2. **98** *Western People,* 29 November 1890. **99** *Freeman's Journal,* 29 October 1890. **1** BL Add. MS 49817 ff. 230–1. Balfour papers, Tuke to Balfour. **2** For a comprehensive account of the 'Fall of Parnell' see P. Bew, *C.S. Parnell* (1980), pp 120–30.

that, apart from being corrupt, existing mechanisms dealing with the relief of distress were ineffective because they lacked autonomy, so he decided not to put the board under the control of a political assembly.[3] As a result, the CDB was empowered to function independently from Westminster and the Castle except in relation to salaries; applications in respect of these were made to the Treasury via the Castle; other correspondence with the Treasury or other government departments could be conducted independently.[4] The board consisted of ten members: two were 'ex-officio' (the chief secretary and a land commissioner), five were permanent, and her majesty appointed three temporary members. In the absence of the chief secretary, the under-secretary acted as one of the ex-officio members; the land commissioner was nominated by the lord lieutenant to represent agriculture and forestry.

The original members were Arthur Balfour, Sir West Ridgeway, under-secretary Fredrick Wrench, the Revd Charles Davis PP, Sir Horace Plunkett, Thomas P. Cairnes, Charles Kennedy and James Hack Tuke. Drawn from widely divergent political and social circumstances, the members were chosen for their individual expertise, and all were very well acquainted with Irish social and economic issues. Sir Fredrick Wrench was an Irish land commissioner and had been carrying out measures under the auspices of the Land Commission and the Royal Dublin Society for the improvement of Irish animal breeds. Charles Davis was employed for his knowledge of marine biology and was involved in improving fisheries in his native Baltimore, Co. Cork, where a local philanthropist, Lady Burdett Coutts, financed technical instruction in fisheries for the local people. Sir Horace Plunkett, an Anglo-Irish aristocrat, had been involved in improving the condition of the Irish peasantry by implementing a system of self-help. He opened the first of his co-operative schemes in his native Dunsany in 1878. Plunkett suffered from tuberculosis, which forced him to move to a warmer climate in Wyoming; while there he 'was taken by the expansiveness and the vigour of American life and business'.[5] He made a permanent return from America in 1888, but his experience there inspired him to devise innovative schemes for Irish farmers, through the widespread foundation of co-operative creameries and shops. Essentially the principles of the co-operative schemes and the CDB were the same. Both advocated government-aided, self-help schemes to ensure long-term rather than immediate relief. Plunkett was selected as a member of the CDB because his efforts had come to the attention of Arthur Balfour.[6] Thomas Cairnes was an accomplished Unionist business-

---

3 P. Cambray, *Irish affairs and the home rule question* (1911), p. 23. **4** Micks, *An account of the history*, p. 14, extract from Balfour memorandum dated 21 January 1892. **5** P. Bolger, 'Horace Plunkett – the man' (1983), p. 36. **6** T. West, 'The development of Horace Plunkett's thought' (1983), p. 40.

man, owning breweries in Drogheda and Castlebellingham and was a director of the Great Northern Railway Company, the Bank of Ireland, and the City of Dublin Steamship Company. He occupied a position on the CDB finance committee and his experience in money management was an inestimable boon to the CDB. A dedicated member of the CDB, he died in 1894 following 'a chill caught in crossing to England in connection with the Congested Districts Board of which he was a most hard working member'.[7] Very little information survives in relation to Charles Kennedy but according to CDB records the Dublinman was a highly respected industrialist and philanthropist.[8]

All the money allocated to the board came from Irish funds. The most substantial source was derived from the Church Surplus Grant. Under the Irish Church Act (22 July 1869) the Church of Ireland lost its official status as the Established Church. Disestablishment, an ameliorative measure designed by Gladstone to 'pacify Ireland', removed a major grievance for Irish Catholics who paid a tithe for the upkeep of the Protestant clergy. The property of the disestablished church was taken into the possession of a Church Temporalities Commission; it sold church property and dispensed compensation to clergymen and other employees for loss of income.[9] It was anticipated that the remaining money would be spent on charitable purposes in Ireland. Gladstone estimated that the property was worth £16 million and that compensation would cost £8,650,000. While no conclusive study has been conducted on the figures, it appears that there were many financial inconsistencies, and, unfortunately, the compensation to all interests, including lay patrons, amounted to over £11.5 million by 1880.[10] In 1891, there was a mere £1,500,000 left over, and the board was allocated the interest, which was a basic rate of 2 per cent per annum and amounted to a sum of £42,250 a year.

The second source placed at the disposal of the board was the Irish Loan Reproductive Fund, which was worth £70,394 (£43,524 in securities, £2,746 cash, and £24,124 in outstanding loans). This fund was already operating to aid fisheries in counties Cork, Galway, Kerry, Leitrim, Mayo, Roscommon, Sligo, Clare, Limerick, and Tipperary. Unfortunately the board was not permitted to extend this fund for projects in the congested county of Donegal, and it continued to be applicable in the non-congested counties of Clare, Limerick and Tipperary. The third source came from a portion of the Sea and Coast Fisheries Fund. Both the reproductive and the fishery funds were considered 'purely Irish' as the money was originally collected by public subscriptions in London in 1822

---

7 Anon., *Thomas Plunkett Cairnes: JP, a memento* (1894), p. 34. He also held a few other prestigious positions, such as president of the Drogheda branch of the Unionist Alliance, the vice-commodore of the Drogheda rowing club and president of the gymnastic club. **8** Obituary, *Irish Times*, 7 December 1907. **9** R.V. Comerford, 'Gladstone's first Irish enterprise 1864–1870' (1995), p. 443. **10** W.E. Vaughan, 'Ireland 1870' (1995), p. 733.

for the relief of distress on the Irish western seaboard. The remaining sum was transferred to the Board of Works in 1874 and 1884 to issue as loans.[11] Valued at about £18,866 (£2,190 in securities, £4,115 in cash and £12,561 in outstanding loans on fishing boats and equipment), this money was only applicable to the maritime districts in counties Donegal, Leitrim, Sligo, Mayo, Galway, Kerry and Cork. It was also permissible for the board to accept gifts of property or money.[12] While the 1891 Act transferred the management of the two fishery funds from the Commissioners of Public Works to the CDB, these fishery funds, amounting to £87,267 14*s*. 2*d*., were not physically transferred to the Board until 1 June 1893.[13] In its first year, the board had a total of £42,250 to spend in any manner it wished. Balfour devised an intricate system of guarantee funds to control the money. This was to ensure that the act would be passed and to protect the British and Irish taxpayer in the case of serious default.[14] The first formal meeting of the board was held on 2 November 1891, at 23 Rutland Square, Dublin. As CDB funds were limited, administrative costs were covered by Treasury money, and the house at Rutland Square was furnished with money 'voted' by parliament (meaning a show of hands agreed to a nominated sum). It was proposed and agreed that the board should employ a secretary and other administrative officers whose salaries were also to be paid out of funds that were voted out of parliament on an annual basis. In other words, the Treasury paid salaried members separately and directly; for example, William Micks, a Local Government Board inspector, was appointed secretary, at a salary of £900 a year.[15]

The initial task of the board was to ascertain which districts qualified for congested status. All necessary data was accessible to the board through the office of the Registrar General – which explains why no major documentation exists on this issue. In accordance with statute, a congested district was an area where the ratio between population and valuation gave a sum of less than 30*s*. per resident. Using statistics from the 1881 census, it was found that a total of 349,516 people were living in areas considered congested. They lived on 3,608,569 statute acres, valued at £556,141 collectively, which worked out at an average valuation of £1 0*s*. 3*d*. per head. There were eighty-four congested districts. They were further divided into maritime and inland districts, as the needs of both types of regions were essentially very different. Generally speaking, the board had powers to improve living standards in the designated districts through the development of agriculture, fisheries, existing cottage-based industries and the creation of markets. In relation to agriculture, the main aim

---

11 Gribbon, 'Economic and social history 1850–1921' (1995), p. 286. **12** CDB, First annual report, 1892, pp 1–3. **13** CDB, Second annual report, 1894, p. 3. **14** RCCI, Appendix to Fourth Report, 1907. Evidence of Arthur Balfour, p. 2. **15** As he currently held office as a civil servant the terms and conditions of his employment were complicated. However, it was dealt with as a separate issue by the board and the treasury. CDB, Minutes of proceedings, 2 November 1891.

was to increase farm size and improve livestock and methods of cultivation; second to this was the development of all industries, including fishing; aid was administered by indirect as well as by direct means.[16] Direct aid meant funds granted by the board could grant funds for specific projects; indirect aid meant the development of infrastructure, which accommodated the creation and supply of markets. Individuals or areas had to apply formally to initiate works, the requests being divided into memorials and applications. A memorial referred to larger-scale works like roads and bridges; memorials were usually presented by a local spokesperson, perhaps the parish priest or a landlord, and sought to benefit an entire region. Applications meant smaller projects and, if successful, benefited the individual.

A series of meetings were held during November 1891 to decide on the best way to deal with applications. To this end it was decided to divide the board into committees, with three members in each, to deal with finance, industries, fisheries and land; two members could form a quorum of any committee.[17] This system was later revised by placing only two members on each committee, except for the agriculture committee, which retained its three members due to the volume of work involved. Committees were limited to inquiry and report unless otherwise specially directed by order of the board. Ordinary meetings were on the second Thursday of every month, but in the event of an emergency the chairman or three board members could summon a special sitting.[18] At these meetings, the board members assessed all requests and decided which warranted attention and deserved funding.

Salary issues were supposed to be the extent of CDB contact with the Treasury but this unorthodoxy was unacceptable to Treasury officials, who endeavoured to revert to the old system – where all official Irish correspondence went to London via the Castle.[19] On 31 December 1891 Micks wrote a personal letter to Balfour from the CDB office at 23 Rutland Square relating to an incident that encroached on the powers of the board. Micks had written directly to the Treasury (without passing through the Castle) asking for instructions on whether the Congested Districts Board or the Board of Works should collect the repayment of loans advanced for fishery purposes. The letter was personally brought back to Ireland by Mr Bergne, a Treasury official, and given to Mr Cullinan of the Castle, it queried whether the letter should have been forwarded to the Treasury via the Castle. To sort the situation out Micks arranged a meeting with William L. Jackson, the new chief secretary. Jackson was heavily influenced by his under-secretary, Sir West Ridgeway, who believed

---

16 CDB, First annual report, 1892, pp 2–3. **17** Aside from annual reports the board kept records for each committee these 33 volumes are housed in the NLI and some copies are held at the library in the Department of Agriculture. **18** CDB, Minutes of proceedings, 2 November 1891. **19** BL Add. MS 49817 ff. 198–9, Balfour papers.

that the Castle should have control over the board's finances. Balfour's chief secretaryship ceased in December 1891; though he remained an honorary member of the CDB until 1907 his official powers ended with his term as Irish government officer. Jackson challenged the independent status of the board and, as chief secretary, he had the power to alter it. Balfour was adamant that the board remain autonomous so he wrote to the Castle reiterating the terms of the act, stating that the CDB was not a government department nor should it be subordinate to the chief secretary except in cases that were specified by statute and in these cases the lord lieutenant had to be consulted. Balfour's intervention ensured that the board maintained independent from normal parliamentary procedures.

During his Irish visit in the winter of 1890, Balfour met Micks who was at the time employed as a local government inspector in Co. Donegal. Coincidentally, Micks had recently compiled a set of sample family budgets for the Commission on Local Taxation, which showed the receipts and expenditure of families in ordinary circumstances in different parts of the country. Balfour thought it was possible, with the level of data contained in the budgets, to interpret the everyday existence of the people (see table 1.1). In a memo circulated at one of the first meetings, Balfour suggested that the board conduct a preliminary survey (including sample family budgets) to help assess the exact condition of the people and to discern the different measures of aid required. He also argued that, the baseline reports, as they are more popularly known, would subsequently act as a measure of the board's success.[20] Six temporary inspectors were employed to conduct the survey; potential inspectors were interviewed by the board and the following were the successful candidates: Major Ruttledge-Fair[21] was appointed to do north Co. Galway and some Co. Mayo reports, Mr Henry Doran did the rest of Co. Mayo and Major Gaskell compiled the remaining Co. Galway reports. Mr F.T.G. Gahan was put in charge of Co. Donegal while Mr James Butler and Mr Redmond Roche dealt with Co. Cork and Co. Kerry. Major Ruttledge-Fair was born in Mayo, Butler, Doran, Gahan and Roche were residents of their respective districts, and, while their is no biographical data available on Gaskell, it appears that all were well acquainted with their allocated areas. The survey began with the northern congested counties from Co. Donegal to Co. Galway, starting with the costal districts.[22] Counties were not treated in order of priority and a possible explanation for the north-south progression is that key figures in implementing strategy (including Balfour and Tuke) had visited the northern areas, and Micks had

[20] Arthur Balfour, Memorandum circulated at a meeting of the CDB, 6 November 1891. [21] In the records the spelling of his surname varies also Rutledge-Fair, Routledge-Fair. The Ruttledge papers are held at the Manuscripts Department in TCD. [22] CDB, Minutes of proceedings, 12 November 1891, p. 1.

served as a local government official in Donegal. Inspectors were paid out of the 'vote', and the salaries were paid through the Land Commission for the duration of their employment.[23] They were permitted to employ the services of poor law officials and other state employees; however, it was stipulated that the inspectors were responsible for the accuracy of information received from respective employees.[24]

Compiling the baseline reports was a huge undertaking; it took over a year to complete and almost five years before all were finally published.[25] Although the work of the baseline inspectors was considered a separate project from normal proceedings, some of the board members helped and advised the inspectors who had little previous experience in work of this nature (Micks compiled the report for The Rosses, Co. Donegal).[26] The inspectors followed a very methodical line of inquiry. Each district was examined under a standardized system of thirty-two questions; officially termed 'headings of inquiry' (see appendix B). It is difficult to ascertain how the 'headings of inquiry' were decided on, but the minutes of proceedings indicate that the input of Tuke was central, as he had conducted a similar line of questioning on his Donegal visit in 1845, in 1880 and again between 1889 and 1890. Major Ruttledge-Fair went to England to confer with Tuke in relation to drafting the questions and instructions for the baseline inspectors.[27] Although the secretary, Micks, submitted some 'headings of inquiry' as early as 2 November 1891, Tuke and Ruttledge-Fair compiled the final draft in February 1892. They were presented to the temporary inspectors at a specially convened meeting on 7 March 1892.[28]

In brief, the first seven questions pertained to land: its location (whether inland or maritime), the average size of holdings, type and extent of crops grown, methods of cultivation, grazing rights, general information on livestock and suggestions for improvement. They also considered the viability of migrating families and their prospects of success, the possibilities of land reclamation and the amalgamation of holdings all received due consideration. Questions 8 and 9 concerned markets and communications; 10, 11 and 12 dealt with employment, rates of pay, migratory labour and cottage-based industry. Questions 13 to 21 examined all aspects of the fishing industry. Questions 22 to 25 concentrated on the local economy of the congested districts and included the specifically requested family budgets. The remaining seven questions endeavoured to determine the actual condition of the resident population on a seasonal basis,

---

23 Ibid., 7 March 1892. **24** Butler initially proposed the use of assistants and it was agreed at the meeting of 12 March 1892. **25** Micks comments in his history that 'the making and printing of these reports occupied more than a year', but this does not correlate with the dates on the reports; the first of the reports was published in 1892 and the last was published in 1897. **26** Micks, *An account of the history,* p. 23. **27** CDB, Minutes of proceedings, 25 February 1892, p. 3. **28** Ibid., 25 March 1892, p. 3.

that is, food consumed, clothing and the condition of dwellings. As six inspectors compiled the reports, inconsistencies occur – some due to the lack of continuity, others presumably due to the fact that the inspectors were not in contact with one another (at least no evidence exists to show they were communicating). At first glance, it seems that there were varying degrees of diligence. For example, Gahan compiled highly-detailed reports of up to sixteen pages on the Donegal districts, while Redmond Roche could only write an average of four pages on the Kerry districts. On closer scrutiny, it is clear that the reports reflect the lifestyles of the people in each district, and the lack of information in some reports is as informative as the elaborate detail contained in others.

As Balfour anticipated, the sample budgets presented the reality of daily life in the congests,[29] that is, congested tracts, and reiterated the need for conciliation. The data pertaining to diet is a striking feature of the reports. Wealth and diet are inextricably linked as national income indicators and the income and expenditure estimates show that the west did not deviate much from the pre-famine mould. In general, the west of Ireland aligns with trends in European peasant societies in that it relied solely on a vegetable diet. Studies on nineteenth-century European peasant societies show that dietary sacrifices were made in order to become more commercialized and better able to participate in the increasing cash economy. Home-grown produce was replaced with a cheaper, exclusively vegetable and in many cases an almost vegan diet (a diet containing no animal produce). Smith and Christian note the same trend in Russia in the late nineteenth century, where poor peasant households sold nutritious produce, which was rarely a surplus, for cash, leaving their own diets deficient as a result.[30] They also state how a high dependency on agriculture on a national level is indicative of a backward or poor economy and that at a domestic level the higher the expenditure on food, the poorer the household. In Russia, agricultural produce accounted for 50 per cent of national income in 1870 and 44 per cent in 1913.[31] In nearly all of the congested districts, agriculture was the primary source of income and food accounted for well over 50 per cent of family expenditure. Taken together, cash expenditure on food, drink and tobacco by families in 'ordinary circumstances' accounted for almost 56 per cent of cash expenditure in Donegal, almost 53 per cent in Kerry, over 54 per cent in Leitrim, Sligo, and Roscommon, over 58 per cent in Galway and Mayo, rising for poorer families in the latter region to over 63 per cent. When on-farm consumption is added, the percentage of income spent on food becomes even more apparent in the household budgets of the west, as it

---

[29] The congested districts were also informally called 'congests'. [30] R.E.F. Smith and D. Christian, *Bread and salt* (1984), p. 356. [31] Ibid., p. 1.

accounted for between 28 per cent and 42 per cent of the value of total consumption in all these regions. Increased monetization had a very negative effect on the poorer households in that it perpetuated the tendency to rely completely on a monotonous carbohydrate diet, a trend that was commonplace all over Europe (see tables 1.1 and 1.2).

When the CDB was founded, the diet in the west was very simple: potatoes, meal flour, and tea were the main articles of diet. Poorer families ate maize when the potatoes ran out until the new harvest (the 'meal months'), or when the potato crop failed. Flour was generally used all year round, except in the very rare instances when people were too poor to purchase it. Crawford notes that (particularly in the urban setting) increased consumption of cereals and other shop goods in Irish diets during the second half of the nineteenth century reduced the relative significance of the potato.[32] Clarkson's analysis of the eighty-four baseline reports notes fifteen items of food consumed. Other than the potato, which was still a staple, bread was mentioned in 78 districts, tea in 70, milk or buttermilk in 62, Indian meal in 58, fish in 58, eggs in 35, oatmeal in 25, bacon in 23, butter in 15, sugar in 12, cabbage in 10, meat in 5 and coffee only in one.[33] While the baseline study of diet still shows a significant dependence on the potato, it also highlights a widening consumption base, which is a sensitive indicator of the rate at which the cash economy was expanding. Irish-grown oatmeal was the preferred commodity but Indian meal was the cheapest and most widely available substitute for potatoes.[34] In 1890, maize (also termed Indian meal) was still used more for human consumption in the congested districts than in other, more progressive parts of Ireland. Its over-consumption caused pellagra (a dietary disease caused by a deficiency in niacin and B vitamins), which, as Crawford argues, became a medical problem in Ireland during the latter half of the nineteenth century.[35]

According to Laura Jones, the diet was not nutritiously deficient if taken in the right quantities and, in her opinion, 'the physical strength of both men and women into middle age was remarkable'.[36] She argues that the people of the Donegal congests were more preoccupied with an adequate rather than a varied diet, but evidence presented throughout the baseline reports tends to contradict this. While the reports make few references to people's health, it is clear from the income and expenditure tables of more prosperous areas that items sold were nutritionally more valuable than the items bought to replace them. To accommodate varying levels of poverty within the congested districts,

---

32 M. Crawford, 'Diet and the labouring classes in the nineteenth century' (1990), pp 89–92. **33** L. Clarkson, 'The modernisation of the Irish diet' (1999), p. 42. **34** Ibid. See also RCCI, Fourth Report, Appendix, Q. 19287. **35** E.M. Crawford, 'Indian meal and pellagra in nineteenth century Ireland' (1981). **36** L. Jones, 'Food and meals in a congested district: County Donegal in 1891' (1981).

returns were given for families in ordinary circumstances and for families in very poor circumstances, for example, in the district of Knockadaff (table 1.2). Using the evidence contained in the Levally report, a rough evaluation of the average diet can be ascertained (table 1.1 provides an example of a more detailed return made in the reports of a family in 'ordinary circumstances'). The sample budget shows a relatively prosperous congested district with varied expenditure; here flour and meal were purchased in equal quantities and the tobacco cost as much as the tea consumed. This district is inland, and no account is made of expenditure on fish. Turf was the only article bartered. Unlike many other congests, cash was paid for eggs, but, in Levally, all eggs were sold 'and groceries bought with the proceeds'. Here the people clearly allowed their diet to suffer in order to engage in the increasing cash economy, and they subsequently purchased nutritionally inferior goods, the glaring example being the £3 sale of oats, which was equal to the sum spent on Indian meal purchase. It is important to note that no clear distinction is made in the use of Indian meal, whether it was for human or animal consumption. However, the baseline reports show that households like Levally with more disposable cash than Knockadaff were still using Indian meal to bridge the gap in the potato season. Another striking feature of expenditure in this congested district is the high level of consumption of meal and flour; which among families in ordinary circumstances in the congested districts of Donegal, Galway, Mayo, Leitrim, Roscommon and Sligo accounted for over 29 per cent of cash expenditure (see tables 4.1 and 4.2). Poorer families in Galway and Mayo spent over 34 per cent of cash income on meal and flour. Clarkson's hypothesis of a link between rising living standards and the decline in Indian meal consumption is not applicable in the congests in 1891; rather it represents further engagement in the cash economy. It is clear from the baseline reports that lifestyles were not enhanced by the increasing cash economy.[37]

The detailed Levally report shows a surplus of almost £6 at the end of the year, whereas the Knockadaff estimates imply that the difference of almost £1 between income and expenditure was left outstanding, indicating that families with less cash were suffering more at the hands of local traders. Ironically, districts deemed to have poorer circumstances (if this is defined as having less cash) had a wider and more nutritious diet than the financially better off in Levally. Knockadaff has an income from fish, so we can presume that some was eaten at home. Regular meals in Knockadaff included butter or milk, and the tradition of making boxty (a potato and butter dish) is mentioned. Butter or milk consumption is not mentioned in the Levally diet. Indeed, all the reports indicate that milk for home consumption was skimmed. Cheese-making, or,

---

[37] Clarkson 'The modernisation of the Irish diet', p. 42.

Table 1.1. Levally, Co. Galway: Annual income and expenditure of a family in 'ordinary circumstances'

Receipts	£	s.	d.	Expenditure	£	s.	d.
Produce sold:				Groceries bought:			
1500 hens eggs	4	10	0	lb tea per week	1	6	0
duck eggs	0	18	0	2 lb sugar per week	1	1	8
8 hens	0	6	8	12 bags flour per week	6	0	0
12 chickens	0	6	0	12 cwt Indian meal per annum	3	12	0
6 ducklings	0	4	6	114 ozs tobacco per annum	1	6	0
8 geese	1	0	0	Oil	0	5	0
28 lb wool	1	2	2	gal. Porter per week	1	14	4
1 ewe	1	4	0	blacksmiths bill	1	0	0
1 wether	1	6	0	12 cwt bran	4	10	0
2 lambs	1	10	0	12 cwt guano	4	16	0
1 bullock/heifer	4	0	0	43 stone seed oats	1	15	0
Pigs sold	9	0	0	21 lb turnip seed	0	1	8
Oat crop	3	0	0	Cabbages	0	0	10
Turf	8	15	0	Bonhams	2	10	0
Migratory labour	8	0	0	Clothing	5	0	0
American money	3	0	0	Rents/taxes	7	10	0
				Total	42	8	6
Total	48	2	4				

On Farm Consumption*

	£	s.	d.				
6½ tons potatoes	15	3	4				
16 cwt oats	6	0	0				
2 tons turnips	1	6	8				
500 hundred cabbages	1	10	0				
2 roods meadow hay	2	0	0				
If 1 acre of potatoes grown							
Add for extra acre	7	10	0				
Total	33	10	0	**Total consumption =£75 8s. 6d.**			

Source: Congested Districts baseline report no. 57. *On farm consumption term used in baseline reports.

cheese consumption is not mentioned in any of the reports. Micheal Ó Sé argues that the main reason for the disappearance of cheese from the Irish diet was that rennet, derived from the stomach of calves and lambs, was used to coagulate milk in cheese manufacture and the people of the west could not afford this expensive raw material. Vegetable-based coagulating materials were also used and widely known, and Ó Sé reckons that it was more likely that people replaced the long tedious process of cheese-making with butter-making because

Table 1.2. Knockadaff, Co. Mayo: Receipts and expenditure for families in very poor circumstances

Receipts	£	s.	d.	Expenditure	£	s.	d.
Calf	2	0	0	Rent	1	10	0
2 Sheep	0	16	0	County Cess	0	2	0
Pig (profit)	2	0	0	Clerical dues	0	6	0
Fish	3	0	0	Meal June/July	2	0	0
Eggs	2	0	0	Flour	1	10	0
				Groceries	0	10	0
				Clothing	3	0	0
				Lights	0	5	0
				Household goods	0	5	0
				Spades	0	5	0
				Tobacco	1	6	0
Total	9	16	0		10	19	0

Source: Knockadaff Congested Districts Baseline Report.

it had a greater return.[38] Traditional Irish flour and meal-based foods, such as soda bread, porridge, oatcakes and flapjacks, are not well represented in the baseline reports, although oats were eaten more in Donegal. Meat-based foods such as stew or traditional black puddings do not figure in the reports, and the consumption of meat was confined to American bacon, which was eaten on festive occasions and is documented as expenditure in just over one quarter of the districts.

The reports show a high consumption of tea in the congests this meant that the west suffered the rigours of indirect taxation. Throughout the nineteenth century, tea had progressed from being a luxury drunk by adults on special occasions to being consumed on a daily basis by adults and children alike. Lysaght notes that, as incomes rose, so too did the taste for strong sweet tea and baker's bread, even in the most deprived areas in the west. Tea was used at a rate of a pound a week per household and sugar was used excessively at a rate of 4 lb per pound of tea.[39] It was boiled, not drawn, and was taken very strong three times a day. Gahan noted from dispensary records that, as a result of excessive black tea consumption, people suffered from stomach complaints and were subject to nervous disorders.[40] The type of tea used was the worst-

[38] M. Ó Sé, 'Old Irish cheeses and other milk products' (1978), pp 83–6. [39] Lysaght, 'When I makes tea, I makes tea' (1987). [40] Gahan, *Glenties*, p. 15, Account of typical daily diet: 'The people take three meals every day, the morning and mid-day meals being most important. For the first, tea, stirabout and bread sometimes a bit of fish, or if well off, a bit of bacon. If very poor,

quality black Assam, which retailed at 2*s*. 8*d*. a pound, or 9*d*. a quarter, and smaller dealers made their greatest profits when tea was bartered for eggs or knitted goods. Apart from groceries, fuel was a big expenditure in Mayo households like parts of Murrisk and other areas that held no turbary rights.[41] In Fanad, the landlords prohibited the sale of turf because in many instances people were cutting up their grazing land and burning the sods. On Clare Island, in Clew Bay, there was no turf for sale and the bogs were difficult to access, but they were 'not altogether out of the way'. Ruttledge-Fair argued that the people, out of pure laziness, preferred 'to cut off scraws, half peat and half clay' near to their homes, which destroyed good grazing land, rather than climb the nearby mountain where there was an abundance of turf.[42] Writing in the 1940s, Evans argued that 'measured by time and labour of cutting, footing, stacking and carrying, turf is an expensive fuel'; methods had not changed since the 1890s, and the baseline inspectors made specific reference to how hard people worked in the bog.[43] The baseline reports do not make specific returns for turf, but they highlight the expenditure in some regions. In Dunfanaghy turf was bartered for lime, while tenants in Spiddle paid extra for turbary rights. But smallholders who had turbary rights had a guaranteed home supply and in some instances a guaranteed cash income. On the Aran Islands, supplies were exhausted, and turf was brought in from the mainland. In the Croaghpatrick and Murrisk electoral divisions, turf was very scarce, it was purchased at Louisburgh and was even brought in boats across Clew Bay from Achill Island.[44] About 200 tons of turf was shipped annually from Buncrana in schooners to Scotland, where it was used for malting brandy, and people received 4*s*. per ton. Other types of fuel were also in use: for example, bog-fir was plentiful in most areas of Donegal and was used for kindling and for firewood. Bogwood was an article of barter in Desertegney, there turf sales were

---

stirabout and tea only. The bread, except in summer, is generally taken dry without butter. The mid-day, or rather two o'clock meal, mainly consists of potatoes and fish, if there is any, or bacon if they can have it. After the potatoes and fish, tea and bread. The evening meal, mainly consists nearly always of tea and bread, or in the cases of the poorest stirabout. The kinds of foods only vary from potatoes to meal when the former are run out. Flour is in constant use and so is tea. A few eggs are eaten, but very few, and a hen or chicken on holidays or any great occasion'. **41** Ruttledge-Fair, *Louisburgh*, p. 3. **42** Ruttledge-Fair, *Clare Island*, p. 3. **43** E.E. Evans, *Irish heritage; the landscape the people and their work* (1967). p. 133. Ruttledge-Fair, *Spiddle*, p. 4. 'As an ordinary day's work at turf-cutting a man is expected to cut, and will cut, ten "cribs". A crib which I counted contained 810 sods. Eight thousand one hundred double strokes of the "sleyne", cutting and throwing out, at fifteen strokes per minute, will occupy exactly nine hours of continuous work. Again, when carting turf to Galway, the cart will be loaded overnight, and those who have the longest distance to go, nearly twenty miles each way, will start at one or two o'clock a.m. and not get home till ten or eleven o'clock at night, walking in and riding out'. **44** Gaskell, *Desertegney*, p. 4.

low because coal was available. The people of Dingle town bought coal in preference to the readily available turf from the large bogs in Ballyferriter. On the whole, turf was the most widespread fuel in the congests, and to reduce costs the inspectors suggested constructing roads to ease the hardship of the people and that all the CDB amalgamated holdings include a strip of bog for fuel.

The expenditure tables also show that very few conducted household improvements. Visitors reported that some lived in squalor, exaggerating their plight to receive more aid. Bennett noted that another reason for simulating poverty was that building a good house or otherwise improving a holding would increase its value and 'his rent might be raised or he might be evicted, and the result of his labours go into the pocket of his landlord'.[45] A small number of inhabitants, mentioned anecdotally, were accused of pretending to be poor by living in circumstances below their means, but there is no evidence in the baseline reports to support this claim. Although not part of the original schemes, the CDB did a lot to improve basic living conditions and housing. Within the congested counties there were varying degrees of cottages (differentiated only by the materials used) that did not fit into census categories. Contrary to the methodology of the census inspectors,[46] the baseline reports divided the housing stock in the congested districts into two classes, 'those with an end room and those that have only one room', and the former were the majority.[47] According to the census, the lowest class of house at this time was one built completely with mud. A visitor wrote the following account in 1903: 'Nowhere in Europe, except perhaps in Turkey and Russia, could a parallel be found to the misery which prevails. As many as 7,683 Irish families, according to the last Census, are living like Kaffirs in mud huts.'[48] Mud huts are not mentioned in the baseline reports, but reference is made to sod huts in the Achill report, an area where Tuke noted the worst class of dwelling during his 1880 visit: 'turf dwellings near the road, which my friends, who were not acquainted with the west, could not believe was a human habitation'.[49] Aalen notes that census enumerators liberally applied the term 'mud cabin' and argues that large, tastefully-built farmhouses tempered with clay were unjustly categorized as mud cabins in the returns.[50]

---

45 Bennett, *John Bull and his other island*, p. 54. **46** For the purposes of surveying the quality of Irish housing stock, the census classified dwellings in four categories. The lowest of the four classes were houses principally built of mud or other perishable materials, with only one room and window. Third class housing was a marginally better abode, usually made of hardier materials and varied from one to four rooms and windows. A second-class house was considered good and had from five to nine rooms and windows. First class housing was the preserve of the wealthy, aristocratic or the professional classes, only a sprinkling of whom resided in the congested districts. **47** Gahan, *Glenties*, p. 15. **48** H.N. Brailsford, *Some Irish problems* (1903), p. 30. **49** J.H. Tuke, *Irish distress and its remedies* (1880), p. 8. **50** M. Fraser, *John Bull's*

As part of the baseline study, the inspectors observed the different types of housing within the congested districts and found a predominance of one or two bed-roomed cottages in greater or lesser degree according to the family means. Location determined the class of house; inhabitants of rural Ireland built homes out of readily available materials, such as timber, sods and thatch for the roof and mud for the floor.[51] In mountainous areas and on some islands, for example Owey in the North Inishowen district, the paucity of materials, and the lack of road access, meant that the houses were one-roomed cabins. Although this type of house existed in almost all districts, it was not as widespread in 1890 due to the major concessions granted to rural Ireland under the labourers acts. The west was not devoid of the social stratification and class awareness of Victorian times, and smallholders, who ranked themselves higher than landless labourers, tended to live in better houses. Therefore the specifications set out for labourers' cottages had indirect influences on raising the standard of smallholders' houses.[52]

The most common style of house had two rooms; it was about 30 feet long, 6 to 8 feet high and between 7 and 12 feet in width from inside wall to inside wall. Poorer-class houses were made of rubble stone-work, set dry, and plastered thickly inside; floors were usually made of mortar or clay, but in very poor cabins, the floor was literally the earth under the house and officially categorized as a mud floor. Better classes of housing had flagstone floors. Some had a combination of clay and stone, which was more of an accident than an intentional occurrence; clay was used to fill the inequalities of the rock surface.[53] Rafters made of sawn bog-deal were used to hang farming implements; hens roosted in some and sometimes a rough loft was constructed above the kitchen.[54] Roofs were covered with thatch; this was made out of strong plant stems such as rushes, or, more commonly straw, the stem remaining from the oat and rye harvest. Thatch required annual repair, which incurred the expense of hiring a thatcher (in the 1890s thatching was not considered a highly specialized skill and there is no reference to a professional *thatcher* in any of the reports). In poorer households, people improvised and secured the roof, as protection against storms, with ropes made of straw or manila patching it with flat stones or bits of wood. In the short-term, thatch roofs were cheap and effective, but, in the long term, they meant continuous upkeep and were unhygienic from many perspectives. While it was water-resistant, thatch had absorbent properties, which ensured that although rain was kept out, the houses were damp and unsanitary

---

other homes: state housing and British policy in Ireland, 1883–1922 (1996), pp 30–3. F.H.A. Aalen, 'The rehousing of rural labourers in Ireland under the Labourers (Ireland) Acts 1893–1919' (1986). **51** J.A. Jackson, *Irish cottages* (1985). **52** Aalen, 'The rehousing', pp 287–300. **53** Gaskell, *South Connemara*, p. 7. **54** Gahan, *Rosguill*, p. 11.

and became breeding grounds for bacteria spores. In turn, this caused numerous types of highly contagious infections (respiratory tract particularly) in both humans and animals.

The term 'cabin' was used by the inspectors for the poorest class of dwelling in the congested counties. A cabin was a small house with one room, 'a wretched-looking bed on the floor at one end and a fireplace at the other'. Cabins were very scantily furnished with a dresser and a few stools and usually there was no table; instead, a 'form' was used to place the potato pot on at mealtimes. In fact, only one report notes the existence of the traditional sugáin chair, 'the seats of which are a kind of webbing made at home of plaited rushes'.[55] There was no chimney, so the smoke either trailed from the hearth through a hole in the roof or out through the doorway. Usually, there was only one door and no window.[56] In Mayo, houses had two doors and the wind direction governed which was used.[57] The better class of house was a very basic, open-plan structure that incorporated two rooms. In some houses a recess was made in the wall, near the fireplace for a bed in the outer room (being the room with the door). The inside room was cleaner, possibly because it was not used throughout the day; it had better beds and a boarded floor; milk and butter were normally stored there. Usually, the couple and the female members of the household slept there. But in some areas the couple slept in the outer room, and the children of both sexes slept in the second room.[58] People were born in the same room as the animals; both sexes occupied one room and very often the same bed. Despite living conditions, which made cohabitation inevitable, the highest level of morality was observed throughout the congested districts. Henry Doran was the only inspector who made a point of highlighting this issue directly in his report on the district of Kiltimagh, Co. Mayo:

> Reflecting on the habits of the people of this and the neighbouring districts, who are born and reared in the same room as their cattle: where brothers and sisters occupy the same sleeping apartment, insensible violation of human decency: living in such foul surroundings, in such close association with the brutes of the field, I have often marvelled how they are so moral, so well disposed, and so good in many ways as they generally are.[59]

An elementary interpretation of the income and expenditure estimates indicates that the resident population were unschooled in basic economics. People did not realize the full value of their produce either nutritionally or economically. Basic living conditions were substandard, but to ensure long-term maximum benefit the board had to rely on indirect measures to encourage fundamental

---

55 Gaskell, *Woodford*, p. 5. **56** Gahan, *Brockagh*, p. 13. **57** R. Nolan, *Within the Mullet* (1998), p. 203. **58** Doran, *Ballyhaunis*, p. 4. **59** Doran, *Kiltimagh*, p. 5.

changes. Apart from farming, industry was completely cottage-based and, as discussed in chapter two, was dominated by women. Improvement in this sphere was at first the only envisaged method of raising cash incomes above a threshold that would lead to a better standard of living.

2

Industries

From the outset, the board was seriously inhibited in relation to industry. It could not introduce major developments because it was not legally allowed to own a company or to compete with private enterprise. The board could give business loans to interested parties, providing that some form of security and reasonable projections were presented. Industrial loans were given at a memorial level, that is, in response to an application made by a spokesperson on behalf of a community, or they were granted to individuals – to purchase looms, for instance. In many respects, a huge burden of financial responsibility was lifted from the board when memorials were successful. The records indicate that the board could not have conducted its industrial works without the co-operation of local clergy in the poorest congests. Memorials, or prospects of them, were few and far between, so the board concentrated on cottage-based industry initially. The extent of surviving domestic industry can be assessed from inquiry headings 8, 12 and 28 of the baseline reports (see Appendix B). These questions examine the regional bias of industry; they assess why industries were not as lucrative or as widespread as they should have been, and also outline early efforts made in conjunction with the board to organize and develop industry.

The baseline reports show that outside of farming and maritime industries, labouring or 'hiring out' was the most important source of paid employment. Available work was very limited within the congested districts, and women fared better than men in finding paid work at home. The main supplementary sources of income were derived from female-dominated, cottage-based industry. Butter churning and poultry rearing were traditionally female enterprises but some men participated in dairy work in the 1890s. By then, spinning, weaving, sewing and embroidery employed women exclusively. David Fitzpatrick argues that based on the census returns daughters were largely redundant in economic terms in the nineteenth century due to the decline in the textile industry.[1] However, the census figures exclude women's work except in specified and

---

[1] Fitzpatrick 'The modernisation of the Irish female in rural Ireland, 1600–1900' (1987), p. 169.

waged occupations therefore his deductions are a too conservative to apply to the west, where most female wages were unofficial. In contrast with the census, specific reference is made in baseline reports and in the CDB annual reports to the importance of female employment, both paid and unpaid. Gaskell marvelled at how industrious the female population of Donegal were, quoting that the people believed, 'If there were only some work or industry by which the men could earn money in the winter it is often said the country would be rich.'[2] Practically all household work, cooking, baking, cleaning and whitewashing, was undertaken by women and, when the men migrated for the harvest season, women reaped the crops at home. Women could earn cash (or in most cases credit) at home, thereby they had direct control over the household money and also rationed food on a daily basis. Throughout the congested districts, women worked particularly hard to ensure a certain income level, poultry-rearing being the most common way of filling the income deficit. In times of hardship, women were definitely more industrious than men; Major Gahan noted that the women of the Glenties district were the 'sole support of the families; the men do little or nothing beyond setting the crop and taking in the harvest'. The average family income in this district was almost £40; of this, almost £19 is readily identifiable as female earnings from eggs and knitting. Other sources of cash income were the sale of sheep, wool, cattle to a lesser extent and corn, all of which involved seasonal care and were no doubt carried out by men and women alike.[3] In general, the reports show that men had a lethargic attitude towards work and preferred to be idle than to engage in 'female' occupations.[4]

In Victorian times, women's engagement in paid work was indicative of poorer circumstances, and, as Joanna Bourke states, 'there was a threshold effect whereby those who reached a certain income level always disliked female employment and, as more households reached this level, more women withdrew from paid labour'.[5] Even within the congested districts, when a certain income level was reached, the people saw no need to surpass it, so money was rarely saved. In the district of Arranmore, Co. Donegal, the people enjoyed a naturally fruitful fishing industry, because families reached a certain income threshold they did not have to rely on the sale of eggs as much as their comrades on the mainland. Inspector Gahan made the following observation: 'The people have more energy, and, although the great profits they reap from the herring fishing has a rather deadening effect on them, from an industrial point of view, still on the whole they seemed to me more industrious than the people of other districts on the mainland.'[6] It is clear from the Arranmore report, which

---

2 Gaskell, *Clonmany*, p. 7. **3** Gahan, *Glenties*, pp 10–14. **4** Documented in various baseline reports also see J. Bourke, *Husbandry to housewifery: women, economic change and housework in Ireland, 1890–1891* (1993) pp 10–26. **5** Ibid., p. 43. **6** Gahan, *Arranmore*, p. 8.

shows a relatively insignificant poultry industry, that women were only industrious when necessary.

Poultry production was an industry common to all the congested districts. This industry cannot be neatly classified; it falls under the auspices of the agricultural department in terms of CDB administration, but for the purposes of this book it is more aptly categorized as a female enterprise. Joanna Bourke belittles the importance of egg money, citing how money derived from eggs bought 'many little items which could not be procured from the husbands' hire'.[7] However, figures from the baseline reports indicate that the poultry industry was a significant element of family income (a return for poultry is given for every district). The smallest documented receipt for eggs in the reports was £1 on the Aran Islands and the highest was £15 in Kiltyclogher, Co. Leitrim, of a total cash income of £35. The true value of eggs in the household budget or on a national level cannot be estimated adequately because of the high level of barter. Indeed, the monetary value of the egg industry could not even be calculated indirectly. Where eggs were used to pay off credit, interest rates must be included; therefore, no reliable figures can be derived. If an area relied heavily on the poultry industry, it indicated one of two things; either the local markets were well organized, or, family circumstances were most certainly at the lower end of the poverty scale.

Kiltyclogher had the only organized local market in the congested districts. Eggs constituted part of the daily diet in this area, which was an exception to the rule in the northwest, and indicative of a family in good circumstances. Poultry meat was far too valuable to be eaten by these producers (salted fish, dried ling or American bacon was eaten on festive occasions) and because the birds were not slaughtered for home consumption there was no feather trade. Therefore the industry had only two dimensions – the rearing of poultry for live-weight sale, and the sale of eggs. Donegal is an excellent example of a congested county where eggs and the live sale of fowl were of considerable importance to household incomes. In Donegal the common procedure was to dispose of the eggs on a weekly basis, on market day. In North Inishowen producers sold their live poultry to shippers at Cardonagh market who exported the fowl to Liverpool and Glasgow.[8] Markets were held on a monthly basis in Moville and on a quarterly basis at six other nearby locations and deliveries were made to various wholesale dealers in Britain within a fortnight of purchase. On average, the eggs were a week old by the time they reached the local dealer who was usually, but not always, the shopkeeper. Only one sixth of all eggs sold in the Donegal region went to the Derry market, which was the main home mar-

---

[7] Cited in J. Bourke 'Women and poultry in Ireland' (1987), p. 294. [8] Gaskell, *North Inishowen*, p. 3.

ket for eggs. Teelin had a choice of markets, as it was well served by the rail network and by steamer, and Derry was the preferred market destination; the area produced 1,089,924 hens' eggs and 80,200 duck eggs in 1891. In Fanad, Brockagh, Glencolmkille and Glenties, the industry was more varied with geese and turkeys being reared as well. An itinerant vendor, known locally as the 'gooseman', bought bought five hundred geese from suppliers in Glencolmkille in 1891. However, hens were the mainstay of the Irish poultry industry; they were low-maintenance, cheap to buy, and they provided ready money.

In general, the inspectors observed an intrinsic lack of understanding of fowl rearing in the northwestern districts, the people did not know how to house or what to feed poultry. The class of hen reared was inferior, described in polite terms by the Fanad inspector, Mr Gahan, as an 'unusual local breed', and the people had little or no knowledge of pedigrees. As a result, breeding was not monitored, and the eggs produced were small and inferior in quality. In the North Inishowen report, the inspector, Major Gaskell, comments that, although the fowl were better bred than other districts, 'there is ample scope for improvements'. In Grange, the industry was in a bad state; 'no attention was paid' to the hens, and ducks were 'for pleasure not profit'. In Spiddle, 'the practice of cutting the tail feathers' made the already small, inferior breeds look even smaller which meant that the people could not engage in live sale. Fowl were fed Indian meal and household scraps and, if left to roam the land, they consumed worms and grubs. In areas where eggs were more valuable, hens were kept inside, mainly to keep track of the eggs, but also to protect them from foxes and vermin. The area from North Inishowen, Co. Donegal, to Kiltyclogher, Co. Leitrim, incorporated twenty-one districts, and the breeds were inferior. There was only one exception. In the district of Clonmany, a young migrant had succeeded in improving the local breed by crossbreeding the existing stock with species brought home from travels abroad.

The Revd J.C. Smith, a Presbyterian clergyman living in Ballaghadereen, was a poultry expert who aided Inspector Doran in collecting information in Galway and Mayo. Smith compiled a separate report on his observations of the industry in counties Mayo, Sligo, Leitrim and Roscommon, where baseline inspectors described the birds as nondescript and small. He emphasized how the deterioration of the breeds was a recent affair. He had conducted a tour in 1888 and maintained that then the fowl 'were a much better class than they are now owing to the effects of continuous in-breeding'.[9] This recent deterioration was not exclusive to Mayo; serious poultry losses also occurred in North Inishowen in 1890. The losses were put down to feeding with undercooked yel-

---

[9] General Report submitted by H. Doran separate from ordinary baseline reports. Appendix A submitted by Revd J.C. Smith, pp 423–5.

low meal, which caused pellagra in humans and cholera in hens. In the Glenties region of Donegal, ducks were more important and hens died from a mysterious disease for which there was 'no cure'. The 'disease' described had all the symptoms of cholera, but no post-mortem examinations were carried out at this time. When Smith conducted post-mortem tests on hens in Mayo, he identified another disease, enteritis, a condition that infected hens only. Tests deduced that bad breeding practice and poorly ventilated housing combined with poor diet (especially Indian meal consumption) caused a tubercular disease that led to a fatal bowel inflammation.[10]

Throughout the reports, a pattern of 'poultry priority' presents itself, and districts clearly varied in their appreciation of poultry. If other cash income sources were available locally, it was reflected in a lower level of care and the stock breeds deteriorated, but if a household depended heavily on poultry the birds were well bred and treated with care.[11] Achill Islanders had a unique respect for their hens and are quoted as saying that 'they would rather lose their cattle than part with their hens'; instead of bartering eggs they bartered turf, which was plentiful. The value of eggs exported from Castlebar and Crossmolina was collectively worth £16,000 a year, and the people received a price 'current to the market reports of the day'.[12] In other parts of Mayo where eggs were plentiful, they were bartered and both producer and trader had little or no respect for the product. A paltry rate of 6*d.* per dozen was paid in Belmullet by the village 'huckster' and because they were not worth selling quite a few of the Mayo districts used eggs for home consumption. In counties Galway and Roscommon people could exchange the eggs for either goods or cash as 'poultry was less thought of than other kinds of stock'.[13] In Kerry and Cork, it was a small-scale industry, and eggs were not bartered but sold to country dealers or shippers.

Carelessness in relation to poultry breeds stemmed from the valuation of eggs in the northwest; poultry products were items of barter. Even in areas where no credit was given, eggs were exchanged for luxury items like tea and sugar. This curious system of 'minute retail'[14] very often meant that the producer was left out of pocket, and inspectors realized that no system was in place to monitor these transactions. In the case of Arranmore, Mr Gahan was particularly concerned about the treatment of the people by rapacious local dealers. He wrote:

> In this district as in others, the credit system mainly prevails for meal and flour. Tea and sugar and small articles are generally paid for as far as possible in eggs or butter. The length of credit charged is about six months. The interest charged is 2*s.* in the pound for one year. Boat loads of seaweed and turf and as stated above, eggs, butter, etc., [are exchanged] for tea and sugar. The great draw-

10 Ibid., p. 420–5. **11** Ibid., p. 425. **12** Gaskell, *Pontoon*, pp 3–4. **13** Gaskell, *Annaghdown*, p. 3. **14** Gahan, *Glencolumkille*, p. 5.

back to the credit system on which people work, is that being as a rule, illiterate, they have *absolutely no check* on the dealer – anything he chooses to put down they must accept, as they have no possible means of checking their account.[15]

On the other hand, Major Ruttledge-Fair found that in Aghagower, Co. Mayo, 'shopkeepers, as a rule, treat their customers leniently, and in bad seasons the amount of credit given is beyond all conception'.[16] Itinerant vendors of commodities such as tea and sugar visited areas that were a long distance from markets, and they usually short-changed the people. Where itinerant vending was competitive, prices were accordingly competitive and fair to the client, but elsewhere there was scope for abuse, and many took advantage. Through their examination of the poultry industry, the inspectors received a unique view of how money was handled in the congested districts. Credit dealings were extensive; local shopkeepers/gombeenmen were usually well informed of their customer's financial situation; this determined the extent of credit given. Some traders sold goods cheaper if they were paid in cash, for instance, Indian meal was sold for cash at a small profit, but when it was bought on credit '3d. per sack is added to the first cost for every month the price remains unpaid'.[17] There were only a few exceptions; in Co. Leitrim, credit was not as extensive because of 'reckless trading' in former years; in some Mayo districts credit was only given for clothes, which were rarely bought.

Despite how disaggregated the poultry industry was, it was well established in the congested counties. The board dealt with it in a very methodical fashion, beginning by upgrading the stock (pedigree fowl were sent to congested counties in 1892). A scheme was initiated in two Galway districts, Carna and Carraroe, and in the Mayo district of Aghagower whereby the people could exchange their male birds for pure-bred cockerels. Unfortunately, the scheme coincided with an outbreak of the fatal 'enteritis' and the delicate pedigree birds perished. On Achill Island a pedigree breed 'throve well', possibly because the pre-existing industry was respected and better care was taken. In this light it seems that the central problem in nearly all eighty-four districts was the large degree of indifference towards poultry farming. The board sent in a poultry expert, Mr Tegetmeier, to investigate the situation; he believed that the majority died of 'hardship, the districts being ill adapted to support purebred fowl, such as had been supplied'. He strongly recommended that in future only farm-bred birds should be purchased and not those bred by poultry fanciers for show purposes.[18] Extra caution was exercised the following year through the introduction of sturdier breeds and by the establishment of four CDB-run poultry

---

15 Gahan, *Arranmore*, p. 6. **16** Ruttledge-Fair, *Aghagower*, p. 3. **17** Gaskell, *Kiltubbrid*, p. 4. **18** CDB, First annual report, 1892, p. 14.

farms, one in Donegal, two in Mayo and one in Skull, Co. Cork. Poultry farms operated on a 'swop' system whereby 'sittings' of purebred eggs were distributed to the wider community from the farms 'in exchange for an equal number of eggs of common fowl'. People received 1*d.* compensation to encourage them to get rid of old batches. An itinerant instructress was employed to tutor the people on poultry welfare, and pamphlets outlining the proper treatment of fowl were distributed. The CDB experience of the poultry industry was very much a learning process, but mistakes were quickly rectified. In 1893 ten more farms were established, which worked out cheaper than distributing large quantities of fowl to the people. In this manner the board could exercise total control over the welfare of its property, and breed out the bad quality domestic poultry. Within two years there was a decrease in the percentage of deaths, and reports indicated an improvement in the quality of eggs and poultry in several districts.[19]

The next most pressing issue was the transportation of eggs, which was haphazard; presentation was poor and there was no quality assurance. Exporters complained that Irish eggs were small and very light (weight determined price and when eggs age they get lighter). They were lighter because 'egglers' held back eggs if they anticipated a hike in prices; the Irish Agricultural Organisation Society (IAOS), which was founded in 1894 to promote co-operation between agricultural producers and buyers, later noted that the women were also guilty of this practice.[20] This was ruinous to the reputation of Irish eggs, which in the normal course of events should have reached their destination within three weeks and be just about acceptably fresh. In Newport, Co. Mayo, 'egglers' held on to eggs for a number of weeks.[21] As a result, Irish eggs did not weigh the standard two ounces; they were dirty and were not packed in cases like Danish eggs, the main competitor on the British market. Irish eggs were packed in straw, which was usually of inferior quality, and rendered the product off-putting to potential buyers. Also the inferiority of Irish poultry breeds meant that the class of egg produced was small, white in colour and thin-shelled, making them aesthetically recognizable as 'Irish'. Irish eggs received a lesser price than the yellow thicker-shelled variety. Even so, bad quality produce had a market among the British poor, but exporters argued that if Irish producers made small efforts (like packing eggs in clean straw) they would get a higher return.[22]

A shrewd businessman, Mr John Lavin, of Castlerea, made a direct application to the board during 1893, requesting financial assistance to set up a daily 'fresh egg traffic' between Castlerea and London. Being humoured at an experimental level, he was supplied with thirty-one laying boxes, which he patented and lent to the local suppliers to fill. This particular district was inland but it

---

19 CDB, Second annual report, 1893, p. 13. **20** G.W.Russell, 'Elections not near. Poultry Societies notice!' (1905). **21** Ruttledge-Fair, *Newport,* p. 3. **22** Gaskell, *Pontoon,* p. 4.

had a pre-existing weekly market where the people sold directly to the exporters, thereby ensuring that eggs were usually 'only a few days old when sold to the first buyer, and about ten days old when they reach their ultimate destination.'[23] As the board had suffered great losses in the infant stages of its poultry initiatives, it was more than willing to lend Lavin money, subject to terms and conditions, to observe his progress from a safe distance, and to extend the operation to other areas if he was successful. Lavin is not mentioned in subsequent reports, but the board adopted his policies afterwards. By 1894 the board had spent £884 3s. 3d. on the poultry industry, which can be roughly divided into nearly £600 on new breeds of hens, £140 on transport, £25 on baskets, £13 in compensation and £40 on commission (presumably to exporters for facilitating the sale).[24] The poultry farms were very successful and totalled thirty in March 1895, most were concentrated in the northern congested districts where the pre-existing industry was more organized. Indeed, the nuns in the convents of Claremorris and Foxford were 'zealously taking up the instruction of the people in the rearing of poultry'. The board, now more confident, extended the expenditure to the purchase of better-bred geese, turkeys and ducks. At this point the purchase of roosters had decreased from the initial outlay of £245 19s. 9d. in 1892–3 to £17 4s. in 1894–5, a clear indication that the control exercised through the medium of the farms was the key to its success. On reviewing the situation, the board established twenty-two more farms in 1896.

The reformation of the poultry industry in the congested districts was perhaps the board's easiest task and relatively inexpensive to transform, bar the trial and error period in the beginning. When the IAOS was established, the CDB loosened its reins over the industry and responsibility for the poultry industry fell naturally under the auspices of the newly formed organization. Joanna Bourke argues that the emphasis the IAOS placed on female employment in this area was a response to allegations that 'its creameries pushed women and girls out of employment, and [it] defended itself against such attacks by declaring that its encouragement of the poultry industry provided the female members of the farming community with an alternative, and more remunerative, occupation'.[25] This assessment does not take account of the extent of the pre-existing poultry industry. Her contention that when female enterprise rose from the level of 'subsistence entrepreneurship'[26] or 'minute retail' to profitable cash-based industry, that men usurped the role of women, is not entirely true. She argues that men became more involved and subsequently displaced women, particularly in the areas of poultry rearing and dairying, but the latter was of lesser significance in the con-

---

23 Mr Doran, *Castlerea*, p. 2. **24** CDB, Third annual report, 1894, Appendix xii, p. 43. **25** Bourke, *Husbandry to housewifery*, p. 184. **26** A phrase Bourke uses liberally throughout her book, *Husbandry to housewifery*.

gested districts.[27] Bourke deals with Ireland as a whole but draws heavily on CDB evidence to support her claim. David Smith criticizes Bourke for her limited use of CDB documents to support her contention that the position of women in waged labour deteriorated in the west between 1891 and 1914. While Smith is equally guilty of limited usage of CDB reports his deductions are more accurate than Bourke's (he highlights how the board recognized, and subsequently used, the traditional roles of women to extend the cash economy in the west).[28] Baseline inspectors identified the bartering of eggs as a major flaw in the western economy; for example, no cash was received for eggs in the twenty-one districts in Donegal. Furthermore the inspectors believed that when women exchanged their eggs for shop goods, they did not receive the full value of their produce. The board set out to redress this issue through the organization of markets and cash payment, and in the process some men were employed. But one thing is certain from the baseline reports: women traditionally dominated this industry and according to the annual reports the board failed in its attempts to employ men in the various poultry schemes. Bourke's argument hinges on the notion that men usurped the traditional role of women, but these positions of authority were new. Women were traditionally the producers and remained so. After CDB intervention, the poultry industry survived as it always had, as a supplement to other farming pursuits, and it never emerged as a large-scale commercial entity. Indeed, Finnola Kennedy notes how poultry production remained a very important income supplement and, in terms of production, an exclusively female industry in the twentieth century.[29]

Other domestic industry

Contrary to Fitzpatrick's census-based assertions, domestic industries, such as weaving, knitting, spinning, sprigging or embroidery, were of great importance to the family income in many congested districts. Again, the full monetary value of these industries cannot be ascertained as many of these products, in the absence of organized markets, were exclusively for home or local consumption. Traditionally, the textile industry had a major commercial stronghold in the north-east, but the reports show that the demand for homespun textiles was waning, due to the influx of imported, mass-produced clothing. By 1890 there were few incentives to card, weave, knit or sew, as all products received a very poor price relative to the volume of work involved. Weaving had lost the pres-

27 Cattle-rearing was limited in the congested districts because the smallholdings could not sustain more than one such large beast. **28** D. Smith, '"I thought I was landed!" the Congested Districts Board and the women of Western Ireland' (1996). **29** F. Kennedy, *From cottage to crèche: family change in Ireland* (2001), p. 72.

tige of former years; the art was becoming unknown and was carried out in only a few of the Donegal districts. Major changes (for example, the invention and wider use of large industrial looms) caused a transition in the Irish textile industry, particularly in relation to weaving (all types of material); it began in the 1760s when merchants started the 'putting-out system'. This practice, which had its origins in the north-east, was a process whereby a merchant acted as a middleman between the raw material and the finished product and received a commission for delegating or putting-out the work. William Crawford traces the origins of this system to the weaving industry, but it became part for the course in other textile industries.[30] It is evident from the baseline reports that 'webs'(the roll of material produced by the spinners and weavers) were produced on a very small scale in the congested counties but were made in two districts in Donegal, eleven in Mayo, fourteen in Galway, seven in Kerry and in all six Cork districts, which proved to the board that the craft had not died out and could be revived.

In a bid to organize and standardize all production, the board initiated technical-instruction classes. The type of instruction given depended on the pre-existing industry, whether it was weaving, sewing or knitting (most of which were female industries); initial outlays included the rental of premises and the payment of teachers to train hands roughened by farm work. After that, the board had to support the various industries by means of small grants until they could support themselves.[31] In very remote and poor areas, the classes were ineffective at first. It was hard to persuade girls, who received better wages as migrants working the fields, to join the various classes for a lesser wage; it was also difficult to change poor time-keeping habits. In some very poor areas, where unemployment was high and girls did not have the money to migrate, classes were over-crowded. A local government board inspector criticized the class held in Ardara, Co. Donegal, for keeping girls (some as young as twelve) for long days in over-crowded conditions. Miss Tierney, the tutor, also encouraged the girls to continue working when they got home in order to improve skills.[32] But in other areas irregular attendance caused some classes to close.[33]

Local clergy were very helpful to the CDB and often provided church property free of charge for the holding of technical instruction classes on condition that the CDB provided suitable equipment. The most successful CDB/church alliance was at Foxford in conjunction with the Sisters of Charity. For some time, the Sisters played a very important role in the development of industry in the extremely impoverished areas of Benada in Sligo, and the Ballaghdereen

---

[30] W.H. Crawford, *Domestic industry in Ireland: the experience of the linen industry* (1972), p. 39. [31] CDB, Ninth annual report, 1900, pp 40–1. [32] M.D. McFeely, *Lady inspectors: the campaign for a better workplace, 1893–1921* (1988), p. 174. [33] CDB, Tenth annual report, 1901, pp 44–5.

and Foxford areas in Mayo. They located their first work in Benada, where they had inherited a property from the Jones family, and they survived on the proceeds from the land rental. During the Land War, when tenants refused to pay rents, the Sisters were forced to return to Dublin in February 1880. Benada was unoccupied for nearly two years until they managed to get an industrial school grant and reopen the convent, which became world-famous for lace.[34] The Sisters also had a convent in Ballaghdereen, in the poor law union of Swinford, reputedly the most under-resourced and under-developed of all the congests. One of the nuns was a member of the Higgins family and her life-long share in the estate was the property of the order. The survival of the Ballaghdereen convent relied on rents from the nearby Ousley Higgins tenants in Galway, and during the Land War rents were not forthcoming. The mother general in Dublin wanted the nuns to leave, but Mother Morrogh Bernard, the nun in charge at Ballaghdereen, insisted they stay. The Sisters were lucky enough to acquire a substantial laundry tender for church vestments for Ballaghdereen. This centre also incorporated a national school and dormitories, which enabled the nuns to get industrial school status in 1886 for seventy-five girls.

While at Ballaghdereen, Mother Morrogh was notified about high levels of poverty in the neighbouring village of Foxford by her friend Mrs Deane, who was a cousin of John Dillon and native of there. Following their mission in 1880, the Redemptorists pleaded with Mother Morrogh to come and help the people of Foxford. It was not until 1890 that the order was in a position to help, and it bought a dilapidated property on the main street for £475. Mother Morrogh opened a spinning and weaving operation in Foxford, intending to maximize the use of the river Moy, its only natural resource. There was a disused millrace for an old corn mill on the west side of the river, but the nun's property was on the east side so a new millrace had to be constructed. An old corn store was used for the small spinning and weaving venture operated by two sisters (named Conroy), who had been trained at Ballaghdereen. Intent on developing Foxford, Mother Morrogh visited a woollen mill at Collooney in March 1891 and on the advice of Michael Davitt she contacted Peter White of the Irish Woollen Mills in Dublin, who advised her to speak with John Charles Smith of Caledonian Mills, Co. Tyrone. Smith visited Foxford and doubted if it could succeed, citing how Arthur Guinness failed to make a woollen factory on the Liffey successful and suggested that they abandon the idea, but he placed himself at their disposal in an advisory capacity for twenty years. Furthermore he also lent his trainee manager, Mr Frank Sherry, and trained the Conroy sisters at Caledon.[35] A small woollen production was started at Foxford with a

---

[34] K. Butler, *The story of Benada* (n.d.), p. 20. [35] The Revd D. Gildea, *Mother Mary Arsenius of Foxford* (1936), pp 90–105.

£2,000 loan secured by Mrs Deane and the mother general of the order secured another loan of £5,000; both agreed to pay the interest on the respective loans.

Mother Morrogh was determined to expand the operation and befriended Charles Kennedy, a well-known philanthropist and a member of the CDB. Being impressed by the work conducted at Foxford, he arranged for a delegation of potential investors to visit the factory on 19 March 1892. The delegation included Mr Burdett-Coutts MP, Fredrick Wrench, land commissioner and member of the CDB, other members of parliament and poor law guardians. The nuns applied for a grant to expand the business at Ballaghdereen, proposing to train local women in domestic service and to transform the existing structure into a hosiery and ready-made clothing factory. Following the satisfactory completion of a questionnaire regarding training, wages, and the administration of the proposed woollen mills, it was agreed that the memorial was feasible and the CDB granted a business loan of £7,000 for the building and fitting of an industrial school in Foxford and £3,000 for the same purposes in the Ballaghdereen convent. The rate of interest was 2.5 per cent and the loans were to be repaid in half-yearly instalments over eighteen years.[36]

The nuns had an advantage over other applicants because they had a proven track record of industrial sucess and access to the necessary security, which in this instance was a re-mortgaged property in Dublin belonging to the order and worth £30,000.[37] Great progress was made in the first year; 43 people were employed at Foxford and 92 in Ballaghadereen. The following year the board awarded a further £1,500 to the Foxford woollen factory and £500 to the Ballaghadereen knitting and under-clothing factory, 'in consideration of the valuable services rendered by the Sisters of Charity in developing woollen industries, and in providing technical instruction'. In 1893 the board formally employed the nuns to provide technical training for boys and girls in the manufacture of woollen goods, hosiery, ready-made clothes and in domestic service. Both factories received capitation grants in return for running the schools. There were many conditions attached to the agreement; firstly, the schools and factories had to operate simultaneously and be staffed accordingly. The board allocated a maximum amount of £4,000 to be paid over three years on a quarterly basis. Quarterly grants did not exceed £333 6s. 8d. but money could be deducted from the school if at any stage there were less than 100 students (deducted at a rate of £3 6s. 8d. per student).[38] The board had the right to inspect the premises and the attendance books whenever it pleased, and the CDB accountant could audit the accounts. Ballaghdereen received half the capitation grant of the Foxford factory; the latter was more successful because it had the

---

[36] CDB, First annual report, 1892, p. 20. [37] CDB, Minutes of proceedings, 13 and 14 October 1892. [38] CDB, Second annual report, 1893, p. 27.

advantage of a good reliable supply of hydropower, being located on a fast flowing part of the river Moy.

Mother Morrogh Bernard seems to have been a good businesswoman and 'was wise in the choice of good expert advisers, especially Mr Frank Sherry, the manager of the factory'.[39] Once the board had issued the loan, the nuns were left to their own devices in relation to instruction, production and marketing but it remained subject to audits because of the grants. Mr W.J.D. Walker, Glenbanna Mills, Co. Down, who had invented a modern handloom, acted as a part-time, salaried adviser to the board in relation to the woollen industry production in Foxford.[40] He reported in 1894 that although production was neither high nor profitable it had great potential. Furthermore he praised the business capacity of Mother Morrogh Bernard, the ladies under her, and the hard-working manager, stating that 'your Board is under the deepest obligation to them, and while your capital has contributed, they are the real benefactors of the area.'[41] Foxford was in danger of losing its capitation grant in 1894, but Mother Morrogh managed to convince the board to extend the grant until 1896. It was strictly speaking still unprofitable in 1896 but Mother Morrogh argued that although the mill had a total financial loss of £632, incurred because the workers were still in training, it had earned £8,000 and ninety-two workers had opened post office savings accounts, saving a sum of £114; with this evidence she managed to convince the board to extend the grant until 1899.[42] In 1900 the board stopped its subsidies.[43] Foxford expanded steadily and all CDB loans were repaid on time, with interest. On 2 November 1910, the thirty-sixth and final cheque for £242 13s. 2d. was sent to the board and the title deeds of the Dublin property, Mount St Anne's, which had been deposited as security of repayment, were returned.[44]

The existence and help provided by the Sisters of Charity was a fortunate turn of events for the CDB. It was very difficult to organize the various other cottage-based industries, which were in competition with highly organized private enterprise. Another instance of collaboration was with the Irish Industries Development Association (IIDA). In July 1893 the countess of Aberdeen, the wife of the lord lieutenant and president of the IIDA, suggested that the association and the CDB liase in the development of home industries. Founded in 1887, the IIDA focused on the organization of home industries; its first year was spent gathering information on the extent of home industries, and in 1888 it bought a depot to display and sell goods.[45] Discussions between the IIDA and the CDB led to the foundation of a scheme referred to in the annual reports as

39 Micks, *An account of the history*, p. 69. **40** P.J. McGill, 'The Irish woollen industry from earliest times to Donegal homespuns' (1949), p. 149. **41** RSCG/H26/30, W.J.D. Walker, Report of Visit to Foxford Factory, 10 December 1894. **42** RSCG/H26/34. **43** RSCG/H26/36, W. Micks Report, dated 13 November 1896. **44** RSCG/H26/40. **45** Bourke, *Husbandry to housewifery*, p. 112.

South Donegal Industries. This was an endeavour to develop and improve the manufacture of homespun tweeds. J.W.D. Walker, of Glenbanna mills, was put in complete charge of the development of the scheme, and his involvement ensured that within a few years Donegal homespun was attracting attention at international exhibitions, and finding international markets. The board lent money to the association to carry out the scheme, providing that the salaries, storage and inspection did not exceed £350 a year. Under the terms of the agreement, the association had to provide technical instruction. It rented depots, furnished them with demonstration looms, spinning wheels, materials and appliances necessary for demonstrating the processes of dyeing, spinning and weaving. The IIDA bought reference books on the textile industry and introduced more modern looms, while the board provided loans to weavers for their purchase.[46] Great progress was made in the tweed industry under the association, and it began buying 'patterns of Harris' to produce more fashionable goods. Goods were stamped with the monogram of the association and an incentive bonus was given to weavers and web owners if they reached the stamp standard.[47] The board failed to encourage more people into the tweed industry and to standardize the quality of webs; efforts to prevent the production of inferior quality goods were not successful. In 1894, the IIDA applied for a loan of £2,500 to modernize the carding of wool, which was still carried out by hand, but the CDB could not afford to lend this amount; a steady fall in price coupled with a lack of investment led to a decline in the tweed industry, and many workers left.[48] The weaving industry employed both men and women, but training in the craft was exclusive to men, partly due to the physical strength required but mainly due to tradition.

In contrast with the better-paid tweed industry, which required skilled craftsmen, women's textile work was poorly paid. For example, shirt-making and sewing was extensive in areas of Donegal, but because merchants controlled the supply of materials (mainly cotton) the output or putting-out system also prevailed. This industry had three dimensions in the 1890s – material cutting (done exclusively in the Derry factory), sewing and the final stage of laundering and finishing. The industry was thriving in the late 1880s and the factory floor could not accommodate the volume of workers necessary for the second-stage work of sewing, so it was carried out partly in depots and in people's homes. The third stage of laundering and finishing for market was carried out in the factories; it was the best-paid part of the work. Rural workers, mainly women from the congested districts in Donegal, were employed to conduct

46 CDB, Third annual report, 1894, pp 18–19. **47** A 'web' was the term used for a woven fabric and was the property of the yarn owner, not the weaver. **48** Some correspondence (dating from April 1892 to March 1897) between the board and the IIDA survives and is held at the Library of the Department of Agriculture, Dublin.

second-stage work or to sew pre-cut shirts along the seams, a task that required no skill and was paid accordingly. Those within a five-mile radius of factories or depots could collect the cuttings, carry them home and get paid when they returned the made-up shirts to the factory or depot. Those outside the 'walking distance' radius were at the mercy of agents that ran rural stations further away from the factory.[49] Donegal agents received consignments twice weekly (by rail or horse van), and work was delegated in order of merit.

One of the prerequisites for becoming an employee was a clean and bright home, which meant automatic exclusion for girls living in the poorer cottages. It was noted in the Brockagh report in 1891 that 'sewing, both by hand and machine, is an extensive and in some parts an extending industry. It is not, however, an industry that at present can reach the poorest classes, as the firms who give out the work and the machines will not let either go into the very dirty little houses where the stuff would only get destroyed'.[50] Areas that had a well-developed shirt-making industry, like Clonmany, enjoyed the facilities of two sewing depots that employed at least 100 families. This facility worked well for those meeting high standards because it was the only form of structured, paid female employment. High levels of cleanliness were observed, and the baseline inspector was very impressed with the effect this industry had on the people; especially since it made them more ambitious, competitive and organized. The area had the proud boast of four girls in the possession of dressmaking certificates; there were even complaints of 'not half enough work'. While payment was always in cash there was a grading system for the finished product, varying from 1*s.* 9*d.* a dozen to 3*s.* 6*d.* and 'higher rates from 4*s.* to 5*s.* being given for special work to the best workers'. The situation in Clonmany was unique, and displayed the high levels of success that industry could rise to in the right hands.[51]

Unfortunately, the number of workers abused by the grading system by far outweighed the numbers treated fairly; that discouraged many young women, who found better remuneration in hiring themselves out as agricultural labourers. In North Inishowen, the business was highly competitive with many agencies and factories. It should have meant very favourable circumstances for workers, but the inspector estimated its worth at only £5,000 for the whole area. This area had the best conditions, according to the baseline reports, but the figure represents a mere 5*s.* a week for fifty weeks for 400 workers. Girls received between 2*s.* 6*d.* and 3*s.* 6*d.* per dozen, and their agents were paid a commission of 6*d.* per dozen shirts delivered. Agents used a system of fines if the garments were late or soiled, so the girls rarely got a full income. In Gartan, where the shirt-

---

49 T.W. Rolleston, 'The Derry shirt-making industry' (1902), pp 418–20. **50** Gahan, *Brockagh*, p. 3. **51** Gaskell, *Clonmany,* pp 4–6.

sewing industry was relatively new, the system differed slightly. Girls had to go to the Letterkenny depot to collect the garments, sign for the amount taken away and indicate deadlines; if these were not met, or if garments were soiled, they risked being fined. Invariably, one girl per household signed up for the work; she was helped by younger siblings who 'finished' the shirts by sewing buttonholes. Girls began 'finishing' as young as six years old and began machine work as soon as they could work the treadles. Help obtained at home made the representative girl appear more industrious and reliable to agents, which in turn strengthened her reputation and ensured more work in the long term. Shirts were mainly hand-sewn, but some girls were fortunate enough to acquire machines at cost price. The 'Singer' normally retailed at £7 7s., on a loan system for 1s. 3d. a week, but to comfortably make repayments and receive a decent wage the girls would have to work all hours; it was estimated that it took sixty hours to complete three dozen shirts by machine.[52] Despite the unfair system of fines, shirt-making was always paid in cash; it was well established in Donegal and did not extend southwards. Even if the board could own or compete with this private enterprise, it had little hope for success against the Derry factories that had a monopoly of the existing markets and an estimated annual wage expenditure of £900,000 in 1900.[53] Due to a lack of funds, the only effort the board could make to aid the girls was to provide technical-instruction classes, and this was not undertaken until 1893 when a sum of £50 was paid to teach girls in Ballyshannon how to operate sewing machines. Legal restrictions prohibited the board from undertaking other direct initiatives in the shirt-making industry.[54]

Apart from shirt-making, a few other woollen-based clothing industries survived; the linen industry had almost disappeared by this stage. Wool, the basic raw material for the carding, weaving and knitting industries, was widely available and cheap in the congested counties. Farms in the congested districts had on average only two sheep; shearings were either used domestically or sold in a raw state. At this stage, cottage-based spinning and weaving operations could no longer compete with the speed of the large-scale industrial looms, and the inhabitants of the congested districts chose the cheaper and more convenient option of sending the wool away. Sheep were shorn twice a year and the value of wool had decreased to a meagre 7d. a pound or 5s. an animal. In the northern districts, it was sent in its crude state to factories in Convoy or Lisbellaw in exchange for cloth, this being usually organized through an agent or the local shopkeeper: 'every 9 lb of clean wool sent 7 yards of material (sufficient for a suit) are returned to the sender, who then pays the reduced price per yard stated on the pattern selected'.[55] Farmers still carded wool in areas where the pro-

---

52 Ibid. **53** Rolleston, 'The Derry shirt-making industry', pp 418–20. **54** CDB, Second annual report, 1893, p. 28. **55** Gaskell, *Levally*, p. 4.

duction of woollen goods (for sale) was still feasible and bought locally. However, it was noted that those who still engaged in carding and spinning were from mountainous regions where the land and the people were poor. Occupants of good land had a higher standard of living and would not work for the miserable returns from carding and spinning.

Although carding and spinning had declined, knitting was still an important home industry in the western and southern congested counties. Sales of knitted goods were declining rapidly, but the craft had survived due to home consumption and a limited local market (socks, petticoats, gloves and stockings being the only items made or purchased). People preferred to buy their outer garments from 'Cheap Jacks', or itinerant vendors of second-hand clothes, who set up stalls at fairs and markets. Migrants bought their clothes in Scotland.[56] In more prosperous areas, clothes were bought on credit in drapery shops that circulated fashionable items from Belfast. This posed a problem for men in Kiltyclogher, whose fashion-conscious wives and daughters secretly ran up bills.[57] In the early 1890s socks were sold from 6*d*. to 8*d*. a pair in Newport and Westport, and local women felt it was hardly worth the effort for that price. A certain amount of work was put out by a few firms in Donegal: Messrs H. McDevitt, B. McDevitt, McGeehan, Gallagher, Kennedy and Pearson. In total 3,600 families were employed. H. McDevitt was the only firm that paid solely in cash, B. McDevitt and Mr McGeehan paid in both cash and kind; the rest paid completely in kind, which meant heavy losses for the people. Knitwear factories bought the wool and paid for the carding and spinning; yarn was then given to agencies that found women to knit the gloves and socks. Agents were usually the local shopkeepers who often abused the payment in kind system, by not giving the full amount in goods. Although the board tried to abolish this system of payment, it could not succeed without the full co-operation of the people, who evidently feared the powerful local shopkeeper. When Inspector Lucy Deane was sent to Donegal in October 1897 to monitor the workings of the 1896 Truck Act (which protected the worker and outlawed the system of fines and payment in kind, specifically in factories), she found it very difficult to find people brave enough to testify against the gombeenman/ shopkeeper.[58]

Technical instruction was also provided in areas where knitting skills were unknown or where the industry was weak. In 1892 the board sanctioned an annual grant of £52 to provide a teacher in Carraroe to instruct the women in the use of knitting machines. From the outset the function of the board in relation to knitting was that of educator and facilitator but its long-term impact was

---

[56] See Glenties, Grange, Rathhill, Knockadaff, Ardnaree and Partry baseline reports; M. Dunleavy, *Dress in Ireland* (1989), pp 163–7. [57] Gaskell, *Kiltyclogher*, p. 7. [58] M.D. McFeely, *Lady inspectors*, pp 78–86.

that it helped the industry to evolve from the basic production of socks and gloves to a wider range of goods such as golf coats and jackets. The demand for knitted golf coats increased in 1911. Machine-knit coats were preferred but hand-knits were still acceptable. Produce was not sold through the board's agents or teachers, but they were bought for satisfactory prices by commercial firms.[59] As the girls were paid directly, the figures never passed through the board's books, nor did the board or its officials know them. The board sporadically appointed teachers on a temporary basis to give instruction in districts where employers and workers wanted to start new kinds of knitting. At Keel in Achill Island, Co. Mayo, assistance of this kind was given in 1914 and the class earned £510 during its first year of work.[60]

While it was not a primary industry, lace-making in the congested districts became very successful. In fact, the industry does not feature in the baseline reports because the main market for Irish lace and embroidery was America, and the McKinley tariff, introduced in 1890, almost destroyed the embroidery industry in the congested districts because it increased the import tax. Prior to this, a lower one existed but 'with rings, corporations, "trusts" and similar corporations of capitalists, the prices to the consumer were screwed up to the point at which the foreigner could not sell his goods in America with profit'.[61] In consultation with the IIDA, the board began crochet and lace classes in Sligo, Donegal and Leitrim in 1894. They expanded rapidly and by 1900 there were twenty-seven classes run regularly, with an average of thirty students per class. Initially wages were low, so a bonus system was used to encourage the girls to stay in the industry while they were training. Bonuses were continued and administered on a scale of loyalty and experience. A bonus of 1s. was given to all girls who attended less than 150 classes if they produced goods to the value of 3s. a week, those who attended over 150 received a 1s. bonus if they earned 5s. 6d. a week and girls who had attended 300 classes had to produce goods to the value of 7s. to get the bonus. Produce from these classes was sold mainly to the Irish Lace Depot, Grafton Street, Dublin, which acted as a facilitator and found markets in Britain (which imported large quantities of lace to the value of over one million sterling in 1896).[62] In 1897 there was a fall-off in the market for Irish tweed but the crochet and lace industries were thriving. Gross earnings of the classes were nearly £4,814 in 1899, twice the amount earned in the previous year, and the depot sent a cheque for £124 out of its profits to be divided among the girls.[63] Those who weathered the initial poor wages and limited incentives were eventually rewarded when Irish crochet and lace gained

---

59 CDB, Twentieth annual report, 1912, pp 28–9. **60** CDB, Twenty-second annual report, 1914, pp 18–19. **61** *Freeman's Journal,* 29 September 1890. **62** CDB, Seventh annual report, 1898, pp 33–4. **63** CDB, Ninth annual report, 1900, p. 23.

international prestige. The tweed industry picked up again in the early 1900s; because of CDB support the tradition did not die out completely in the slack periods, and in 1908 homespun workers in South Donegal alone earned over £11,000. In those days homespun was sold from boxes or benches on the public street at the local monthly fairs at Ardara and Carrick, but if it rained the market was ruined. The board provided money to build a market-house, known as 'The Mart', at Ardara, which was officially opened by Cardinal O'Donnell in 1912. The building was also used for measuring, inspecting and storing.[64] By 1913 the monthly fairs at Ardara and Carrick in South Donegal were recording an increase in sales of home-woven tweeds but the tweed industry was more organized in the northern districts due to the existence of a supportive friendly society. A society member, Mrs Kennedy, circulated information leaflets to the local spinners and weavers to ensure they were familiar with current patterns and dyes.[65] The existence of the society ensured that all the tweed was sold at fair prices.[66]

By the turn of the century, the board had facilitated many industrial projects in the congested counties. Samples of lace, crochet, hosiery, basketwork and Donegal carpets were sent to the viceregal lodge in the Phoenix Park for the royal visit in April 1900. In a letter from Colonel Arthur Bigge, the board learned that the queen 'was greatly pleased to see these proofs of the evident admirable results of the endeavours of the board' and that she made several purchases from the exhibits.[67] The lace industry was extended in 1902 when curtain factories were started at Carraroe and Gorumna Island. The board employed one German and two French instructresses to teach the girls a very specific style of Renaissance lace curtains. Pupils were trained to teach so that they could start new centres elsewhere.[68] Fair progress was made in the first year and there was a good demand for the curtains, which were sold through Mortons, an English-based firm, which also exhibited and facilitated the sale of Donegal carpets. Mortons had opened the first Donegal carpet factory in 1898, and in 1905 they proposed to build two more factories in the Rosses in Donegal employing between 150 and 200. They received a loan from the CDB on the strength of their success in the other Donegal factories at Killybegs and Kilcar.[69] Because the company guaranteed when the industry first started that the board would not suffer any financial loss, it had no rights to audit or examine internal records of the carpet factories. Again the board was not aware of what wages the girls earned.[70]

Lace and crochet industries enjoyed continued success because there was a steady demand for appliqué and Limerick lace from 1903 to 1907 as trim-

---

[64] McGill, 'The Irish woollen industry' (1902), p. 179. [65] CDB, Twenty-second annual report, 1914, p. 20. [66] CDB, Twenty-third annual report, 1915, p. 23. [67] CDB, Tenth annual report, 1901, p. 47. [68] CDB, Twelfth annual report, 1903, p. 36. [69] CDB, Fourteenth annual report, 1905, p. 34. [70] CDB, Twenty-second annual report, 1914, pp 19–20.

mings for dresses. It was noted in 1903 that progress was hindered and production stunted in home industries because the best workers saved money and emigrated, lace industry workers in particular. As a result, the demands of Paris and New York wholesalers, the main customers, were not met. Home industries also suffered through the irregular and unpunctual habits of workers, which led to delays, unfilled orders and the subsequent failure of this trade to expand. In 1905 the turnover of the industry classes, exclusive of sales made by workers direct to local buyers, was £12,000. The board believed that it would have been considerably more but for absenteeism, and blamed poor school attendance in early life for the bad time-keeping.[71] The success of the Irish lace industry hinged on international fashion trends, which incidentally created a huge demand for crochet in 1906. In spite of the 'irregular attendance and the want of steady industrial habits', total receipts in 1905/6 amounted to £21,573. That year the value of classes in seven districts of northwest Mayo exceeded the total poor law valuation.[72] By 1906 Irish lace had gained such an international reputation that the board proposed that all producers adopt a recognized stamp to guarantee the authenticity of the articles. It noted a growing practice of inferior-quality counterfeits being sold as Irish.[73] Prices were paid in accordance with quality, the more intricate the design the higher the price, and this should have acted as an incentive for girls to keep up with modern fashion trends. Despite its efforts, the board found that the girls were too lazy to learn new crochet designs, guipure in particular, and this jeopardized the reputation of the industry. Crochet patterns were difficult to learn and time-consuming. The girls were unwilling and slow to change to patterns that they could not produce with expert speed, and unfortunately earnings were production based.

In November 1898 the board extended its technical instruction to include the role of women in the home. It conducted domestic economy classes to educate the women in cookery, laundry, housewifery and dressmaking. Courses continued for four months and at the end the girls received a certificate.[74] It is apparent from the course outline that the ultimate aim of the classes was to provide training for young girls planning to enter domestic service outside the congested districts because employment of this kind was limited in the west (see appendix C for a breakdown of areas girls were trained in). While the board did not discriminate against 'grown girls' or married women, it preferred a realistic approach to employment in the sector; therefore spaces in these classes were granted to young girls. Older women were at a disadvantage in the job market: Breen notes that there was little incentive for employers to give jobs to older

---

71 CDB, Fourteenth annual report, 1905, pp 33–4. 72 CDB, Fifteenth annual report, 1906, p. 26. 73 Ibid., pp 25–6. 74 CDB, Twentieth annual report, 1912, pp 30–1. 75 R. Breen, 'Farm servanthood in Ireland, 1900–40' (1983), pp 88–102. For an account of servanthood in urban Ireland

servants at higher wages when there was an abundance of girls available.[75] Interest in domestic training classes was so high that the board had to further extend operations by employing Irish-speaking instructresses for Gaeltacht areas.[76] Sixteen of the girls attending the course at Sneem, Co. Kerry, lived an average distance of four miles from the classroom and some walked over nine miles a day for four months during the winter.[77] Another girl, who walked sixteen miles a day, managed to attend 72 out of a total 81 course days. Demands for trained domestic servants in Ireland surpassed the supply because the young women emigrated as soon as they completed training. Higher wages and better conditions were available abroad in the early 1900s and the inspectors noted that people of the west were more inclined to go to America than to seek employment in Ireland. In fact, at the turn of the century most Irish newspapers were advertising assisted emigration packages for Irish domestic servants to colonial destinations. Institutions such as the IAOS, the Department of Agriculture and Technical Instruction and the United Irishwomen supplemented CDB efforts in relation to female industries; the United Irishwomen founded in 1911, aimed to reconstruct rural life specifically using the traditional role of women.[78] The board began co-operating with 'the United Irishwomen in giving practical house-to-house instruction to women in their own homes in household management.'[79] When the DATI was founded in 1899, it was decreed that the board would continue to bear the cost of aiding industrial classes in the congested districts and if the department decided to start classes in neighbouring non-congested areas it would have to meet the entire cost.[80] In time, the DATI aided these classes but condemned them as being 'a plaster on the sore' used to compensate areas that complained of unjust treatment by both the board and the department.[81] The board had very different views, believing it was wiser to start home industries in poorer areas where the women were more inclined to make a concerted effort to make an industry self-sufficient. The board was especially proud of the progress made in relation to domestic training and the immediate impact it had on the homes. When the department suggested that the responsibility for domestic economy classes should be transferred to it in 1914 (but the payment of teachers' salaries should still come from CDB funds), the board was unwilling to transfer this duty unless it had a firm guarantee that they

---

see M. Hearn, 'Life for domestic servants in Dublin' (1990), pp 148–80. **76** Gaeltachts are indigenous Gaelic-speaking regions. **77** CDB, Tenth annual report, 1901, p. 45. **78** H. Plunkett, 'The United Irishwomen' (reprinted 1986), p. 25. While Plunkett contended that the United Irishwomen was not a branch of the IAOS but had 'come in to complete our work at the point where we believe it to be at once the most important and the most perfect'. **79** CDB, Twenty-third annual report, 1915, p. 20. **80** CDB, Tenth annual report, 1901, pp 44–5. **81** G.W. Russell, 'How not to start rural industry' (1909).

would be continued. The DATI could not guarantee their continuity so the classes subsequently remained under the auspices of the board.

Lace and crochet industries began to decline in 1912, due in part to changes in fashion, Austrian competition and a lull in the American market. By then, Irish workers were keen to adopt new methods, but the fickle nature of the fashion industry was a disincentive for the board to invest in machines. Ironically the reputation of well-finished Irish lace was so high it meant that handmade lace would always have a market. The countess Dudley, a philanthropist and wife of the then lord lieutenant, took an interest in the lace curtain industry and promoted it among her friends, who sent considerable orders to Mortons or its agents. But the outbreak of war marked the end of luxury purchases, and the fashion industry no longer required a high volume of lace and crochet. Attendance at the lace-making classes fell because the girls found higher wages knitting, using colourful, embroidered stitching which had become the latest fashion trimming. When the earnings dropped to £11, 680 during 1914–15, the running of 33 classes became uneconomical and the board shut them down. The key to the success of the lace and crochet industries was the intense attention it received from the board, but the board neglected the further development of other industries. From this the board realized the dangers in relying too heavily on any one industry and concentrated on developing various new ones. Mr Gilbert Phelan, the inspector of industries, tried to anticipate demands from his knowledge of the fashion industry.[82] Using the base locations of the lace and crochet classes, the board began new endeavours and was fortunate enough to receive a contract for knitted goods from the Naval Office during the war; again the value of this work is unknown as these wages did not pass through the board's accounts. Earnings in the female industrial classes increased during wartime in the absence of foreign competition, and in 1917 Irish crochet was fashionable again. The lace industry was dwindling, but button making was proving a reliable source of income.[83]

In stark contrast with the intense manner in which the board concentrated on female industry, relatively few measures were taken to aid male industries. This is partly due to the fact that the board could not compete with private enterprise but mainly due to the fact that it was forced to develop pre-existing industries; few of which were male-dominated. All the baseline reports and the Mansion House reports of 1879 indicate that, judging by the class of furniture in houses, the men were incapable of woodwork, and carpentry was not a traditional industry in the congested districts. A survey of all the CDB records show that outside of agriculture and fisheries only a few measures were taken

[82] CDB, Twenty-second annual report, 1914, pp 18–20. [83] CDB, Twenty-fifth annual report, 1917, pp 18–19.

to develop male industries. Carpentry classes are mentioned in the first annual report when a grant of £20 was given to provide classes for boys in Cashel National School, Co. Galway. The same year, barrel making or cooperages were started to facilitate the cured fish trade, but only minor efforts were made to enhance other industries for men such as carpentry and basket making.[84] In 1894, the board indicated how it still provided classes at Carna in conjunction with the Board of National Education. By 1914, only three carpentry instructors were employed in what was then termed 'manual instruction'. These classes taught young men how to make rough household furniture and farm implements and how to carry out simple repairs on timberwork.[85] During the war years, these classes ceased and toy-making classes began in Galway for boys.[86] Following the war, there was a demand for furniture, and the board sent a carpentry instructor to make the necessary furniture with the aid of local boys in Galway. The board sold the furniture (bedsteads, tables, chairs, dressers and chests), at a shop it opened in Galway, at cost price of materials, and when general income levels increased the board found it impossible to supply all the demands promptly.[87]

To minimize costs in the fishing industry and provide practical training for local men, the board endeavoured to manufacture necessary fishing equipment at home. Boat building was started in the industrial schools via CDB grants. Local carpenters and boat-builders were commissioned under the instruction of a Scottish shipwright to build Zulus at Carna and Roundstone, Co. Galway, in 1897 with the object of producing a boat for less than the cost of buying it abroad. The board bought wood superior to that normally used by local builders and the boats cost £220 to build, excluding the shipwright's salary. It was decided that the industry was economically viable because of the employment it created and savings made on delivery costs (£14 to deliver a boat from the Isle of Man, Co. Down or Co. Wicklow and £40 from Scotland).[88] As much as possible, centres were founded in areas where there was a tradition of boat building or where there were pre-existing industrial schools such as Baltimore and Killybegs.[89] The industrial schools received grant aid from the board, and by

---

84 CDB, Fifth annual report, 1896, p. 23. Only one CDB-sponsored industry failed completely. It was an experimental 'straw bottle envelope factory'. A local committee started the factory in Kiltyclogher, Co. Leitrim, with a £200 loan from the board. Wheaten straw, the basic raw material, was not grown locally; the managing committee decided after a year that it could not be profitably run and the board was refunded. The other marginal failure was in 1904 when the board began an experimental floor mat factory in Glenbeigh, Co. Kerry, supplying four handlooms specially made for this work. The sale of mats was not monitored but the board's investment was put to great use after as a base for instruction in weaving. **85** CDB, Twenty-second annual report, 1914, p. 20. **86** CDB, Twenty-fifth annual report, 1917, p. 20. **87** CDB, Twenty-seventh annual report, 1919, p. 10. **88** CDB, Seventh annual report, 1898, p. 31. **89** CDB, Tenth annual report, 1901, p. 42.

the turn of the century some centres were taken over by private enterprise. By March 1902, the CDB yards had produced 26 decked fishing boats, 18 nobbies (a style of decked boat), and 8 Zulus.[90]

To reduce costs in the cured fish industry, cooperages were founded at various locations such as Teelin and at Burtonport to make barrels for the cured mackerel and herring industry and to train young men in barrel making. Prior to this, barrels were mainly imported from Scotland. For example, the Cork/Kerry region imported almost 100,000 Scottish or English barrels a year for the pickled mackerel trade. The Northern cooperages were run directly by the board and even made slight profits, but the main objective was to train coopers. Barrel-making equipment was not readily available in Ireland; both wood and iron were brought to the assembling points by the CDB vessel, the *Granuaile*. By 1897 the Teelin and Burtonport factories were thriving, with demand exceeding output and good quality barrels made either 3*s*. 6*d*. or 4*s*. each. The board was not concerned with making a large-scale industry out of the cooperages. It was still limited by statute in relation to competition with private enterprise, so in areas where small independent cooperages were in competition with the CDB, it charged more for barrels in order to give competitors a head start.[91] In the Cork and Kerry region, the cured fish industry operated more independently of the board than the northern areas but the board still provided subtle support for the south. The board's efforts in relation to curing stations and cooperages in the south was minimal but it brought eight coopers from Kerry to Teelin in 1898 for training. They received a wage of 15*s*. per week and the board covered their travelling expenses.[92] In the southern districts the board gave loans to the coopers to buy the material and ensured that local dealers stocked the requisites. For example, McCowens of Tralee assisted the local barrel-makers by importing the staves, headings and hoops, and the board provided loans to Kerry coopers to buy the equipment.[93]

Despite intermittent successes at later stages the CDB technical instruction classes for men were not as successful as female classes. Unfortunately no follow-up reports were conducted when the board was dissolved in 1923, but the twenty-seventh annual report conducted a regional analysis of the poorer regions in Mayo for *The Times* special Irish supplement.[94] This report incorporated a comparative study of Erris, Lettermore, Swinford and Glencolumbkille in 1891 and in 1919. Lee argues that the board's methods of locating industry in these

---

[90] CDB, Eleventh annual report, 1902, p. 37.   [91] CDB, Nineteenth annual report, 1911, p. 38.
[92] CDB, Seventh annual report, 1898, p. 32.   [93] CDB, Twentieth annual report, 1912, p. 27. The board hoped to lend money to a local entrepreneur to undertake the running of a cooperage in the South but the only proposal received was from a local fish-curer; negotiations were unsuccessful on the grounds that a fish-curer would only make enough to suit his own requirements.   [94] *The Times*, 4 November, 1919.

remotest areas were ludicrous, but evidence from the report referred to shows that the opposite was true.[95] These areas were deemed the poorest and, as Tuke commented, Erris was 'the culminating point of man's physical degradation'.[96] The inhabitants became destitute when the potato crop failed and every year had to rely on government relief or charity when potato supplies ran out.[97] In 1891 the people in the parish of Pulathomas handled the least money and were the poorest inhabitants in the congested district. A total of 528 families or 3,052 persons were in poverty in the parish, and half of them were destitute. In Pulathomas, few opportunities had existed for male employment, but lace and crochet making, established by the board, provided a wage of a pound a week to each girl. The board distributed thread and yarn; the work was carried out in the girls' homes; the finishing and packing was done at the school; and the produce was sold through the board's teacher. As a result of CDB help, the quantity of homegrown food doubled, living standards rose far above the bare subsistence levels of 1891 and through the development of female enterprises, which generated a cash income, the cycle of debt was broken. That the CDB instructors marketed both agricultural produce and textiles helped to enforce a fair system for textile workers and eliminated the role of the gombeenman in the process. Because women received cash payments, the board set a precedent that enabled women to realize the full monetary value of their work. In turn, this allowed families in the congested districts to engage in the widening cash economy.[98] Consequently one of the board's greatest achievements was ending the truck system of payment for textiles.

Limited funding and legal constraints confined the board in its industrial development and forced it to use pre-existing structures and skills in the various industries. Bourke insists that home industries enhanced by the CDB, the co-operatives and the DATI intended to mould the west into an idyllic Irish rural community. It was not within the means of any of these groups to begin any new industries on a wide scale and she fails to acknowledge the extent of pre-established home industries that are well documented in the baseline reports and in the various preliminary investigations of the IIDA.[99] Bourke uses the annual reports very selectively, stating that 'receipts from home industries increased more slowly than expenditure. In 1904, and drastically in 1906, it was forced to cut expenditure on home industries.'[1] Expenditure was cut when industries became unfruitful and the board economized when giving loans to individuals who had very little collateral to offer as security, but between 1900 and

---

95 J. Lee, *The modernisation of Irish society, 1848–1918* (1979), p. 125.   **96** CDB, Twenty-seventh annual report, 1920, pp 6–7.   **97** Ibid., p. 6. For a more detailed account of life in Erris, see S. Ní Eineacháin, 'The Congested Districts Board in Erris, Co. Mayo – Part 1' (2000), pp 90–117.   **98** CDB, Twenty-seventh annual report, 1920, p. 10.   **99** Bourke, *Husbandry to housewifery*, pp 112–36.   **1** Ibid., p. 121.

1905 varying sums of money, as high as £880, were lent to 290 individuals to buy spinning wheels, improved looms, knitting machines and carpentry tools for the board's manual instruction classes.[2]

Contrary to what Bourke implies, incomes did surpass expenditure. While it is very true that receipts increased slowly, this was something the board had anticipated. It was also noted that female earnings were 'more prudently spent than the earnings of men in such employments as fishing. It is true that a small portion is spent on personal finery, but not to any extravagant or reprehensible extent.'[3] During the year 1919/20, £111,802 was paid to women for work done at the board's female industrial classes in comparison with £80,359 paid in the previous year. In Donegal, payments by commercial firms and co-operative societies exceeded the payments made at the board's classes.[4] Technical instruction classes were a fundamental element of altering life in the congests, but in spite of relative success the CDB classes never became self-supporting and could not even contribute toward the teachers' salaries. Bourke misinterprets the basic object of the board; it was not a capitalist institution; it was more concerned with raising living standards and improving overall social conditions, and it succeeded in its endeavour by using the traditional role of women in the west. She also fails to observe the fact that income from technical instruction was re-invested in modernizing equipment and therefore not declared as a profit. CDB classes gave women a cash income, which made them more aware of the value of their work, an important factor in abolishing payment in kind and in raising morale.

[2] CDB, Fifteenth annual report, 1906, p. 27. [3] CDB, Twentieth annual report, 1912, pp 28–9. [4] CDB, Twenty-eight annual report, 1919–20, p. 14.

3

Maritime industries

'It has been estimated on excellent authority that an acre of the best land will produce in the year one ton of corn or three cwt. of meat; the same area of good fishing ground will produce the same weight of food in a week.'[1] This was an internationally, well-accepted hypothesis from at least the early 1800s, but Ireland had a poor representation of full-time fishermen compared to other European countries. Evidence of foreign interest in the fishing rights of Irish territorial waters as early as the fifteenth century shows that they were rich fishing grounds, but at the close of the nineteenth century fishing was a supplementary income to agriculture, even though the sea was a more fruitful provider than the land.[2] The baseline survey found that there was no domestic or, what is also referred to as a 'natural' market for fish; it was a marginal food source, having gradually disappeared from the Irish diet. Fish was an important component of the Irish diet at one stage and Louis Cullen argues that, in the early nineteenth century, when food purchases became a symbol of social status that fish had no commercial outlet. He also claims that shellfish was the least valued of all fish and eaten only by the poorest people.[3] Indeed, Aogáin Ó Rathaille, the seventeenth-century Gaelic poet, accounts for his own consumption of shellfish as a symbol of his reduction to abject poverty.[4] The reasons for the displacement of fish as a valuable food source are deeply rooted in prohibitive legislation that began as early as 1535, when it became mandatory for all vessels fishing in Irish waters to pay a duty and register in the customs books. This law was rigidly enforced, and the expense involved in the industry along with high taxes deterred Irish participation on a commercial level.[5]

---

1 Revd C. Davis, *Deep sea fisheries of Ireland* (1886), p. 9. **2** A.E.J. Went, 'Foreign fishing fleets along the Irish coasts' (1949), pp 17–24. As early as 1306 a Scottish vessel was seized off the Irish coast for illegal fishing. An act was passed in 1465 to prohibit the large numbers of Dutch and Spanish crews fishing in Irish waters. **3** L.M. Cullen, 'Population growth and diet' (1981), p. 96. **4** D. Corkery, *The hidden Ireland* (1977), p. 178. **5** Went, 'Foreign fishing fleets along the Irish coasts' (1949), pp 17–24. The 1465 act was not enforced or obeyed fully but a 1535 act made it mandatory for all ships to pay revenues to the crown: 13*s*. 4*d*. for vessels of twelve tons or more and 2*s*. for smaller vessels. King Philip II of Spain paid a royalty of £1,000 in 1553 to the Irish

Salt taxes introduced in the early eighteenth century had a major impact on the value of Irish fish and also played a part in the decline of the industry. In the late seventeenth century, salted herring was an important element of the peasant diet, and Ludlow highlights that domestic consumption of salted herring was higher than exports. Dungarvan was the only Irish centre where salt was extracted from sea water but to comply with new regulations, salt had to be refined from rock sources, and this type was imported mainly from Portugal. Salt was required as a preservative for food, so the duty had severe repercussions for the poorer classes, who were unable to cure meat and fish for home consumption (eating incorrectly, cured fish and meat was unsafe and caused stomach trouble and, in extreme cases, violent nausea). The extra expense of salt taxes placed a strain on small curing operations that bought less salt and produced less cured foods. These taxes were repealed in 1722. Ludlow asserts that the duties did not cause any overall damage to the industry, but they did cause a thirteen-year absence of salted fish from the peasant diet and thus the habit of eating fish was broken.[6]

Throughout the eighteenth century, men from the east coast of Ireland participated to some degree in the commercial fisheries, but the industry did not emerge on a commercial footing along the west coast. Boats remained small and catches were primarily for home consumption. John F. Burke, a nineteenth-century economist, argued that the decline in the Irish fishing industry during the 1790s could be attributed to the political and agrarian unrest. He believed that rumours of a French invasion caused many to abandon the fisheries in favour of the political movement, which coincided with unfruitful fishing seasons. Burke used herring export figures to support his claim; the average annual value of which was £22,000 in 1781–9 but only amounted to £3,000 in 1790–8. He also highlighted that this was not a reflection of a decrease in the domestic demand for fish, for Irish herring imports rose from £11,500 to £61,000 in the same period.[7] In an attempt to revive the Irish industry at the beginning of the nineteenth century, the government introduced a bounty system. The scheme, which had limited success, encouraged fishermen to modernize equipment and

---

treasury for permission to fish off the north coast of Ireland for a term of twenty-one years. During that term Sir Humphrey Gilbert reported to the queen that 600 Spanish fishing vessels availed of the opportunity to fish, using Baltimore and the Blaskets as centres for the industry. He also mentions Spanish complaints of cables being cut by the natives. In the reign of Charles I the Dutch were granted fishing rights in Irish waters for the sum of £30,000, and in 1650 Sweden was granted the same rights and under the same conditions. By the eighteenth century England had imposed a series of bounties on fish taken from Irish waters and offices were built to centralize the collection of these dues. See also W.S Green, 'The sea fisheries of Ireland' (1902), p. 370. **6** C.G. Ludlow, 'A history of salt in Ireland' (1993), pp 173–4. **7** J.F. Burke, *Outlines of the industrial history of Ireland* (n.d.), p. 141.

buy bigger boats to sustain large catches, and the number of men fishing increased from 36,159 in 1820 to 64,771 in 1829. At this stage, the Irish commercial fisheries were owned by, and involved, fishermen from the east, who travelled in large vessels to the west coast of Ireland (where fish was more abundant) and gained maximum benefits from the bounty system. In essence, the bounty system did not apply to those who used small canoes, so the era of bounties further displaced fishermen from the west. Generally speaking, the bounties had a transient effect on the industry, the total payment amounted to £87,989. However, the bounties were counter-productive they caused price inflation; they created an artificial market that collapsed when the bounties ceased in 1829 and ultimately caused the commercial value of fish to plummet.[8]

Clarkson's independent analysis of Irish diet in the early nineteenth century shows that while the Irish ate more fish than the English, they purchased twice as much meat as fish, indicating that, by then, fish had declined in popularity.[9] Clarkson and Crawford attempt to cover the history of fish consumption in Ireland but deal with it very briefly; they conclude that, while fish consumption in Ireland was always low, fish was eaten more than meat or bacon. Indeed, the extent to which fish was consumed cannot be fully ascertained because of haphazard market facilities and the lack of evidence.[10] However, there is enough alternative data to show that in general, the dietary habits of the Irish peasant changed in the early part of the century, shifting from meat and fish to vegetarian.[11] For example, the workhouse diet was predominantly vegetarian and did not include fish.[12] This pattern comes into alignment with other European, peasant societies that were moving away from natural markets in order to participate in the increasing cash economy.

John de Courcy Ireland attests that, by the time the famine occurred, the taste for eating fish had ceased to exist; to support his claim he draws an analogy between Ireland in famine times and contemporary experiences of United Nations' agencies in famine-stricken areas; 'it is very difficult to induce an unlettered populace suddenly to alter its diet even to save its life'.[13] According to evidence from the commissioners of the Board of Works, responsible for Irish

---

8 Green, 'Sea fisheries,' p. 372.   9 Clarkson, 'The modernisation of the Irish diet' (1999), pp 32–45.   10 Browne, 'The ethnography of Inisboffin and Inishshark' (1898–1900), cited in Clarkson and Crawford, *Feast and famine: a history of food and nutrition in Ireland, 1500–1920* (2001), p. 234. They mention Charles Browne's observations of Inishbofin and Inishshark where he links the prevalence of rheumatoid and bronchial disease with the 'extent to which fish and potatoes enter their dietary', but offer no evidence to support his claim.   11 Clarkson and Crawford, *Feast and famine*, p. 106. They refer to other data on fish consumption found in poor law union records that pertain to workhouse diets and a few urban studies that show the consumption of herrings.   12 J. O'Connor, *The workhouses of Ireland: the fate of Ireland's poor* (1995), p. 101.   13 J. de Courcy Ireland, *Ireland's sea fisheries: a history* (1981), p. 49.

fisheries in autumn 1846, when 'impending famine was certain and deaths from starvation had occurred, large supplies of fish were allowed to rot on the shore or were spread on the adjacent fields as manure'. Commissioners of Public Works reported in 1847 that country people would not eat fish without potatoes.[14] Numbers engaged in the fisheries had been in steady decline since 1829, and the famine both accelerated and intensified this trend. People sold fishing gear, and in some cases vessels, to buy food.[15] Following the famine, extreme poverty 'led to boats being sold or left unrepaired, equipment neglected, and Atlantic coast fishing villages decimated; as emigration continued, the number of boats and men diminished steadily'.[16]

Grimshaw notes that the Irish industry declined steadily and persistently during the thirty-year period 1861–90. The numbers fishing halved from 45,839 to 22,384 by 1885. Both during and after the famine a significant number of Irish fishermen emigrated, notable numbers of fishermen from Dungarvan went to America and Newfoundland where they 'introduced the system of long line fishing, which has ever since been practised'.[17] During the same period, English and Scottish fisheries were thriving; the cruel irony was that their success hinged, to a large degree, on the fruits of Irish waters. In 1875 Irish boats accounted for only 29 per cent of the total number at work in Irish waters; these vessels were privately owned by individuals, small groups and most operated on a part-time basis. On the whole, Irish fishermen were disheartened with the condition of the fisheries, which could not compete efficiently with the rest of the British Isles, and as a result many emigrated (see table 3.1). Incidentally, this system was later re-introduced by the CDB into the west through the instruction of Scottish fishermen. Although emigration played a significant role in the declining numbers, those who left the west were not full-time fishermen. Holdsworth, a contemporary expert, commented that fishermen from the west 'belong to the class who only fish occasionally, when seaweed-cutting, farming, and other occupations fail them'.[18] He also observed the paucity of equipment and lack of market 'in very many cases when fish appear on the coast, these men have few means of catching them, and when fortune favours the fishermen, there is frequently no way of disposing of their catch to their advantage'.[19]

Fishing as an occupation could not earn parity with farming in Ireland despite the fact that in many respects, with adequate, well-administered funding, the fisheries had a better chance of solving the poverty problem than farm-

14 RCCI, Fourth Report, Appendix I, 1907. **15** Davis, *Deep sea fisheries of Ireland*, p. 20. **16** Gribbon, 'Economic and social history, 1850–1921' (1996) p. 287. **17** Green, 'Sea fisheries', p. 373. **18** E.W.H. Holdsworth, *The sea fisheries of Great Britain and Ireland: an account of the practical working of the various fisheries around the British Islands* (1883). p. 191. See also J.C. Bloomfield, *The fisheries of Ireland* (1883). **19** Holdsworth, *The sea fisheries of Great Britain and Ireland*, p. 5.

ing. Irish politicians devoted practically all of their time to land issues to the detriment of industry; indeed, attempted fishery revivals in the late nineteenth century coincided with events of the land question, which dominated the public consciousness. Irish fisheries remained the 'Cinderella of Irish industries', due to inconsistent government support: aid given in 1819 was reduced in 1824 and eliminated in 1830; seven fish-curing houses built in 1847–8 were closed in 1850, just as they were beginning to be efficient.[20] In 1849 a select committee reported on the fisheries but nothing came of their findings, in 1852 a Donegal MP, devised and introduced a fisheries bill, which received huge support in Parliament but failed to become law. In 1864 Mr John A. Blake MP endeavoured to implement another fisheries bill but it was withdrawn in favour of a different bill that was made law in 1869.[21] Articles appeared frequently in the *Irish Builder* regarding the poor state of the fisheries and the extent to which Ireland trailed behind the rest of the United Kingdom.[22] At the end of the nineteenth century, the cured fish figures from the Isle of Man was four times the Irish quantity and most, if not all, of the fish was taken from Irish coastal waters. Evidence exists to support the claim that most fish sold in Irish markets was caught in Irish waters by Manx fishermen, who sold it to British curers who in turn sold it to the Irish market.[23]

Table 3.1. Numbers engaged in fishing (Ireland)

Period	*Vessels and boats*	*Men and boys*
1861–65	10,713	45,839
1866–70	9,265	39,274
1871–75	7,472	29,126
1876–80	5,880	22,126
1881–85	5,968	22,384

Source: T.W. Grimshaw, *Facts and figures about Ireland, part one* (1893), p. 39.

To ameliorate circumstances, three inspectors were appointed under the 1869 Fisheries Act to deal with the Irish industry; but according to Davis, their time was spent making rules for salmon fisheries and had no influence on the deep-sea fisheries. They had no public money to spend on the industry until 1874, when Isaac Butt, leader of the Irish Parliamentary Party (IPP), managed

---

[20] Gribbon, 'Economic and social history' p. 287. [21] Davis, *Deep sea fisheries of Ireland,* p. 20. [22] *Irish Builder,* 15 February 1876, p. 54. [23] Burke, *Outlines of the industrial history of Ireland,* p. 329.

to secure the Irish loan reproductive fund for the improvement of the Irish fishing industry. This fund amounted to £43,000 and a further sum of £30,000, the remnant of a fund in the hands of the Society for Bettering the Condition of the Irish Poor (SBCIP), an English charity founded during the famine of 1822, was also placed at the disposal of the inspectors to provide loans to all Irish fishermen for building boats and buying gear.[24] The industry was so disjointed that the money was wasted away; for example, harbour construction (a crucial stage of development) was under the supervision of the Board of Works and the fishery inspectors had no say in where they were located. Thomas Brady, one of the three fishery inspectors, voiced his concerns about misappropriation of funds in relation to marine works as early as 1867. Usually, a landlord would subscribe or petition for marine works either on his land or for the benefit of his tenants, meaning that the subscriber gained personally, albeit in an indirect way. Brady argued that locations were selected and constructed with the interests of the subscriber in mind, rather than for the general interest.[25] Fewer works were constructed in the congests because a percentage of the total cost had to come from rates, which were predominantly in arrears. After Butt acquired the funds, The *Irish Builder* reported that the fisheries continued to be:

> sadly neglected by our own countrymen, and [...] our people have often been starving, with a mine of available wealth almost under their feet. We do not dare to touch upon the troubled sea of Irish politics and show the shortcomings of Irish Members of Parliament; but we could wish that some of these persons would perform an act of practical patriotism by devoting their attention to our fisheries and waste lands.[26]

In the absence of government support, some individuals endeavoured to aid their localities and a small number of important works were carried out with money acquired through private means or through the influence of local gentry. At the end of the eighteenth century, Mr William Burton Conyngham established a herring fishery at Burton Port and on the Island of Innismacdurn, Co. Donegal, by donating money for equipment, and the government gave grant aid amounting to £30,000 to construct salt factories, stores and other buildings. In 1783 the fishery earned £40,000, but in 1793 it failed altogether and the proj-

---

24 Trustees for Bettering the Condition of the Poor of Ireland, *A summary of the state of the Irish sea coast fisheries* (1872), p. 26. In 1822 a large sum of money was collected in London through private subscription for the relief of distress and part of this money later became the Sea Coast and Fisheries Fund. This fund was used to provide loans to fishermen if they could provide an adequate security bond. The loans were used to buy larger boats and were of great benefit to men who would normally have used small sprit boats and canoes. Men who acquired larger vessels were more inclined to engage in full-time commercial fishing. **25** *IB*, 15 July 1883, p. 197. **26** *IB*, 15 February 1876, p. 54.

ect was abandoned.[27] The Donegal herring industry continued for a while on a smaller scale, but poor sales in the 1830s finished it completely. This industry was further damaged from 1850 to 1880 when herrings practically disappeared from Irish waters. As Hargreave argues in his description of the fishery on the Island of Arranmore (off the coast of Co. Donegal) periodical support had a harmful long-term impact on any area:

> Many of the islanders have always fished for lobster, herring, cod and plaice but except for two boom periods between the 1780s to 1793 and 1891 to 1921 the fishing industry has drifted between near extinction and short-lived revivals. Indeed, throughout much of the nineteenth century, the collection of seaweed and carrageen moss was probably more important than fishing. Conditions between and after the boom were never bright.[28]

Another philanthropist, Lady Burdett-Coutts, started to aid the industry about 1880 by providing money on loan to the fishermen of Cape Clear, in West Cork, to develop a herring fishery.[29] Her venture proved very successful.

> The 'Capers' – as the inhabitants of Cape Clear are called – have in their short experience of four years become the most skilful, the most daring and the most successful of the fishermen of all nationalities who come to the fishing grounds. The periodical victims of starvation now earn sometimes £100 in a lucky night; they now have cheque-books; houses with good slate roofs are springing up.[30]

When Manx men fishing for herrings at Kinsale reported that there was an abundance of mackerel off the south coast, Lady Burdett-Coutts then proceeded to donate money to the mainland fishermen to develop this new fishery. The fresh mackerel industry required different equipment, but it was very profitable and it soon surpassed the cured herring industry in importance. When Lady Burdett-Coutts began lending money, a substantial-sized commercial boat with nets cost on average £650. She lent between £250 and £350 to the intending owner or owners, and the outstanding sum was paid in increments to the boat-builder interest free. The money was invested in the people under the watchful eye of Fr Charles Davis PP, the terms of repayment were lenient (10 per cent annually of the amount lent, with no interest) and as soon as the annual repayments were met, the capital was reinvested in the community industry. Part of the Baltimore fleet moved further along the Cork coast to Castletownberehaven, then on to Valentia on the Kerry coast, from there it progressed northwards to Smerwick, Fenit, and up as far as the Shannon, all of which later became important fish-

---

27 CDB, Fifth annual report, 1896, p. 18. **28** C. Hargreaves, 'Economic and social conditions on Arranmore in the nineteenth century' (1962), p. 104. **29** *IB*, 15 July 1883, p. 197. **30** *IB*, 15 October 1884, p. 311.

ing centres. The service industry surrounding this fishery also flourished; for example, boat-building began to thrive (but mainly off-shore and particularly in the Isle of Man).[31] Efforts to copy the success of Cape Clear and Baltimore along the west coast were unsuccessful because of financial difficulties. For example, Fr Bernard Walker, a parish priest in Burtonport, attempted out of his own finances to restart the herring fishery in 1883, for which a Miss Skerritt provided boats for tuition off the Connemara coast but the scheme failed. Contemporary critics viewed the success of the Baltimore industry as a model for Irish potential, but it only succeeded because of the generous risk capital provided through external sources.[32]

By 1890 the art of fishing was practically extinct along the west coast; those deriving an income from seafaring were boatmen rather than fishermen. A more profitable income could be earned by using the boats to transport goods, so money was not invested in fishing equipment. Throughout the nineteenth century, the natural markets of the west, which promoted a self-sufficient economy, were permeated by the spread of a cash economy that did not value fish. Domestic fish markets were not very significant, and fish was such a poorly valued commodity that fishermen were lucky if it was accepted as an item of barter. This makes the extent of fish consumption in the west particularly difficult to monitor. Most coastal dwellers had small canoes or currachs, and probably caught enough for personal use.[33] These vessels were not registered, they were too light for any weight levy to apply, and the fish caught was not officially traded. Using Cullen's argument that fish consumption was a symbol of low social status and given that the west contained some of the poorest regions, we can assume that a certain amount of fish was consumed.[34] All the maritime baseline reports indicate that fish was cured and used as a relish with potatoes, and that fresh fish was not as popular.

It appears from the baseline reports that the seaweed industry in the northwest was much more significant than the fisheries, so much so, that the board investigated the possibility of its development as a cheaper form of maritime industry. Seaweed was an important industrial raw material; in its crude state

---

31 S. Fitzgerald, *Mackerel and the making of Baltimore, Co. Cork, 1879–1913* (1999), p. 7. **32** Green, 'Sea fisheries', pp 369–86. **33** Currachs (also curragh) were very simply constructed using a light wooden frame for the top sides, strengthened by a keelson curved upwards at each end to make the stern and sternpost. The ribs were pieces of cask hoop cut to give the requisite curve to the bottom. Narrow batters were nailed to the outside to make the floor. Tarred canvas was then nailed to the outside for water-proofing and three or four pairs of light oars propelled the canoe. Holdsworth, *The sea fisheries of Great Britain and Ireland,* p. 5. 'These curraghs float like bubbles on the water when empty, but with four men in them, and each using a pair of oars, they are easily managed, and will go through a great deal of bad weather. They are about twenty feet long and four feet wide, and are used for the line fishing.' **34** Cullen, 'Population growth and diet' (1986), p. 96.

it contains iodine, and burning common seaweed creates a substance known as kelp, which was a valuable alkaline source. Raw seaweed also contains potash salt, a natural form of fertilizer necessary for nurturing crops on poor soil; it was also used in glass and soap manufacture, during the American and French Wars. It was extensively available along the western seaboard, but its value was only fully appreciated in the northwest where people earned sizeable cash incomes from the sale of raw seaweed and its by-products. All shoreline tenants gathered seaweed for personal use as a fertilizer, and, when the occasion arose, surplus was sold to inland farmers. At the end of the nineteenth century, inland seaweed sales had declined considerably because of the widespread availability and use of guano and artificial fertilizer. The baseline reports indicate that those who still relied heavily on the sale of seaweed inland were exceptionally poor and sometimes carted it ten or fifteen miles for the sake of a cash income.[35] According to John de Courcy Ireland, the tradition of kelp making was first developed in the Aran Islands early in the eighteenth century. He also claims that in 1754 a group of Irish fishermen from the west brought the idea to the Hebridean island of Uist and were responsible for founding its flourishing industry.[36] However, the kelp industry flourished more in Scotland, where chemical companies began to manufacture kelp as a source of alkali at the beginning of the eighteenth century. In the absence of an Irish chemical company emerging, Ireland's function as kelp producer was to fill up the requirements of the Scottish manufacturers when they had bought up all the native stock. But the industry never reached its full potential because the market crashed following the Napoleonic wars, and in 1830 it was discovered that alkaline substances could be produced synthetically.

The fall-off in the alkali market did not decimate the seaweed industry, for in 1812 a French chemical manufacturer named Courtois discovered iodine and in 1815 a French scientist, Davy, found that marine organisms contained iodine, further scientific advances showed that iodine; had medicinal qualities as an antiseptic and was useful in the treatment of goitre. This discovery helped to maintain the Irish seaweed gathering industry until the 1890s. The international demand for iodine was filled by the kelp-burners of Ireland (where it was confined mainly to the west coast), Scotland, Brittany and Norway. A few small-scale iodine factories were founded in Donegal and Galway, but they could not compete with the large and long established Scottish firms. Traditionally, there was a strong economic link between the northwest and Scotland, mainly because of daily goods ferries and a strong social link through migration. It was observed that two or three Scottish firms monopolized the Irish kelp trade, each taking a

---

[35] Gaskell, *South Connemara*, p. 5. [36] J. de Courcy Ireland, *Ireland and the Irish in maritime history* (1986), p. 178.

certain length of the northwest coastline and never encroached on one another's jurisdiction. This continued well into the twentieth century; North Inishowen kelp was still imported by the Paterson company of Glasgow in the 1930s.[37] Prices were kept abnormally low due to lack of competition; they were particularly low in Donegal until a local iodine industry began at Ramelton in 1880. Then people received fair market prices but Scottish firms, whose interests were in jeopardy, paid the manager £300 to close, and by 1891 the industry in Donegal had reverted to old standards and the average price paid for kelp was as low as £3 a ton. Further decimation of this industry occurred when it was discovered that nitrate deposits contained iodine, and Chilean and American mining companies flooded the world market.

According to the reports, kelp was made in twenty of the maritime districts, all in the northern counties of Donegal, Galway and Mayo, and it was of the utmost importance to the economy of sixteen of these districts; in Fanad it was said that the seaweed was as important to the kelp-burners as the saving of hay to the farmer, and it was mainly conducted by women.[38] Landlords in Glenties, Belmullet, Louisburg and Letterfrack charged a rent for the shoreline and a royalty of almost 25 per cent of the income received from seaweed. In the southwest it was undervalued, rent was not charged for the shoreline and kelp was not made. Where seaweed gathering and burning was a thriving industry it was gathered either from the shore or from boats. The harvest occurred twice a year in April and September, when the weed parted from its stem and set adrift. The April harvest had the highest calibre weed; it drifted in to exposed shores but not into the bays. In this respect, the islanders had a major advantage over mainlanders who had to tear it off the rocks using 18-foot long poles (which had a short crosspiece fixed at one end for cutting) and had to drag it through nearly twenty feet of water onto land. When there was a storm, seaweed was driven ashore; whole families went into the water to save it, but it was usually women

---

37 Maghtochair, *Inishowen: its history, traditions and antiquities* (1935), p. 144. **38** N. Ó Dómhnall, *Na Glúinte Róssanacha* (1952), p. 113. Is mór an tógáil intinne na mná agus na páistí a fheiceáil ar an obair seo, ag scíordadh anon agus anall leis an gcuraigh, ag deanamh sciste ar carraig, ag luchtú na feamaí, ag cleasaíocht chun an chladaigh, ag cur an lasta i dtír, ag imeacht arís ar luas fá choinne ualaigh eile. Tuilleadh daoine ar an gcladach ag spreagh na feamaí báite, ag deanamh moll den feamaí tirim, ag freastal na háite … Ach cé gur shúiniúil a bheith ag amharc orthu ní fheadadh duine gan smaointiú gurbh fhearr é da mbeadh na páistí ar an scoil agus na mná ag déanamh oibre ba cineálta thiocadh lena nadúir.' Ó Dómhnall's account pertains to the early 1900s in the Glenties, Co. Donegal. It roughly translates: It is a wonderful sight to behold the women and children at this work, going forward and back, making heaps of seaweed on the rocks, skipping down to the shoreline, bringing it to dry land, off again with speed to get another load. Others on the shore spreading the drenched weed, gathering the dried weed…Although it was wonderful to observe one could not help but to think that it would be better if the children were at school and the women doing work kinder to their nature.

who carried it in crates or creels to the grass or sand above high-water mark.[39] Some kelpers sailed out 10 or 15 miles from the Aran Islands to where the ribbon weed was also found; it was gathered when the water was at a certain level (the last three hours of ebb tide and at the first three hours of floodtide). Boatmen had their families waiting for their arrival ashore; these unloaded the boats and spread it out to dry while the kelpers rested. Regardless of how it was harvested (from boats or from the shore), gathering typically continued for two or three days. Once ashore, it was spread as evenly as possible to dry. At least two hot summer days were needed to dry it enough to make kelp; if it rained the weed had to be re-gathered and covered because rain washed out the valuable salts.

When it was dried, it was burned in a 'rude kiln' made out of earth and stones and fuelled with turf. The burning process was tedious and required constant supervision; weeds were placed directly on the kiln; as each piece burned and turned bluish black in colour, it was removed and replaced by another; once it cooled it was moulded into rectangular shapes or stacked in heaps until the agent/dealer came around to test it.[40] The test itself was simple; kelp was placed in a glass, and sulphuric acid poured over it to determine its purity (this was judged by how fast the acid changed colour, it indicated the levels of iodine in the kelp and determined the price). People complained that the test was unfair because it was conducted behind closed doors and was based on a small segment.[41] Suppliers counter-argued that the whole amount was not necessarily consistent in quality, while the agents complained that stacks of kelp were often adulturated with sand and stones.

As it was reaped differently in each region, inevitable inconsistencies occurred, which had an impact on the monetary value of the end product. For example, it took nearly twelve boatloads of seaweed to make a ton of kelp. Only 3 to 4 lb of iodine was derived from one ton of kelp, and this yield was only attained if the weed received careful treatment. Produce was rarely consistent: for instance, Rosmuck kelp was made from ribbon weed and was not as rich in iodine as the same weed grown in the open sea. Inconsistencies in produce were reflected in pricing, which had a knock-on effect on production levels. In Louisburgh, Co. Mayo, where a considerable amount was made, the average price paid was £4 10*s.* per ton. Two agents were employed in the area, and the landlord received a royalty of one fifth of all kelp sold. On the Aran Islands, two thirds of the population burned kelp, and £4 was received per ton. Carna families were paid £5 a ton due to the higher calibre of kelp produced. Higher prices of £7 to £8 a ton were paid in some Aran centres. In the South Connemara

---

39 M. Luddy, 'Women and work in nineteenth and early twentieth-century Ireland' (2000). Luddy remarks that 'in the absence of a horse or donkey women were used as beasts of burden': p. 48. **40** Gaskell, *South Connemara*, p. 11. **41** Gaskell, *Fanad and Rosguill*, p. 5.

region, kelp also received a higher price because the native red weed had higher contents of iodine than ordinary ribbon weed. Scottish kelp manufacture was more sophisticated at this point, and there was limited scientific knowledge of maximizing the use of seaweed; manufacturers knew to advise the use of red weed as opposed to black weed, which grew on the rocks above low water mark. They also encouraged burners to use the long fibrous stalk (the best part of the weed), but many used the inferior flat end band to fill quotas.

Although kelp-burning was considered an industry worth investigating in the baseline reports, its importance in the congested districts was declining by the early 1890s; its sole purpose was to fill the shortfall in the Scottish market, and this was not a certainty. The board sought advice from a representative of a chemical firm near Glasgow, who stated that Irish kelp did not produce maximum yield because it was incorrectly burned. He argued that a minimum average of 10 lb of iodine should be derived from one ton of kelp but properly burned kelp should yield 20–22 lb of iodine; he advised the board to conduct further scientific tests to help correctly calculate the commercial value of the various weeds and that the people should make kilns with an iron grating at the bottom, to maximize yield. He also advised residents to open a manufacturing plant operated on a co-operative principle to ensure that profits of the industry stayed in the district.[42] According to statute, the board could not own or compete with private enterprise; it could give loans, but because nobody expressed an interest in opening a manufacturing plant the board could do very little for the Irish kelp burning industry except monitor the behaviour of the Scottish agents. The board contemplated building a kiln in Rosmuck to experiment on the best way of getting a pure iodine product; this in turn would prevent adulteration and standardize the product; but prices fell and the project was not undertaken.[43]

Kelp burning was filed under miscellaneous matters in the annual reports of the CDB and was only included if there was an unusual occurrence, such as a particularly profitable year. In 1906 the board reported that the industry was of considerable importance in some coastal areas of Mayo and Galway, but was of more significance to the island communities, which had not benefited as much from other CDB supported industries. On the Islands from Aran to Inishkea off the Galway coast and the Islands of Tory, Inishboffin and Gola off Donegal from £3 10*s*. to £4 10*s*. per ton was paid for kelp and £1 10*s*. was paid for selected kinds of dried, unburnt weed. Some families sold from two to four tons of the burnt kelp and their receipts were estimated at £10 or £12 for each family. The report noted that the quantity of kelp was above the average of former years but does not mention whether this was due to better planning on the part of workers or more favourable weather conditions.[44] In 1906, the board

42 Gaskell, *Rosmuck*, p. 10. **43** CDB, Seventh annual report, 1898, p. 34. **44** CDB Fourteenth

noted receipts of £1,180 on the north coast of Donegal and £2,400 in Galway. But at this point fewer skilled people worked in the industry and the quantity of burnt kelp had decreased.[45] Traditionally, kelping was a family-run industry in Ireland but due to the impact made by American and Chilean competition few new workers had joined and learned the craft. Indeed, newcomers were not welcome in some areas: Fanad kelpers were 'very strict as to their rights to the seaweed and a stranger coming to take the seaweed from a kelp burning district would be forcibly made to desist from gathering it'.[46] In 1911 the board subsidized various small-scale, kelp-burning experiments, using specially prepared kilns, and had satisfactory results; it was willing to continue with the experiments but, by then, kelpers had found easier ways of obtaining cash incomes and it was too late to revive the industry to its former glory.[47] At this stage, scientific research had found that the quality of iodine produced from the manufacture of Irish seaweed was a higher calibre than that produced from the nitrate refuse, which had been comparatively cheap for the previous fifteen years. Competition on the iodine market from the US and South American mines had decimated the Irish kelp burning industry but did not have the same impact on seaweed gathering. Scottish agents continued to purchase the dried or unburned seaweed from Irish gatherers at fair prices as they were certain of an unadulterated product. In relation to its maritime development, the board had little option but to engage in the fisheries and its service industries.

The condition of fisheries in the maritime congests

It is difficult to categorize the fishing industry in the west in the latter half of the nineteenth century. It was not a commercial industry, and, it was not a cottage industry, although it helped agricultural workers.[48] The extent of fisheries on the west coast, with the exception of a few areas in the south, did not qualify for industrial status. Residents of maritime districts did not have money to invest in modern fishing gear; this dissuaded them from becoming full-time fishermen, but efforts in the fisheries also kept them as part-time farmers. However, in most instances the board found that fishing was secondary to agriculture.[49] To raise the maritime districts out of the 'at risk of distress' category it was necessary to establish an alternative industry to agriculture, and in the

---

annual report. 1905, p. 40. **45** CDB Fifteenth annual report, 1906, p. 32. **46** Gaskell, *Fanad,* pp 5–6. **47** T. Dillon, 'Iodine and potash from Irish seaweed' (1930); CDB, Twentieth annual report, 1912, p. 30. **48** J.O. Moore, *The possibilities of Irish agriculture and allied industry* (1912), p. 116. **49** P. O'Neill, *A social and cultural study of crofter life on the West Donegal seaboard* (1940). See also V. Pollock, 'The seafishing industry in Co. Down, 1860–1939' (1988); N. Campbell, 'The CDB and the development of fishing in South-West Donegal 1890–1923' (1997).

absence of mineral reserves full-time fishing was the most obvious option. In all the northern districts, boats and gear needed to be up-graded and methods modernized. The situation was marginally better in Kerry and Cork, where decked boats and seine nets were in use. Outside of Baltimore in Cork and the Claddagh in Galway Bay (the latter was not considered congested until 1909), no mackerel fishing was carried on by means of nets, and no other class of sea-fishing existed on a commercial scale. In his book, Micks commented that Dingle was the only place where receipts per family from fishing exceeded £40 a year, and Inishowen, Valentia and Baltimore being the only places where receipts per family were above £20 a year. These estimates are not from the baseline reports but they indicate the general pattern of fisheries as they existed when the board took charge. On his travels as a CDB employee, Micks observed that 'from Lough Foyle to the mouth of the Shannon there was not a single boat that could carry a sailing boat's full train of nets'.[50] This was partially due to the absence of piers, suitable boats and gear, but chiefly to the lack of capital and technical skills.

The fishery department was made up of the Revd William S. Green, Fr Charles Davis and Mr Tuke. Green was appointed chief fisheries inspector because of his long experience, Davis for his role in the mackerel fisheries in Baltimore, and Tuke for his interest in Donegal and his general abilities. The fishing industry was divided into freshwater (or inland) fisheries and sea fisheries; the CDB dealt exclusively with the latter. For administrative purposes the industry was split into two zones, the first zone comprising Donegal, Mayo and Galway, the second Kerry and West Cork. Financing the fisheries needed careful consideration; the board hoped that if it kept expenditure within strict commercial limits, that when, and if, private enterprise or local co-operation took its place, the fishermen would be accustomed to an honest price, and trained workers would be used to receiving a fair wage. Concentrating particularly on the northwest, the board began by setting up stations; used primarily as storage depots and for curing fish but also as CDB centres for giving technical instruction, loans and selling goods. Stations at Downing's Bay, Iniscoo, Malinbeg, Teelin, Cladnagearagh, Iniskea and Dooagh were all operated directly by the board. Stations at Bunowen, Inisboffin, Inver and Portacloy were operated on a semi-independent basis (between the CDB and private individuals), but due to administrative difficulties these joint effort stations were discontinued in 1894. To combat the possibility of the misappropriation of fishery funds, the board did not lend money; instead it bought the boats, kitted them out and leased them as a package to the fishermen: 'In no case do the board advance cash to borrowers. They either purchase what is required and hand it over to the fisherman or

---

50 Micks, *An account of the history*, p. 35.

arrange to allow him to purchase where he wishes and then pay the account direct on proof of delivery, usually in the presence of the local representatives of the board'.[51] Loans were secured by a mortgage or on a guarantee given by the borrowers and their sureties. The Irish loan and reproductive fund (which partially financed the fishery department) was first made available to the board on 1 June 1893; it was used primarily for buying boats and gear. By December 1893 only 315 applications for loans had been received, of which 111 were granted, 118 were still under scrutiny, and 87 applicants were not entitled to money due to outstanding loans. The expense involved partially explains the lack of interest; for example, an average boat considered suitable for mackerel and herring fishing, with complete trains of nets, cost between £300 and £600.[52]

In 1892 parts of Kerry and West Cork had a sea-fishery already operating on an independent commercial basis. Transit and markets were good, but landing accommodation was substandard, so the board organized the building of roads and piers to be built on behalf of the people, for example on the Blasket Islands (where a road and a boat slip was built and a corresponding slip was built on the mainland). Any work conducted in the congests was supervised by CDB appointed engineers, but needed approval from the county surveyor.[53] Work was carried out directly by the board under the advice of marine engineer, R.C. Parsons, and all marine works in the congested counties were made of concrete. Until then, piers were built out of inferior quality materials, such as pencil (a light shale-like stone) and pebbles, neither of which were durable. The cost of roads, bridges and marine works was borne by the Treasury, and maintenance costs were administered under the grand jury laws, with money derived from cess payments. From Donegal to Galway, transit and market facilities were considered defective, and poor packaging was also a problem. When the Inishowen fishermen transported their fish by train to Moville (a major trading centre), it was so poorly packed that it bruised in transit, and was sold at a disadvantage in British markets compared to fish carried by sea.[54] To minimize damage and to speed up the delivery process, the board subsidized a steamer service between the Aran Islands and the mainland. Steamer services were too expensive for wider use, but the RDS-owned vessel, the *Fingal*, was available intermittently for the rest of the coastline but only in emergency circumstances. Transporting the goods entirely by steamer to destinations such as London was unfeasibly expensive, so instead the Midland Great Western Railway Company of Ireland brought it from the west to Dublin (the dispatch depot for the British market). Realizing the industry's potential, the rail company scheduled special trains at fixed rates and in some cases even made a special siding at the point

---

51 Ibid., p. 21. 52 F.S. Sheridan, 'The congested districts' (1915), p. 18. 53 CDB, Second annual report, 1893, p. 29. 54 Gaskell, *North Inishowen*, p. 10.

where the fish were brought ashore from the CDB steamer.[55] Co-operation from rail companies was necessary until such a time that the local markets for fresh fish became more significant and this did not occur until the turn of the century.[56] In the case of cured fish, where rapid transit to market was not a priority, steamships and sailing vessels could be chartered as necessary to take pickled or dried fish to market.[57] An exception to this concerned a successful smoked-haddock industry that had emerged in Teelin: a good quality article was produced but it failed to meet market demands because the cost of carriage was too high; the venture was abandoned.[58]

Co. Donegal had 21 congested districts, all of them were dependent on agriculture; 17 were also maritime, meaning they had a shoreline. Teelin was the only northern district where whole families were engaged solely in fishing, and its baseline report notes the many disincentives to engage in fishing on a full-time basis – from the paucity of equipment in use, to how hard the whole family had to work. At Teelin there were usually two takes of fish a day. Men rowed out to their lines at 7 a.m. (they would have been set the previous evening about 4 or 5 p.m.) each line holding about sixty hooks baited with cuts of herring; as they were hauled in, the fish was unhooked and thrown to the bottom of the boat. Lines were then recoiled in the basket but were often so twisted that it took the men hours to unravel them. After the catch was taken in, the lines sorted and new ones set; they still had to row four miles home, which meant reaching Teelin about midnight. In many cases the boat used was not crew property and its owner received a share of the fish caught.[59] Donegal was in dire need of an alternative industry to agriculture: previous attempts of starting and restarting commercial fisheries had failed, so old loans were in arrears and the board inherited them through the fishery funds.

Curing fish on a commercial level was new to the west so Micks was sent to the Shetland Islands to observe the curing procedures and to recruit instructors to work for the board. On his travels, he met Alexander Duthie, a Scottish fish merchant, who agreed to come to Ireland for six months to help the board organize the fishery in Donegal. Duthie had been involved in a scheme to convert crofters on the western coast of Scotland into full-time fishermen. The venture failed because the crews were given expensive boats and gear without sufficient instruction; loans went unpaid and the depreciated equipment was repossessed. From his experience in Scotland, Duthie organized a special shared loan system for Donegal fishermen whereby the cost of the boat and gear was repaid through a deduction of one third of gross earnings. The manager of the

---

55 CDB, Second annual report, 1893, p. 17.   **56** CDB, Tenth annual report, 1901, p. 34.   **57** CDB, First annual report, 1892, p. 15.   **58** CDB, Second annual report, 1893, p. 23.   **59** Gahan, *Teelin*, p. 9.

fishing station had to keep the accounts of each boat and retained one-third of the annual earnings for repayments. The balance was divided equally among the crew, and eventually, the six-crew members became joint owners. In this respect, the fishermen did not have to manage their own financial affairs and this was a key factor in the success of the Donegal fisheries.[60] Under the shared loan system a crew of six men could own a small Scottish deep-sea boat at the end of a good year with profit (in the case of *St Colomba* £84 2*s*. 1*d*. or approximately £15 each).

Table 3.2. Cost of a small Scottish deep sea boat, *St Colomba*

	£ *s. d.*		£ *s. d.*
Cost of boat	80 0 0	Nett earnings from	
Cost of nets	62 10 8	10 months fishing	251 9 7
Cost of lines	11 18 4		
Cost of repairs	12 18 6		
Total	167 7 6		

Source: CDB, Fifth report, 1896, p. 16.

In Cork and Kerry the board also provided boats and gear on a shared loan system but the men managed the money themselves. An individual loan system was favoured in Galway and Mayo; one man took out the loan, and payments were made by means of fixed half-yearly instalments. This system was unsuccessful; the board found 'that in the counties Galway and Mayo it is a question of time when we either have to take back the boat and gear and make a loss, or come down on the borrower and his sureties upon their personal undertaking to repay.'[61] When the fishermen could not meet the repayments, the board repossessed the boat and wrote off the outstanding debt. In Donegal there was no financial loss to the board except in the event of a wreck, and this was covered to a large degree by insurance (provided by Scottish firms) from 1899 onwards.[62]

Providing a technical instruction service was a central and fundamental part of the fishery department's work. In many areas of Donegal, Mayo and Galway the board had to start the industry from scratch, which meant literally making seafarers out of farmers. It began by employing Scottish instructors to teach the men how to fish, then it initiated the secondary industries necessary to service a commercial industry. Scottish instructors spent the full year in charge of the vessel, teaching local fishermen how to use long lines and how to handle the

[60] CDB, Nineteenth annual report, 1911, p. 28. [61] Ibid., p. 29. [62] CDB, Ninth annual report, 1900, p. 37.

trains of nets.[63] A Miss Skerritt, who had previously been involved in the Revd Walker's 1883 fishery revival in Burtonport, gave the board two boats in 1892 for the purpose of training men to fish. Practical instruction in fishing was carried out to a large degree, and instructors received an annual salary of up to £100 to train crews. In 1892 eighteen boys were trained, some progressed to become skippers in 1893, and all continued to train others. By 1893 a further 100 new hands received instruction and all participated in the mackerel fishery. Provision of instruction, one of the costliest overheads in the fisheries department, was borne completely by the board until 1898; then it tried to devise a fair system of contribution from the fishermen. Instruction on net mending was also provided in conjunction with the Board of National Education, which provided half the cost and allowed its staff to be used for management and inspection.[64] Net-mending instructors were employed to give classes after school hours, and usually three quarters of the classes were national school pupils; on the Aran Islands eighty boys and girls were trained in the craft. When the pupils were proficient enough, they were employed to mend share-boat nets.[65] Repairs were carried out under supervision, and the local fishermen paid for the service. This instruction was extended to incorporate mounting new nets, 'thus saving for the local fishermen the money that hitherto went across the Channel in payment for mounting and barking the nets'.[66] Incidental to its work in fisheries, the board facilitated the improvement of communications by giving the necessary local guarantee for the extension of posts and telegraphs. The board could argue a strong case for maritime areas, stating the relevance of telegraphs to developing fisheries.[67] In 1902 the board was also involved in outdoor relief in the construction of small lighthouses under the sanction of the Commissioners of Irish Lights. This ensured the safe return of boats at night and extended the working day. The lighthouses were strategically built on Inisboffin and Deer Islands. Fishery lights were also erected along the coast, starting with the more dangerous areas in the northern maritime counties where thirty-day 'Wigham' lights were used.[68]

Prior to the intervention of the CDB, currachs were the only vessels in use in the northern congested districts. Currachs were the only generic style of boat suitable for the entire coastline; for example, on the Aran Islands there was no natural shelter; the islands were frequently hit by squalls and the fishermen needed boats that could be easily lifted on to dry land.[69] In areas where there

63 CDB, Fourth annual report, 1895, p. 14. **64** P. Kane, 'Aran of the fishermen' (1898), p. 245; CDB, Fourth annual report, 1895, p. 18. **65** CDB, Thirteenth annual report, 1904, p. 35. **66** CDB, Second annual report, 1893, p. 23. **67** For an account of the Aran Island telegraph see Harvey, pp 236–49. **68** CDB, Thirteenth annual report, 1904, p. 35. In Kilronan an acetylene light, the latest technology, was used and plans for the same were in progress for Derrynane. **69** CDB, Seventeenth annual report, 1908, p. 26.

was no harbour accommodation, the crews had to haul their boats high up on a steep shore every time they used them: 'This entails much labour on the crews and wear to the boats. The crews consist of five men only, and work must be hard, the distance over which the boats must pass being from 50 to 100 paces from the water's edge at low tide.'[70] The board tried to introduce Scottish deep-sea boats but found them unsuitable for the Aran Islanders or the Arranmore fishermen of Donegal, it also discovered that Greencastle (open) yawls could not go to sea in rough weather. A decked sailing boat, the 'Zulu,' was larger, and deemed more suitable for herring fishing at Downing's Bay. In South Aran, Greencastle yawls were worked on a share system along with six or eight-oared curraghs built by the islanders. Catching different species and sizes of fish required various types of equipment; in other words a boat decked for mackerel fishing could not part-take in the herring fishery. Each time one fishery was proving more profitable than another, the board had to make financial allowances to buy equipment and to alter technical instruction. Such was the case in 1895 when the herring fishery off Scotland was poor and the demand for Irish herring soared. The Irish industry was not organized in time, and the board found it difficult to keep up with the demand because of a labour shortage in the factories to process the fish. While the fishing industry was male-dominated there was a certain degree of female employment, but it was confined to the secondary industries at fish-curing stations for gutting or curing. Because it was irregular, work at the curing stations was paid on an hourly basis (it depended on the arrival of boats, the weather, the quantity of fish caught and whether it was partially cleaned on deck).

Both the fresh and cured fish trade required good-sized vessels to increase the take and decent landing accommodation to facilitate these larger vessels. The fresh fish trade was more expensive because the essentials (ice, ice-hulks and packing boxes) were costly and the trade relied heavily on quick transportation to market by rail or boat, but fresh fish had a higher market value than cured or dried fish. In general, the board paid for repairs, freight of fish to market, sales commission and the large working expenses of the stations, such as ice hulks, packaging, rent and labour. Natural ice was imported from Norway; it had to be pre-purchased and housed, which added to the cost, and in poor seasons the ice was wasted.[71] The cured fish trade only flourished when the fresh fish demands were met, but the board had to facilitate this industry by building sheds and stores, hiring fish curers and purchasing salt. The curing plants were

---

70 Gaskell, *Desertegney*, p. 6.   **71** CDB, Seventh annual report, 1898, p. 28. Later when commercial refrigeration became more widespread the board considered manufacturing ice to reduce overheads but were advised against the venture by a Mr Banfield, an expert in the field of ice manufacture.

not equipped in time for the 1893 season, nor had they sufficient storage space; artificial drying rooms were incomplete and wet weather hindered the process. Curing fish was a complicated process and if incorrectly done the produce inevitably rotted. Trained fish curers from the Shetland Islands, others from the east of England, the south of Ireland and Norway were employed to teach people in each CDB station how to cure fish properly and to standardize the quality of the produce. To this end Alexander Millikin, a Scottish fishery officer, was invited to supervise the operation. Where people were uneducated, they were brought to other areas to train and to watch successful ventures in operation. Mayo men were taken to Donegal to observe CDB operations and on their return were experienced enough to take positions of responsibility in curing stations.[72] Using the curing stations as centres the board could act as an umbrella body for the fishermen and merchants could observe the work being carried out and be guaranteed of a high quality product. One such merchant, Mr C.W. Hobbs, was so impressed after a visit to the stations that he began to trade directly and exclusively with the board, which was easier than dealing with the individual fishermen. Hobbs was guaranteed a consistency in produce, which was difficult at the best of times, considering the fact that ruthless salt traders were selling adulterated and inferior quality salt.[73] Both Hobbs and Crawford, a Belfast merchant, specifically praised the efforts of Alexander Duthie in relation to developments in the fisheries. Merchants visited the various stations by sea on the RDS-owned *Fingal,* and on the advice of Crawford the board built a steamship in 1895. The *Granuaile* was built at a cost of £10,250 and was used to conduct the board's work along the entire west coast.[74]

In 1893 the board tried to establish a mackerel fishery in the northwest. The southern fresh mackerel trade was thriving at this time, notably in Baltimore, where Lady Burdett-Coutts was providing vessels and gear on a loan system. Galway Bay was selected as a starting point because it had existing transit facilities. At this time the Galway fishermen were oblivious to the fact that it was possible to catch mackerel during springtime. Mackerel did not come inshore in spring, and local vessels were too small to venture great distances from the mainland.[75] Seven crews from Arklow were hired to prove to the Aran fishermen (the term 'Aran fishery' in CDB records refers to fishermen who used Aran as a centre of trade; they were not necessarily from the Aran Islands) that catching mackerel for the fresh fish market would be profitable enough to repay the loan and provide a comfortable living. Each of the Arklow crews received a bounty of £40 to test uncharted waters a good distance from the shore. When

---

[72] CDB, Second annual report, 1893, p. 24. [73] CDB, Fourth annual report, 1895, appendix xxv, p. 50. [74] Ibid., p. 18. [75] A.E. Murray, *A history of the financial relations between England and Ireland from the period of the restoration* (1903), p. 434.

the boats arrived, low sea temperatures and stormy weather prevented progress, but by the end of the ten-week season, the total number of mackerel caught was 299,480 and each of the Arklow boats made an average of £316.

The success of the Arklow men enticed many others into the mackerel fisheries. Aran became such an important centre that it was necessary to employ an agent to market the Aran produce in London, Mr W.W. Harvey of Cork, the official CDB mackerel agent from 1892 until 1894, paid an average price of the combined markets of Manchester, London, Liverpool, Birmingham, Leeds, Bradford, Nottingham and Sheffield, minus 6s. 9d. per half box (which he charged for freight, a commission for English salesmen, tolls, ice and packing). The board provided the ice-hulk and boxes and also paid the managers' wages; Harvey purchased the ice and paid for all other labour.[76] His payment was the remaining sum, which was a net profit of 'at least one hundred pounds'.[77] At this point the board was suffering heavy losses and in some respects begrudged Harvey the payment for work that could easily be carried out by a CDB employee. In 1895 the board took over sales and transferred Harvey's duties to Mr Shimmin, who previously worked as an inspector. For the fishermen the deduction remained the same, and a further charge of 2.5 per cent was made for supervision and management. Because they received a daily telegram from the markets as proof of the price, the Aran fishermen were happier with the new arrangement. That was the first year that the board did not lose money in promoting the fishery (it had been a heavy expenditure in previous years). When all expenses were paid, a sum of just over £58 was left over but it was weighed against the losses of earlier years.[78]

While the fishermen appeared to be content with the board's operations, independent observers voiced complaints; an article appeared in the *New Ireland Review*, criticizing the board for its policies on the Aran Islands. The author, the Revd P. Kane, praised the board for starting a new industry on the islands, he acknowledged that the board was a non-profit organization but implied that the CDB tried to discourage other buyers in order to break even. He took issue with the fact that the board refused to sell ice to the dealers, citing a case where a Dublin merchant purchasing Aran mackerel had to transport the fish without ice. In Dublin the boxes were opened and packed with ice before being sent on to London. Furthermore he argued that the board was underpaying the fishermen by charging too much for freight, and accused the board of paying lower than the average London market price. 'On 2 May 1894 the value allowed for the fish taken by the CDB was £14 13s. 4d., £9 2s. 3d. was deducted for transport and the fishermen received £5 11s. 1d. for their efforts. This amounts to over one third of the London market value.'[79] Kane condemned the board for

---

[76] CDB, First annual report, 1892, p. 16.   [77] CDB, Third annual report, 1894, p. 13.   [78] CDB, Fourth annual report, 1895, p. 14–5.   [79] Kane, 'Aran of the fishermen', pp 242–5.

using a contradictory policy, claiming that on the one hand it was trying to entice men into the commercial fisheries on very favourable terms (loans for equipment etc.), yet the actual remuneration provided by the board was frugal.

By this time a number of resident fishermen had become well established under the board's supervision and began negotiating prices with other merchants. They were not under any obligation to the board and were free to sell to the highest bidder. Arklow men, who were initially introduced by the board and were revered by the Aran locals, were conducting successful independent sales.[80] To further facilitate the growth of the industry and possibly in light of Kane's criticisms, the board fixed its fresh mackerel price for the entire 1898 season at low prices, thus encouraging fishermen to go elsewhere. Competition at the height of the season caused huge losses to the board but was a direct advantage to the fishermen, who obtained good prices all through the season. It became clear that if the board did not occasionally enter the field as buyers, independent merchants would be less inclined to give good prices; it was quite happy to operate in a 'fall back' capacity for those who were unsuccessful with other merchants.[81] If there was a glut in the market, the board bought the surplus to 'prevent fish being sacrificed', from 1898 on, figures given as average earnings in the CDB reports are an incomplete indicator of the level of commercial fisheries because fishermen began to deal with other merchants.[82] By 1900 the spring mackerel fishery was particularly well established at the Aran and Galway centres, but the CDB offered continued support by issuing circulars to fish merchants negotiating contracts. It suggested that firms interested in buying the Aran catch should give the fishermen a fixed scale of prices during the season. The board consented to lend its ice-hulks and supply fish boxes to firms offering the best prices. Fishermen would sign agreements with a firm selected by the CDB; these bound them to accept a fixed scale of prices, and gave the firm exclusive buying rights.[83] That year recorded disappointing yields in the mackerel fisheries in Cork and Kerry, barely producing one-third of the previous year's catch. Consequently, the prices were higher and the merchant who fixed his price in accordance with the 1899 prices benefited greatly.

To err on the side of caution, the board always tried to ensure a variety of fisheries were in operation so that regions did not depend exclusively on any

---

80 Ibid., p. 235. 'Anthony Murray, obtained, I was told, £81 for 4,100 mackerel. They commonly ran up to £1 per 120, in April that year. The enterprising owner of the "Veronica", Mr Marshall, called the "Mackerel King", who knows where and how to shoot his nets, was able to send home £250 this same year to Arklow, and this, after all expenses were paid, including his own keep and that of his men. This was in the early season, the prices were good, the sale having been effected in some cases at least, if not in all, to buyers dealing directly with the men.' **81** CDB, Seventh annual report, 1898, p. 22. **82** CDB, Fifth annual report, 1896, p. 21. **83** CDB, Tenth annual report, 1901, p. 31.

Table 3.3. Profit and loss statement, Blacksod mackerel fishery, spring, 1899

Expenditure	£ s. d.	Receipts	£ s. d.
Rail charges	508 13 1	Sales of fresh fish less commission	1,526 15 9
Special rail charges	65 13 9	Sales of cured fish	524 18 1
Coal for steamer	84 13 4	Sale of ice	19 12 7
Purchase of fish	1,261 17 0	Miscellaneous	9 9 4
Freight on returned empties	26 0 6		
Purchase of ice	155 11 0		
Subsidies to Arklow	80 0 0		
Depreciation of boxes and sundries(total cost £593 16s. 2d.)	197 18 9		
Hulk (total cost £228 19s. 8d.) at 10 per cent	22 18 0		
Management and labour	204 18 8		
Incidentals	14 18 9		
Salt and barrels	114 2 3	Balance (being net loss to Board)	£1,015 9 4
Charter of steamer	359 0 0		
Total	£3,096 5 1		£3,096 5 1

Source: Ninth annual report of the CDB (1900), p. 28.

one type. In 1896, when the pickled mackerel industry was in jeopardy, the board had tried to market the product at home and on the Continent, but the results were unsatisfactory. The main market for cured or pickled mackerel was in the United States, a significant portion of which was an Irish-American sympathy gesture, so the CDB organized a label of origin. However, this export was subject to a tariff, which was paid directly by the fishermen. In 1896 an impending revision or new tariff left 'large stocks of pickled mackerel unsold, and an uneasy feeling existed that a practically prohibitive duty might be imposed this year on pickled mackerel.'[84] As it transpired the new American tariff was not raised significantly; however, the predicament could have resulted in the loss of the American market the problem of regional over-dependence re-emerged. By 1898 the board had sublet its curing stations, but it continued to oversee negotiations between fishermen and merchants, and channelled its energy into marketing the cured produce. If a season was unproductive and very little fish was sent to the stations, it was cheaper for the person leasing the station not to

84 CDB, Sixth annual report, 1897, pp 19–20.

Table 3.4. Cost per barrel of sending mackerel to America

	s.	d.
Cost of barrel	4	0
Salt	3	6
Labour in curing	3	6
Freight, commission and duty in America	18	0
Cost of fish at 4s. per hundred	9	6
Total	38	6

Source: Tenth annual report (1901) p. 39.

open; and, in the winter of 1899–1900, the board opened nine stations for curing cod, ling and glasson but an active demand for fresh fish resulted in three stations receiving no fish for curing.[85] In 1899, merchants at Aran, Cleggan, Donnloughan and Roundstone cured 3,142 barrels of mackerel, all of which were sold to the American market and obtained a good price. Sometimes sales of a late, slow season surpassed those of a good season, but when familiar waters were unproductive the board undertook the cost of experiments 'in order to induce experienced fishermen with properly equipped boats to risk the uncertainty of an untried fishing ground'.[86] The board opened a new curing station at Blacksod Point in 1899, two Arklow crews were employed to test the waters there for a bounty of £40 each per season and a constant price of 14s. per hundred for the fish. The Arklow crews were successful and provided evidence of rich fishing grounds off Blacksod bay, but the station showed a loss of £1,015 for the board that year (see table 3.3).

The cured or pickled mackerel trade with the US flourished until 1900 because mackerel had left American costal waters. In 1900 they returned in large shoals and this led to a drop in price from $14 to $9 a barrel. Considering the cost of barrelling the fish, Irish fishermen began to question whether it was worth catching it for cured export (see table 3.4).

Nine dollars was equal to 37s. 6d. and when the merchants noted the fall in prices they declined to open the curing stations. The CDB was prepared to open curing stations and buy mackerel at 3s. 6d. per hundred, but the fishermen were not willing to accept the price. The situation improved in the following year and the prices recovered to $15 per barrel but only half the number of barrels was sent, partly due to bad weather but mainly due to caution. At Clifden only £8 was earned for 26 boxes. In Roundstone the earnings fell from £1,450 in 1900 to £1,005 in

[85] CDB, Ninth annual report, 1900, p. 36. [86] Ibid., p. 27.

1 Woman collecting fish, *c*.1892. Tuke 4
Photographer: Major Ruttledge-Fair
Reproduction: Courtesy of the National Library of Ireland

2 Women carrying baskets of seaweed, *c*.1892. Tuke 43

Photographer: Major Ruttledge-Fair
Reproduction: Courtesy of the National Library of Ireland

3 Members of the CDB receiving directions from a local woman, *c*.1907.
CDB 95.

Photographer: Robert J. Welch
Reproduction: Courtesy of the National Library of Ireland

4 (*above*) View of unsanitary house in Monivea, Co. Galway, *c*.1906–1914.
CDB 9

5 (*below*) New dwelling house in Monivea, Co. Galway, *c*.1906–1914.
CDB 11

Photographer: Robert J. Welch (1859–1936)
Reproduction: Courtesy of the National Library of Ireland

6 Downings Pier, Co. Donegal, *c*.1914. CDB 47

Photographer: Robert J. Welch (1859–1936)
Reproduction: Courtesy of the National Library of Ireland

7 (*above*) Downings Pier, Co. Donegal, *c*.1914. CDB 46

8 (*below*) Curing fish, Downings Pier, Co. Donegal, *c*.1914. CDB 48

Photographer: Robert J. Welch (1859–1936)
Reproduction: Courtesy of the National Library of Ireland

9 Curing fish, Downings Pier, Co. Donegal, *c*.1914. CDB 71

Photographer: Robert J. Welch (1859–1936)
Reproduction: Courtesy of the National Library of Ireland

10 Nurse visiting a family, Arranmore, Co. Donegal. CDB 55

Photographer: Robert J. Welch (1859–1936)
Reproduction: Courtesy of the National Library of Ireland

1901 and £495 in 1902.[87] In 1901, the board cured a mere 252 barrels in Blacksod; this was only when the fresh fish prices fell too low to merit the cost of icing and transport to English markets. In its second year Blacksod began to make progress; 9 large and 13 small boats were involved in the fishery; 11 of the small boats belonged to the Inishkea islanders, and 277,323 mackerel were caught.[88] The board continued to market pickled mackerel elsewhere in an effort to reduce the reliance on the American trade, which hinged on whether or not mackerel visited its shores. The DATI inquired into prospective markets for cured mackerel in Germany and South Africa, but was unsuccessful.[89] Barrels of herring were given for free to various inland towns in Ireland, but the reports subsequently received were not encouraging, 'being generally to the effect that there was little demand, and although we offered a further supply at 35*s*. while the cost to us was 55*s*., only twelve traders applied at this price, and they took only thirteen barrels'. Efforts to sell the Downings produce to vendors of cured herrings in Ireland failed because cheaper, but inferior, Norwegian herrings were already available.[90]

All ventures were started on an experimental basis, and because the board bought the equipment, it suffered the losses when boats and gear were damaged or outdated. The board had to act as a fall-back agency, and this required huge working capital; for example, in Teelin long-line fishing in the winter of 1901/2 was a failure. Some fishermen earned nothing at all because fish (cod, ling, glasson, conger and skate) abandoned the normal fishing grounds. To top it off, the winter herring fishery was also a failure for the Teelin men. The board reacted the following spring by employing six large Scottish vessels on a bounty system to find profitable fishing grounds off the Donegal coast. Between 28 April and the end of May, when dog-fish prevented further fishing, 918 barrels of herrings were caught by the six boats. Some of the local boats tried to join in, but the grounds were about sixteen miles north of Horn Head and the smaller vessels, and as a result could not safely participate. In this case CDB intervention showed the potential earnings from larger vessels, and as a result many were equipped for the autumn fishery, which was worth £35,000 and another £5,000 was paid to people working onshore for curing and marketing. Donegal responded well to help, and the 1901 autumn figures eclipsed those of previous years and compensated for losses in the spring.[91]

It was very expensive for the board to support the fishing industry, and the high cost of technical instruction was a huge drain on funds especially the cost of tuition. Instructors were employed as skippers of CDB share-system decked boats and yawls, eighty of which were employed in Donegal, Mayo and Galway.

---

87 CDB Twelfth annual report, 1903, p. 20. **88** CDB, Tenth annual report, 1901, p. 40. **89** CDB, Tenth annual report, 1901, p. 39. **90** CDB, Eleventh annual report, 1902, p. 32. **91** CDB, Eleventh annual report, 1902, p. 25.

Relations between the people and their instructors were always amicable, and it appears that an Irish-Scottish 'meitheal' system existed with regard to the fisheries.[92] Crews became dependent on their Scottish instructors, and very few would go to sea without them, especially when the weather turned stormy and in the short winter days 'they would not take the risk of proceeding to sea without instructors'.[93] This was an advantage to the board because the instructors reported on the ability of crews to work and maintain the expensive gear.[94] By 1897 the fishermen were profiting enough to afford to contribute towards the cost of tuition.[95] From 1898 to 1899 the number of instructors employed was 63, and their wages amounted to £4,000. It was found that the crews took advantage of their services by leaving the instructors to do all the repairs, so the board decided to get the crews to contribute to the cost of wages.[96] In 1900 it was decided that a new crew could avail of free tuition for two seasons; in the third season they would give 10*s*. a week or one ninth of the earnings, and if further instruction was needed in the fourth season the men paid 20*s*. a week, and the charge rose to 30*s*. a week in the event of a fifth. This system encouraged the fishermen to learn more in the free seasons. In stark contrast with the situation in 1891 when all the instructors were Scottish, it was also reported in 1901 that out of 77 instructors 44 were Irish. The board paid £5,330 for instruction in 1902, but under the new system £1,143 was repaid by the crews. Rules were stricter for the following year; in the case of ordinary CDB boats, instructors were provided free for two spring seasons, two autumn seasons and one long line season. Donegal share boats paid one ninth of net earnings and the existing Connemara share boats also paid one ninth, or two ninths if they did not mend their own nets.[97] Although the fishery from 1902 to 1903 was generally considered a failure, £4,469 was spent on instruction; the fishermen contributing £953 toward this cost.

Problems within the industry

Large investments were necessary for the board to aid participation in the fresh fish industry, and large risk capital was necessary for the successful running of

---

92 'Meitheal' is a term normally applied to a system where neighbours helped each other to bring in the crop.   **93** CDB, Twelfth annual report, 1903, p. 33.   **94** CDB, Thirteenth annual report, 1904, pp 24–5. In the summer of 1903 ninety Scottish girls were employed curing herrings at Downing's Bay along with twenty girls from the Rosses district, County Donegal, and all the boys and girls available in the Downing's district. Girls from the Rosses district were employed in Scottish curing stations in Wick and Peterhead during July and August. The deal included free lodgings, travelling expenses, they were paid 3*d*. per hour, with a bonus for each barrel of herrings gutted and packed. Burtonhead coopers were also employed at the Scottish herring fishing. **95** CDB, Seventeenth annual report, 1897, p. 19.   **96** CDB, Ninth annual report, 1900, p. 37.   **97** CDB, Eleventh annual report, 1902, p. 35.

a cured fish trade. The only other possible method of carrying on the trade was by co-operation among the fishermen in all branches of the trade, but the prospects of this happening were slim in the short term.[98] The board relied heavily on local initiative for lasting improvements and hoped that the people would organize themselves voluntarily.[99] Only one such local initiative emerged: Aran fishermen founded a Co-operative Fishing Society to deal with the low fish prices between 1910 and the beginning of the war. A Fr Farragher, in conjunction with the IAOS, founded a co-operative system modelled on a Manx society, which had failed because it attempted to apply co-operative principles from start to finish. In the Aran society all equipment belonged to individual fishermen and co-operation began only at the sale stage, proceeds being divided on a proportionate scale based on the catch of the respective crews. The society promoted 'personal skill and industry to the greatest degree', and claimed to prevent 'the slackness that would be natural if the total proceeds were divided otherwise among members of the society'.[1] This society received financial support from the board and continued until 1923 when it wound up voluntarily; the outstanding debt to the CDB was written off.[2]

It was difficult to get people to engage in the fisheries full-time. Connacht in general, and Connemara especially caused most concern for the board, as it contained some of the poorest and most populated maritime districts. In a recent article Angus Mitchell accuses the CDB of 'woeful neglect' of the Connemara district, but in fact a very concerted effort was made to aid this area with particular emphasis on establishing commercial fisheries there.[3] Ireland had a long tradition in the field of marine biology research but a survey of the fishing grounds on the west conducted by the Royal Dublin Society in 1890 incorporated a new dimension. The lengthy research gave affirmative results; it showed that from the plankton (basic fish food) to the shoals that fed on them, the Irish coast was a guaranteed rich annual producer; it also stated that 'no place seems so admirably suited for a fishing station as the Aran Islands.'[4] Despite all the physical evidence and the equipment provided by the CDB, the numbers of fishermen from the Connemara region were lower than anticipated. The board even paid Irish-speaking fishermen from Donegal to train the Connemara men but it made no difference: they continued to fish in currachs for local trade. Connemara men, had no regard for the tuition provided by the board, possibly because it was free, and they did not seem to care for investment in the future. As early as

---

98 CDB, Third annual report, 1894, p. 17.   **99** CDB, Twenty-first annual report, 1913, p. 17.   **1** CDB, Twenty-fifth annual report, 1917, p. 18.   **2** CDB, Minutes of proceedings, 8 May 1923, p. 3.   **3** A. Mitchell, 'An Irish Putumayo: Roger Casement's humanitarian relief campaign among the Connemara Islanders' (2004), p. 75. This article outlines Roger Casement's involvement in the collection of a fund in aid of poor areas in Connemara in 1913.   **4** Green, *Sea fisheries*, p. 384.

1894, the third annual report of the CDB noted heavy losses in Connacht because the fishermen would not modernize their ways. Because curraghs were unsuitable for catching cod, ling and glasson, the Connemara men could not engage in year round fishing.[5] Although the board was most lenient in terms of loans to the Connacht fishermen, it was disappointed 'that more practical fishermen were not sharing in the fishery'.[6] In contrast, Donegal fishermen working out of the Malin head curing station had, with less training, made almost £3,362 in 1895, nearly £1,300 more than the previous season. Over two thirds of that amount went into the pockets of the fishermen and their families, either as payment for fish or for the labour in cleaning, salting and drying it.[7]

Efforts to improve the fisheries in the South Connemara district were in direct competition with the turf industry, which traditionally had a guaranteed market on the Aran Islands (where there was no turf). This work was conducted in daylight hours and transported in hookers, which were cheap sailing vessels. In contrast, the fishing industry was conducted in high-risk, expensive boats; a lot of the work was done at night, and there was no guaranteed wage. The counter attraction of the kelp trade was another reason why Connemara fishermen were slow to start fishing for mackerel, because the seasons coincided in both spring and autumn. In 1899 a gale drove five of the CDB decked vessels ashore in Connemara and four men were drowned. The tragedy had wider implications as it put a stop to all fishing whilst the search lasted, and after that people were slow to fish in larger vessels in unfamiliar waters.[8]

When Connemara men did fish, they preferred to engage solely in the fresh fish trade, so curing stations were not sustainable along their coastline. However, the board was obligated to store salt and barrels in the Cashla and Kiggaul stations and to train local men to cure, in case of a glut in the fresh fish market. When the boats belonging to Connemara men were unsuccessful in the mackerel season, repayments were not met. Audits showed that if the money was managed right, there was enough to support the fishermen, to maintain boats and gear, and also to repay the loan instalments.[9] It was also noted that when the part-time, haulage boatmen/ farmers did engage in the fisheries, they went for more obscure types of fish or crustaceans, which had a limited or luxury market: 'Persons who are not acquainted with the resources of the people may be astonished to hear of such a ready-money market in a district supposed to be reduced to semi-starvation. Many families along the coast make an addition to their income by lobster fishing, their annual receipts varying

---

5 CDB, Third annual report, 1894, p. 16. **6** CDB, Fourth annual report, 1895, p. 17. **7** CDB, Fourth annual report, 1895, p. 13. **8** J.M. Synge, *Collected Prose II* (1982), pp 136–7. Synge notes the distress drowning caused to the Connemara Islands. **9** CDB, Fourteenth annual report, 1905, p. 27. **10** CDB, Twenty-first annual report, 1913, p. 10.

from £3 to £10 a year.'[10] The CDB labours were almost wasted on the Connacht men and, in 1905, the board failed to find a suitable crew for a boat, under a special share system devised for the Connemara coast. Even when the board had firmly established a fishery in Cleggan, the Connacht men were easily disheartened and lacked commitment. 'Most of these crews gave up early to go to England for the harvest, as they do every year, even when fishing is good and promising well, and if the fishing season is late some of the crews break up before it closes.'[11]

Nearly all of the boats supplied to the South Connemara fishermen were in serious arrears by 1906; in three cases the mortgage was foreclosed and the boats repossessed. In twenty-one other cases a collector received the proceeds of the fish caught and credited the board with a fair proportion of the earnings. Irrespective of the arrears in 1906, the board provided two instruction boats for South Connemara and two instructors were allotted to each boat; the 'crews did not, however, turn out very satisfactory, as some of the men were frequently absent, and in the case of one of the boats three different crews were used during one season.'[12] The board made another very concerted effort in the spring of 1907 by putting six boats aside especially for the South Connemara region. An agent was sent to recruit crews but he could only find enough for one boat on the share boat system. The crew delayed their arrival and decided at the eleventh-hour to renege on their agreement. Subsequently, the board received an ultimatum from a representative of the South Connemara fishermen demanding temporary contracts, 6s. a week 'grub money' and a share of the earnings. The board could only guarantee a market for the fish and could not provide a grant-in-aid system for when seasons were late or unproductive. In this instance, there was sufficient alternative, albeit short-term, employment available in the district in 'relief works'. South Connemara fishermen had repeatedly proven themselves untrustworthy, but the CDB continued support, placing a resident inspector in Clifden to monitor the progress and habits of the fishermen. In the following year the board abandoned its instruction scheme in the region due to constant changes in crew-members and unsatisfactory results. It re-offered a boat with forty practically new nets to a crew selected from one of the islands; 'but they (the fishermen) refused unless we agreed to supply them with special nets, which in our opinion were unsuitable, and unless we made structural alterations in the boats, which were not considered advisable. The boat was accordingly transferred to another district'.[13] The establishment of various commercial fisheries, especially the spring mackerel fishery, opened up many previously unexplored possibilities, and even the remotest parts of north Mayo

11 CDB, Seventeenth annual report, 1908, p. 19.   12 CDB, Fifteenth annual report, 1906, p. 21.
13 CDB, Seventeenth annual report, 1908, p. 20.

became centres of trade. Connacht fishermen were last to avail of CDB help, they received loans on better terms and were the first to give up if the season did not bode well.

CDB retreat from fisheries

As early as 1894 the board was hopeful that its assistance in the cured fish trade would no longer be required and that private enterprise would naturally adopt this potentially profitable business.[14] By 1900, it was making an intense effort to retreat from its obligations to the fishermen and was issuing public notices inviting tenders for a lease on its curing stations. From 1903 onwards it reduced the budgetary allocation to the fisheries, and central administration focused more on land issues. Brian Harvey estimates that spending on fisheries went from 30 per cent of annual CDB income between 1892 and 1900 to between 3 and 8 per cent in the succeeding years. In contrast, he notes that spending on land purchase went from between 6 and 12 per cent of the budget prior to 1900 to 60 per cent in 1901, and in later years it went as high as 95 per cent.[15] Harvey fails to mention that extra Treasury allowances to the CDB were specifically pre-assigned to land purchase. Of course, the loans derived from old fishery development funds were continually used for that purpose, but the manner in which this money was spent (in loans to fishermen etc.), no longer required such close scrutiny.

Gradually, the board tried to isolate itself from all aspects of the fisheries; but it also intervened when equipment became outdated or when service industries were in trouble. For example, when it transpired that the Teelin cooperage was badly located (because the neighbouring Downing's Bay area emerged as a more important centre) the board opened a new and more conveniently located centre at Downing's Bay. It was worked by four Scottish and two Irish coopers, previously employed at Teelin; the various other CDB cooperages were self-supporting.[16] This industry received substantial CDB subvention due to the disproportionate engagement in the fresh fish industry.[17] The same applied to

---

14 CDB, Fourth annual report, 1895, p. 14. A Cork firm of fish merchants were the first to express an interest and a proposal was submitted to the board in 1897, indicating their interest in managing the spring mackerel fisheries at Aran and Cleggan but the proposal did not amount to anything. **15** B. Harvey, 'Changing fortunes on the Aran Islands' (1991), p. 248. **16** Expenditure on cooperages up until March 1903 was £12,983 and receipts had well surpassed this. **17** CDB, Twentieth annual report, 1912, p. 27. In 1908 the *Granuaile* brought three cargoes of staves, headings, iron and wooden hoops from Fraserburgh and Peterhead to Ireland. Two of these loads were sold to the coopers in Cork and Kerry, who paid for the materials partly in cash and partly on a loan system. The other cargo was for the boards' cooperages at Downings Bay and Burton Port.

boat building. Centres were started up in conjunction with industrial schools and pre-existing craftsmen. However, this industry continued in a sporadic manner as it depended on the abilities of the trainee shipwrights. Only one boat was ordered from the Kilronan (on Inishmore, the largest of the Aran Islands) yard in 1906, which failed to produce it in time for the summer fishery, and the board had to buy a second-hand Scottish vessel instead. Kilronan closed in 1907 when three of the shipwrights emigrated to America. The premises and gear were rented at a nominal fee to one of the remaining men to conduct repairs only.[18] The viability of the shipyards depended on location; while shipbuilding at Kilronan was considered uneconomical (because the cost of delivering timber was too high), the Killybegs plant was still in operation even after the advent of the motorboat because it was in a thriving fishing region. The board granted £300 in 1906 to construct a new shed at the yard so that building could continue all year round. In 1907 four Zulu boats were designed and built at the Killybegs industrial school; they were 36 feet on the keel and made a price of £160 each.[19] This represented the most successful year for the board in boatbuilding, and the Killybegs yard even installed a 60 horse power engine on one boat. In 1908 eight Zulu boats were built for the board, four at the industrial school at Killybegs, at prices from £225 to £227 10s., complete and ready for sea.[20] Meevagh, the yard beside Downings Bay, progressed to building motors, it had a shed equipped with saws and lights worked by steam, which enabled work to progress in the short winter days.[21] A wooden steam drifter was built at Meevagh in the following year, and an Arklow fishing boat was fitted with a petrol motor bought with £900 lent by the DATI. It 'commenced herring fishing at Killybegs in February and met with more success than any other boat engaged in the fishing on that part of the coast'.[22]

The extent to which the CDB could aid the commercial industry had stabilized from the turn of the century until the advent and wider use of the motor boat. Technological advances posed a crisis for the board: it had to either take on full responsibility for the loans necessary for the new motorized equipment or withdraw its efforts. Considering the revolution in the global industry, the board decided that providing expensive steam-boats to part-time fishermen was impractical and decided its funds would be more wisely spent in purchasing

---

Efforts to get local timber firms to supply the small cooperages on favourable terms were not successful. 'Ordinary business terms for repayment were hardly suitable to such small tradesmen, whose sales were rather uncertain and who find it difficult to hold their own with machine made barrels that have caused the cutting down of prices'. Most were closed in 1911 due to insufficient demand and the introduction of machine made barrels. **18** CDB, Sixteenth annual report, 1909, p. 26. **19** CDB, Seventeenth annual report, 1908, p. 27. **20** CDB, Eighteenth annual report, 1909, p. 18. **21** CDB, Twentieth annual report, 1912, p. 26. **22** CDB, Seventeenth annual report, 1908, p. 24

lands for resale to tenants.[23] Scottish steam vessels first entered Donegal costal waters to fish in 1907; before long foreign competition was high even at Downing's Bay, which had emerged as the most important CDB station. When the fishing industry was powered by wind, the fishermen of the west, with CDB aid, were able to compete equally with other countries. Although it was still possible to make a profit using a sailboat, harsh weather conditions prevented the vessel from leaving the shore, when it could fish it was last to return and received 'fag-end' prices. 'As the reaping hook cannot compete with a modern corn-cutting machine, it is obvious that the sailing-boat cannot remain as effective on the same fishing grounds when the steam or motor vessel appears.'[24] By January 1911, over 120 Scottish and English steam-drifters were engaged in the herring fishery and their ability to stay out in adverse weather conditions encouraged the Donegal men to petition the board for steam vessels.

Because the DATI was helping to finance the power vessels, an advisory committee was set up following the 1909 Land Act to ensure that the CDB and the department worked in tandem in relation to fisheries.[25] The board did not withdraw efforts completely and received a loan from the development commission fund to acquire five steam-boats and ten motorboats.[26] Only full-time fishermen could apply for a loan for a motorboat; those who wished to pursue fishing as a part-time occupation limited themselves to the use of decked vessels. Sailboats could still earn £50 a year, which along with other income sources provided a comfortable standard of living. In 1908 the board also tried to introduce the use of a steam drifter following the receipt of applications from several crews in the congested districts. The drifter was ordered from a Glasgow firm and a crew entered into arrangements with the board to fish on the Irish, Scottish and English coasts under a modified form of the share system. The new system made allowances for coal, running expenses, salaries for a skipper, engineer and fireman; one-fifth of the earnings went to the crew and the balance was to go toward the repayment of the boat and gear. When the boat was nearing completion the crew pulled out and the board could not find a replacement, 'the people being apparently averse to leaving home for such long periods' and the board suffered a loss of £275.[27]

In 1912 the Irish fresh mackerel trade slumped because this fish was no longer the novelty it had been twenty years earlier and the British market was saturated by produce from Cornish steam drifters. Inevitably prices were lower and the board had not succeeded in acquiring a European market for pickled

---

23 CDB, Twenty-third annual report, 1915, p. 14. **24** CDB, Ninteenth annual report, 1911, p. 30. **25** CDB, Nineteenth annual report, 1911, p. 34. **26** D. Hoctor, *The department's story: a history of the Department of Agriculture* (1971), p. 52. The 1909 Development Fund Act granted £54,000 for the development of fisheries over five years. **27** CDB, Seventeenth annual report, 1908, p. 27.

mackerel. The board formally disclaimed all obligations relating to marketing fresh fish in 1906 so it could not justify its re-intervention in the fresh fish industry.[28] The only alternative was to properly conquer the US cured herring market, which was already supplied by the Norwegian fishermen. Until this point, all Irish mackerel on the American market was so considered inferior in quality that the highest prices received were lower than the fourth-grade Norwegian produce. Due to this inferiority, a prejudice existed against all Irish exporters, even though there was nothing wrong with Irish mackerel. CDB-cured produce was of a very high calibre and attracted buyers from afar: in November 1902 a fish merchant from New York visited Downing's Bay to buy cured herring for the US market, 'a proof of the high, reputation which the Downing's Bay fish have attained'.[29] A Norwegian trader came to Cleggan in 1905 in a steamer equipped with barrels and salt and hired a staff of local female curers for the herring season. The mobile curing station paid better wages than the Irish stations, and the fish, which was caught in Irish waters and cured by Irish women, was probably resold as Norwegian produce.[30] In fact, most Irish merchants sold fish to dealers in Liverpool, which was resold as British merchandise and received a higher price.

Norwegian methods, equipment and marketing surpassed all Irish attempts; the Norse fishermen went out in large boats to the Dogger Bank in the North Sea, where they remained for about eight weeks, returning only when all the barrels were full. Prolonged fishing periods in the North Atlantic required vessels large enough to carry the barrels and a committed crew.[31] While Irish fishermen caught mackerel with nets, Norwegian fishermen used large numbers of lines, worked by booms run out of slow-moving, sail boats. As each fish was hooked, it was taken on board, split, cleaned and immediately put into a barrel of brine.[32] The board hoped that by standardizing the mackerel, adopting the Norwegian method, and observing the American market requirements, it would attain a higher market status for Irish goods.[33] A Norwegian fisheries expert was employed to assess the CDB curing stations and methods in the west. He agreed that the quality of Irish mackerel was very high, considering that the

---

28 CDB, Sixteenth annual report, 1907, p. 16. Independent trade was encouraged and facilitated by the board since1903, when it began to sell ice to the smaller merchants to enable them to compete on a par with the larger firms that could afford to import it independently (costs had reduced considerably and by 1912, with wider use of refrigeration, artificial ice was bought in Dublin and was sent in wagonloads as required to the Galway stations). **29** CDB, Twelfth annual report, 1903, p. 25. **30** CDB, Fifteenth annual report, 1906, p. 18. **31** Ibid., p. 23. The US market made very specific requirements in relation to size; standard sized barrels had to contain fish of the same size to suit retailers. **32** CDB, Twentieth annual report, 1912, pp 24–5. **33** Report by the Chief Inspector of Fisheries 'A Government brand for fish cured in Ireland for export' (1906–7), pp 716–25.

methods of curing were primitive, and advised that mackerel should be cured immediately after the boats landed because mackerel deteriorates rapidly after it is caught (the blood congeals and it darkens the colour of the flesh). Irish barrels were not strong enough to endure the rough handling on the way to the US, so the two-hoop barrel was replaced with a four-hoop barrel on which 'CDB' was stencilled. From 1912 the CDB had adopted all the methods used by the Norwegians, and had gained equal market status in America by 1914. The Norwegians only cured and sent autumn mackerel to America, but the board even managed to market the smaller spring mackerel there. Although the spring label obtained a lower price, it did not interfere with the high reputation of autumn mackerel.[34]

In 1912 the board had a fleet of 73 sailing boats that were still in operation under the share system. One third of the catch went to the board for the management and upkeep of the boats and equipment. Power-fishing boats had revolutionized the industry in other countries, and in reality sailing boats could no longer compete. In 1912 the board bought steam drifters costing £3,000 and motorboats costing £1,250 on behalf of the fishermen. But to warrant the expense, the board had to keep them in use all year round, which meant that the crew had to commit to longer periods at sea to follow the shoals to the north of Scotland or beyond.[35] The purpose of buying these new boats was to keep up with technological advances; the crews did not have the option of becoming eventual owners because the length of the mortgage time was too long and the repayments too high.[36] By this time the CDB marine works were also outdated, and, as Pollock notes, harbour provision for large, wind-independent boats was 'at best inadequate and at worst abysmal' and this contributed to the lack of engine power in the sea fisheries.[37]

The industry was badly hit by the outbreak of World War One, when many trained fishermen enlisted, attracted by a guaranteed wage. In Galway nearly all the crews were broken up because the young men of the Claddagh, the fishing quarter of the town, joined either the navy or the army.[38] Those who remained at home were either too old or too young for military service; as a result, very few Galway boats fished, with re-arranged crews, during the first year of the war. The small amount of fish caught meant that there was no need for the service industries, and the board noted 'great suffering and destitution among many of the fishermen's families in "the Claddagh" only for the liberal

---

34 CDB, Twenty-second annual report, 1914, p. 11. **35** CDB, Twentieth annual report, 1912, p. 20. **36** CDB, Twenty-third annual report, 1915, p. 14. **37** V. Pollock, 'The introduction of engine power in the Co. Down sea fisheries' (1991), p. 1. **38** CDB, Nineteenth annual report, 1911, p. 32. The Claddagh was not considered congested until 1909 and nearly all the residents were full-time fishermen. The market facilities were generally quite good, local demand was high and the evening catch was delivered in time for a train service to Dublin for sales the following day.

allowances paid by the Admiralty and the War Office to the wives or mothers of those on active service'.[39] The most devastating effect of the war on the Irish fishing community was that Lough Swilly, being used as a military base, was closed for commercial fishing. This left the curing industry without work, and rail companies stopped operating services between Derry and smaller ports in the west. Mackerel fisheries had huge potential during the war, but statistics still showed the lack of participation in the northwest. The total value of mackerel caught in 1914–15 was £55,679. Kerry fishermen earned £30,065, Cork earnings amounted to £17,423, Galway, including the Aran Islands, only earned £5,234. In Donegal, Mayo, Sligo, and Clare the earnings in the mackerel fishing were small.[40] In 1917 the incomes of all congested districts fishermen were high because steam vessels that normally intercepted shoals going to more shallow waters were engaged in wartime duties. Even inshore fishermen with small vessels profited greatly, indicating the low levels of deep-sea fishing conducted by the Irish. A total of £162,106 was made out of the mackerel and herring fisheries, nearly £100,000 of which was made in Kerry and Cork. Other methods of fishing by long-lines, hand-lines, trawls and trammel nets used to catch the less plentiful and less popular fish such as turbot, brill, sole, cod, conger, haddock, hake, ling, plaice and whiting, realized sales amounting to £20,658 in the same year. The board noted that by 1914 local fish consumption had risen considerably but no returns were made for the value of local sales making the CDB annual estimates incomplete because statistics collectors did not visit various small locations.[41]

Micks disregards the war years when dealing with fisheries under the board, stating that the 'profiteering harvest' gave an unrealistic picture of progress made under the CDB.[42] This is true to a certain extent, but it must be weighed against the fact that at British markets prices for the more common fish were fixed by the food controller and as a result mackerel and herring received 3d. per lb less than the prices set for coarse fish. The fishermen of the congests protested strongly, specifically in relation to fixed mackerel prices and the cost of bringing heavy freights to market. No heed was paid to their protest because 'the Food Controller was obliged to fix a low price for the fish caught in the largest quantities'.[43] Micks does not emphasize that the relatively exorbitant prices paid to Irish fishermen during the war were subsumed by the inflated costs of materials. Prior to the war a motorized fishing-boat cost about £1,100 and the market was competitive; by 1918 the cost had risen 33 per cent and fishermen competed fiercely when a boat came up for sale.[44] In the four years

---

39 CDB, Twenty-third annual report, 1915, p. 14.   **40** Ibid.   **41** CDB, Twenty-fifth annual report, 1917, p. 17.   **42** Micks, *An account of the history,* p. 54.   **43** CDB, Twenty-sixth annual report, 1918, p. 13.   **44** Ibid., p. 14.

between 1914 and 1918 mackerel nets quadrupled in price and the cost of herring nets tripled. Fuel costs, determined by the Ministry of Transport, were high during the war and by 1921 the cost of transporting fish had increased 120 per cent as compared with 1914. Fishermen also had to pay higher insurance premiums to indemnify them against war risks and high costs interrupted the board's steamer services between Galway and Aran and between Sligo and Belmullet. In 1919 only £258,052 was received for the catch in the congested districts, literally the same sum as the previous year although the cost of freight had risen.[45] When the war was over and board duties returned to normal, the board resumed its support of the fishing industry, but most of the equipment was outdated. Powerboat ventures were carried out only on an intermittent and experimental basis until the dissolution of the board.[46]

In all, the CDB did manage to create a commercial fishing industry in the west of Ireland between 1893 and 1923. Before the board began its work, the commercial fishing industry was confined mainly to the east coast; in 1890, with the exception of Baltimore, Dingle, Teelin and the Claddagh there were no full-time fishermen in the congested districts. While the board withdrew finances gradually from 1903 onwards, a CDB support network was in place. In general, it was not very successful in the fisheries; policies were well planned but a combination of external factors, mainly a lack of commitment from the people, led the board to retreat in its efforts from 1912 onwards. It did succeed in some areas, and by 1923 successful commercial fisheries, with full-time workers, were operating from centres in Donegal and on the Aran Islands. Families earning between £8 and £10 per annum in 1891 were earning at least £40 in 1919, and those who engaged in full-time fishing using powerboats were earning in excess of £100.[47] Although the board focussed more on land issues from 1912 onwards and no major innovations were introduced to the fishing industry, it continued to support the industry via loans until 1923. The Gaeltacht Commission reported in 1925 that there were about 1,000 full-time fishermen in Ireland including 300 stationed in the congests. Of the 12,000 part-time fishermen, 10,000 were from the west, as a direct result of the board's efforts. The extent of its support became more evident after the board was dissolved because its systematic instruction and technical training was not replaced by a Saorstát measure. The Gaeltacht Commission noted that many left the occupation in the absence of support between 1923 and 1925.[48]

---

45 CDB, Twenty-fifth annual report, 1917, p. 21. **46** CDB, Twenty-eight annual report, 1920, p. 20. Technical education also broadened to include power-boat maintenance and boys were sent to the Pembroke Technical School at Ringsend, in Dublin, to learn how to drive and maintain a marine motor. Later this scheme was extended when the board opened a school for motorcar driving in Galway. **47** Ibid.,12. **48** Saorstát Éireann, *Report of Coimmisiún na Gaeltachta*, pp 46–9.

4

Agriculture under the CDB

To fully appreciate the impact the CDB made on agriculture it is necessary to trace how the prevailing conditions in 1890 evolved. Since the famine, two major transitions had occurred: subdivided holdings were consolidated, and there was a regression from tillage to more intensive cattle rearing. In broad terms, Ireland contained two separate economic zones because rampant subdivision of holdings had reduced farms to subsistence levels, especially in the west. There, subdivision can be traced to post-Cromwellian times when section 10 of the 1703 penal law (to prevent the further growth of popery) required that the already small and poor holdings be divided equally between all sons on the death of their father.[1] The various laws and land confiscations meant that by 1800 Irish Catholics owned a mere 5 per cent of Irish land.

When the Act of Union became law in 1801, the central political base shifted from College Green to Westminster. The political representative class, many of whom were landowners, moved to London (for some the move was only when Parliament was in session but a percentage moved permanently) thus the pre-existing process of absenteeism accelerated. Absentee landlords employed an agent or, on smaller estates, a reliable tenant, to collect rents, and before long landlords had little or no knowledge of how their lands were managed. From at least 1800 onwards, middlemen or gombeenmen rapidly assumed the position of rent collector, leading to changes in spending; Irish rent was predominantly spent in England and middlemen usually rewarded themselves with a healthy commission.[2] In simple terms, middlemen gained control of spending in their respective areas and in many cases this strong financial footing helped them become the local trader cum loan officer. Some landlords remained but

---

[1] Sheridan, 'The "congested districts" of Ireland', p. 4. See M. Cronin, *A history of Ireland* (2001), p. 82. During the Cromwellian plantation when Irish Catholics had a choice of 'hell or Connacht'. As a result of this legislation the west became overpopulated. Even if the lands were efficiently farmed to produce maximum yields relatively small profits were made because the penal laws also required that two-thirds of gross output from farms worked by Irish Catholics should go as rent to the landlord. [2] S. Clark, 'The importance of agrarian classes: agrarian class structure and collective action in nineteenth century Ireland' (1982), p. 14.

socially there was less incentive for this class to reside in the congested districts. They were reduced to a mere sprinkling by the end of the nineteenth century and in their absence further subdivision was endemic.[3]

By the time the famine occurred, the population had swelled and numbers dependent on subdivided holdings (particularly in the west) had reached unsustainable levels. It is impossible to gauge exactly how many conacre plots or small farms there were in the country because land was registered in the name of the owner, not the tenant. Agricultural statistics were first compiled in 1847 and that survey noted 530,545 holdings in Ireland ranging from one to thirty acres. But the figure does not include holdings of less than an acre, nor are provisions made for farmers with two or more holdings of varying valuations because he was 'returned' as having one holding (the valuation was the sum of his holdings).[4] Ó Gráda notes how the statistics (excluding random errors) were conservative because the value of turf was not included in the aggregate estimates.[5]

Subdivision and subsequent over-dependence on smallholdings was considered a primary cause of the 1847 famine, and the consolidation of farms was perceived as the best method of preventing a recurrence. Consolidation was facilitated by the various land acts since 1870 but they were devised in a way that excluded smallholders from land purchase schemes. In the absence of capital the only way consolidation could be achieved among the poorer classes was through a shift in inheritance patterns – one inheriting son as opposed to dividing the holding between all children. Land tenure patterns changed only slightly in the west in the 1840s and the 1850s except for the fact that the grazing rights were dissolved (they were previously held in common). When smallholders were dispossessed of lands, grazing rights were also confiscated; the rights were not passed on to the next occupier, and large tracts of commonage became available to a new class of tenant occupier that came to be known as a rancher or grazier. Both terms are used interchangeably, but in the case of the west they signify two distinct classes. A rancher, to use David Seth Jones' loose definition, was someone who occupied a minimum holding of 150 acres, valued at a minimum of £50, whereas a grazier occupied a smaller amount of land. He notes that after the famine it was English and Scottish ranchers that took occupancy of farms in the west for grazing.[6] He also comments how there was no link between the rancher/grazier and the peasant community and that this is clear

---

3 L. Kennedy and D.S. Johnson, 'The union of Ireland and Britain, 1801–1921' (1996), p. 35. **4** HC 1921 (1) vol. xli, p. 101. These statistics were compiled on an annual basis by the census office from 1847 until 1900 when the duty was assigned to the Department of Agriculture. The only effort made to enumerate holdings under one acre was in 1919; however, the venture failed as the onus was on farmers to sign returns and post them back to the DATI. **5** C. Ó Gráda, *A new economic history of Ireland* (1988), p. 113. **6** D.S. Jones, *Graziers, land reform and conflict in Ireland* (1995), pp 144–5.

from the land ownership pattern.[7] Usually ranchers did not reside in the areas where they acquired lands and therefore did not contribute to the local economy. Solow reiterates this point, arguing that graziers had abandoned tillage so that they did not even create seasonal employment.[8] Ranchers were regarded as a semi-gentry class; they held positions on the local magistracy, the board of guardians, etc. and engaged in upper-class pursuits such as hunting, but they were unlikely to live in the congests all year round. In the 1870s the 'eleven-month system' (eleven-month tenure contract) became widespread; this was a money-spinner for landlords and those who could afford the tenancy, namely graziers.[9] Graziers were more common in the congests than ranchers; they were mostly likely to be shopkeepers with extra cash who, under the eleven-month tenure, could engage in cattle dealing (these shopkeeper-graziers were also known as jobbers). According to Hall, the Bank of Ireland willingly lent money to graziers and ranchers.[10]

Consolidation stratified Irish farming during the period 1850 to 1891, and in rural terms four distinct classes emerged nationally, (1) landlords and occupiers of more than 100 acres; (2) occupiers with 30–100 acres, (3) those with less than 30 acres of land (these usually had a second source of income) (4) the landless labourer. As well as the Protestant ascendancy landlord class, by 1860 ranchers were to be found in the first class.[11] Solow, using evidence provided by Hooper, contends that this new class of occupier of '30 acres men' had emerged by 1851 and argues that this class contributed little to the agricultural economy (that they played no part in increasing the density of livestock or tillage farming from 1854 to 1912).[12] The third class of occupier had under thirty acres and landless labourers ranked lower than tenants. This tiered system also applied in the west, where holdings averaged about four acres, the third class occupiers were the most common and there were few paid labourers. Harvest work was carried out through a *meitheal*[13] system (a system of co-operative help) or it

---

7 Ibid., p. 153. **8** Solow, *The Irish land question*, pp 110–11. **9** Jones, *Graziers, land reform*, p. 237. Landlords were better off dealing with graziers as they did not have to comply with land acts or extend any tenant right. For example, William Henry Mahon inherited an estate in 1893, which incorporated lands in Sligo and Mayo; it had 282 smallholders, all of whom had held tenant rights on land valued at £1,000. From 1893 to 1908 Mahon gradually leased the untenanted lands, valued at £1,400, on the eleven-month system for a higher return to 15–18 tenants. **10** F.G. Hall, *The Bank of Ireland, 1783–1946* (1949). **11** Jones, *Graziers, land reform*, pp 3–17. **12** Solow, *The Irish land question*, p. 109. Jones, *Graziers, land reform*, pp 60–1. In contrast with Solow, Jones argues that, besides ranch enterprises, it was occupiers of between 30 and 100 acres who increased their dry cattle herd by 71 per cent from 1861 to 1912. He figures that this class of occupier benefited more from the cattle trade than ranchers, but he is careful to distinguish between this new medium-sized tenant farmer class that emerged in the 1840s and smallholders in the congests **13** A. O'Dowd, *Meitheal: a study of co-operative labour in rural Ireland* (1981). See also O'Dowd, *Spalpeens*, p. 210. O'Dowd defines *meitheal* as a working group.

was conducted by nomadic labourers in lieu of lodgings and food.[14] By the end of the nineteenth century, the indigenous bourgeoisie in the west comprised priests, the shopocracy and middling tenants or 'thirty acre men'.[15]

Partly as a result of low prices, census returns from 1850 to 1890 show a mass retreat from agricultural occupations in the non-congested portions of Ireland, where farming was more profitable and the impact of graziers was more notable. While it is believed that the famine played a big part in the reduction in numbers it was more to do with the decrease in tillage and a subsequent lack of employment. Solow notes that tillage decreased dramatically on larger farms between 1854 and 1874, and that this was true for small farms between 1874 and 1912. The main fall-out from this was that the concentration of people working the land fell from five million to two million.[16] These figures are probably more representative of the declining numbers of landless labourers because the retreat from agriculture caused a reduction in the cultivated area of the country, which dropped from four million acres to two million acres.[17] Hans Staehle offers another theory on the reduction of Irish crops, arguing that the decrease in labour-intensive tillage was more closely related to emigration than to ranching and that the shortage in manpower led to a decrease in tilled land.[18] Cullen subscribes to Staehle's theory, blaming emigration for a labour shortage, which resulted in a further fall in tillage acreage.[19] However, Solow's contention seems more convincing – namely, that bad weather conditions in the 1870s resulted in disappointing yields (crop failure in some areas) and caused a dramatic decrease in tillage. For example, in March 1877, when farmers should have been tilling the soil and planting crops, it rained for twenty days; and in April it rained for twenty-four days. That August, when farmers were trying to reap the harvest, it rained for twenty-seven days and crops could not dry.[20] The estimated value of Irish crops declined steadily, from £36.5 million in 1876, to £32.7 million in 1878, reaching a low of £22.7 million in 1879.[21] Grimshaw notes an earlier 'disastrous crop failure' in 1870, which depressed the state of commerce and agriculture

---

14 For an account of nomadic labourers or the origins of the Irish Travellers see J. Helleiner, 'Gypsies, Celts and Tinkers: colonial antecedents of anti-traveller racism in Ireland' (1995). See also G. and S.B. Gmelch, 'The emergence of an ethnic group: the Irish Tinkers' (1976); J. MacLaughlin, *Travellers and Ireland: Whose country? Whose history?* (1995). M. McCann et al., *Irish Travellers: culture and ethnicity* (1996). **15** L.J. Taylor, 'The priest and the agent: social drama and class consciousness in the west of Ireland' (1985). **16** For an account of those who abandoned agricultural occupations see D. Fitzpatrick, 'The disappearance of the Irish agricultural labourer, 1841–1912' (1980). Also Breen, 'Farm servanthood in Ireland, 1900–1940' (1983). **17** T. Kennedy, 'Fifty years of Irish agriculture'(1899), p. 404. **18** H. Staehle, 'Statistical notes on the economic history of Irish agriculture, 1847–1913' (1951) p. 448. **19** Cullen, *An economic history of Ireland*, pp 135–7; Kennedy, 'Fifty years', p. 404. **20** Solow, *The Irish land question and the Irish economy*, p. 121. **21** Ibid., pp 125–6.

and reduced the material condition of Ireland to 'an almost irrecoverable state'.[22] This fall-off in tillage had a huge impact on seasonal employment in terms of internal migration and encouraged more external migration.

Regardless of national trends, tillage was not a viable option in the west because profitable tillage required large tracts of fertile land. Indeed, Crotty argues that Irish climatic conditions were more suitable for grassland farming as opposed to tillage or crop-growing and that 'land broken out of pasture for tillage', deteriorated rapidly.[23]

International trading encouraged through *laissez faire* policies and the repeal of navigation acts in 1849 (which removed import taxes in Britain and gave rise to free trade) provided an impetus for the transition from labour intensive tillage to animal production. Wider availability of cheap American or Russian grain reduced the demand for Irish agricultural produce and the limitations of the Irish rail network did not help: it cost 70*s.* to send a ton of eggs from Cavan to London while it cost only *20s.* to send a ton of eggs from Canada to London.[24] Lee explains that high transit costs arose from a lack of risk capital despite the fact that Irish rail construction was considerably cheaper that British rail or Irish canal construction.[25] Indeed American produce reached not only British, but even the Irish market; in times of cash shortage, imported maize meal replaced local oatmeal as a supplement to the potato diet, which was still standard in western areas particularly in the Northern districts. A combination of bad weather, market trends and transit costs should have decimated the western smallholder but they filled the low-paid market niche and survival was also facilitated by lower rents. Solow shows in her book *The Irish Land Question and the Irish Economy* that when Irish tillage farmers changed to stock-rearing, large numbers left their farms and landlords reduced rents, rather than have untenanted lands.[26] In a later article, she adds that landlords of poorer lands were employing valuators to assess rents on holdings and that these were instructed to set rents at a value 'that will let the tenants live'.[27] This was not

---

[22] Grimshaw, 'Irish progress during the past ten years, 1881–1891' (1891), pp 582–3; T. Barrington, 'A review of Irish agricultural prices' (1927). [23] R.D. Crotty, *Irish agricultural production: its volume and structure* (1966), p. 24. He notes that the only method of countering the harmful effects of tilling Irish land was to sow grass periodically. But this was a luxury enjoyed by wealthier farmers who could afford to render a field unproductive for at least one season and did not apply to the smallholder in the west [24] Kennedy, 'Fifty years', p. 401. Remoter parts of Ireland were at a great disadvantage; for example, whereas it cost 22*s.* to send a ton of butter from Tralee to Cork (eighty-three miles), the rate on the Belgian state railways for the same distance was 7*s.* A ton of flax could be brought from Belgium to Belfast through Hull for 18*s.*, while it cost 22*s.* to transport the same amount from Donegal to Belfast. [25] For wider discussion on the Irish rail network see J.J. Lee, 'The construction costs of Irish railways' (1967), pp 95–109. See also J.J. Lee, 'The provision of capital for early Irish railways' (1968). [26] Solow, *The Irish land question,* pp 168–9. [27] Solow 'A new look at the Irish land question' (1981), p. 312.

Table 4.1. Average income and expenditure of families in ordinary circumstances in nine districts in Donegal

Receipts	%	Expenditure	%
Cattle	14.99	Clothes	16.01
Pigs	11.42	Flour	15.23
Domestic industry	10.9	Meal	14.14
Eggs	9.74	Tea	11.66
Hiring	7.84	Tobacco/alcohol/snuff	10.06
Migratory labour	7.7	Stock purchase	8.82
Corn	5.35	Rent	6.24
Sheep	5.05	Agricultural costs	4.4
Fish	4.81	Sugar	3.80
Butter	4.72	Household	3.2
Miscellaneous	3.92	Fishing costs	2.77
Turf	2.75	Clerical	1.77
Horse	2.75	Co. cess/dog licence	.99
Kelp	2.75	Other food	.9
Labour	2.2		
Hay	1.37		
Fowl	1.24		
Wool	.46		

On-farm consumption as % of value of all goods consumed = 41% (meaning 41% of all farm produce was consumed at home)

Compiled from CDB Baseline Reports from districts of Rosguill, Gartan, Dunfanaghy, Tory Island, Rosses, Glenties, Killybegs, Lough Eask, Ballyshannon.

only a response to pressures from tenant rights groups; falling market prices also played a part, and tenanted land was more valuable than untenanted. She also argues that there was a competitive land market in Ireland, and that tenants were often guilty of raising rents by bidding against each other at auctions (but this applied only in the case of larger holdings). Judicial rents (those set by land courts) were also low because they were set in accordance with the Griffith Valuation, which was based on yields in 1837. Aggregate estimates shown in tables 4.1 and 4.2 indicate that rent amounted to between 6 and 13 per cent of family expenditure but a general survey of individual returns shows that rent was only between two and ten per cent of household expenditure in Donegal, Mayo and Galway.

Although rents were lowered between 1879 and 1890, the general transition (encouraged through an increase in ranching) to more intensive cattle rearing further weakened the position of the west, and very little money was invested in farms, bar the basic minimum to replenish stock. In turn, this meant that in

Table 4.2. Average income and expenditure of families in ordinary circumstances in ten districts in Leitrim/Roscommon/Sligo

Receipts	%	Expenditure	%
Cattle	22.17	Flour, meal, bread etc.	31.26
Pig	21.25	Clothes	19.9
Remittances/labour	19.01	Rent	13.54
Eggs	10.58	Tea and sugar	10.61
Butter	10.46	Bacon and fish	7.48
Oats	7.38	Agricultural Costs	5.74
Potatoes	5.06	Tobacco	4.13
Straw	1.62	Pig	3.91
Fowl	1.32	Household	2.4
Sheep	.89	Alcohol	.59
Wool	.26	Clerical dues	.44

On farm consumption as % of value of all goods consumed=34.49%

Compiled from CDB baseline reports from districts of Kiltyclogher, Kiltubbrid, Ardnaree, Tubercurry, Ballaghdereen, Dunmore, Boyle, Tumna, Castlerea, Moore.

later years returns were low.[28] Dry cattle exports quadrupled between 1850 and 1914. The number of Irish cattle rose from 3,957,000 in 1881 to 4,240,000 in 1890 but, according to Jones, the beef herd was increased by a reduction in the domestic slaughter of beef calves rather than by an expansion in the cow population.[29] Because cattle were increasingly slaughtered abroad, the numbers engaged in the provision trades (for example, butchering and leather tanning) dropped significantly.[30] The Irish could still participate cheaply in the poultry and dairy industries but in the latter half of the nineteenth century the Danes and Dutch increased their hold on the British market for dairy, poultry and pork products.[31] By 1890 Irish butter had a poor reputation and it continued to fade because adulteration was common; the main centre for Irish butter was Cork

---

28 Grimshaw, 'Irish progress', p. 591. Griffith's Valuation was based on fixed principles concerning land. It varied in relation to buildings annually. The average rateable valuation for 1880–5 was £13,828,000 and increased by a paltry £119,000 in 1885–90. Towns of 10,000 inhabitants and upwards had an average valuation of £2,110,000 in the first half of the 1880s and £2,201,000 in the second. This reflects how little emphasis placed on investing money, particularly in buildings and households; as a result, returns in later years were low and banking capital was only marginally higher in 1891 at £7,190,000 than in 1881 at £6,954,000, an increase of 3.2 per cent.   **29** Grimshaw, 'Irish progress during the past ten years', p. 584; Jones, *Graziers, land reform and conflict*, pp 44–5.   **30** Gribbon 'Economic and social history, 1850–1920', pp 267–8.   **31** Ó Gráda, *Ireland*, p. 255.

and it was noted for selling poor quality butter.[32] The active demand for meat in Britain throughout the industrial era ensured that beef production was the main Irish niche in the British market.[33] At the peak of its nineteenth-century development, the cattle industry was valued at three quarters (£37 million) of the value of Irish agricultural output when it stood at £49.5 million.[34]

With increased foreign competition in the British market, the role of the Irish farmer was reduced to that of beef and dairy producer. In general terms, calf prices rose steadily after 1850, by 1890 it was profitable for the small farmer to rear calves and then sell them to the store graziers in the east.[35] A three-tier pattern emerged in the cattle industry in terms of profitability: the west was the breeding ground; the east was the rearing area; and Britain was where animals were fattened. Staehle cites the work of an anonymous author in the *Statistical Survey of Irish Agriculture* (1900), who claims that Scottish farmers literally gave up breeding cattle as they could be acquired from Ireland relatively cheaply, and fattened afterwards on Scottish pastureland.[36] The western smallholder was confined to breeding calves because the land could not sustain larger beasts: 'It may be taken as certain that the small holdings will not support large cattle' was the general conclusion of all the baseline inspectors, who also noted that cattle born in the congested districts were generally inferior breeds. If they survived the winter, calves were kept for twelve, or in some cases eighteen, months, during which time they grew but did not fatten and were then sold to Co. Meath and English buyers.[37] Apart from it being impossible to fatten the animals in the congests, if western smallholders tried to sell mature animals transport costs to markets were too high. The bigger the animal the higher the cost; moreover animals lost condition in transit, which reduced the eventual price.

Within the national economic framework the position of the western smallholder was considerably weaker than the eastern smallholder. Lands that would have been categorised as 'waste' in other parts of the country were in permanent use in the west and the qualification for congested status was that at least twenty per cent of holdings in a county had be 'uneconomic'. Using census returns, Jones shows that the number of congests in the east was negligible compared to the west: 'In the grazing districts of Meath and in parts of Westmeath, for example Trim, Navan, and Mullingar, "uneconomic" holdings comprised

---

[32] Solow, *The Irish land question*, p. 151. [33] Crotty, *Irish agricultural production*, p. 12. Irish cattle were exported live as 'lean stores' to England to be fattened and killed there. These store cattle or yearlings reared for beef were kept for one winter but, outside of drovers, the industry only provided employment for labourers and this was usually limited to seasonal employment to harvest fodder for the winter. [34] Solow, *The Irish land question*, p. 172. [35] For analysis of cattle prices see M.E. Turner, *After the famine: Irish agriculture, 1850–1914* (1996), pp 95–125. [36] Staehle, 'Statistical notes' p. 457. [37] Gaskell, *Desertegney*, p. 2. See also Ruttledge-Fair, *Knockadaff*, p. 2.

less than 6 per cent of the land area'.[38] The labourers in the east held lands of less than two acres but their land was fertile and they could survive better than their smallholders in the west. Holdings that were considered farms in the west were equal in size or yield to cottier holdings in the east, but the cottiers in the east were not considered farmers. Farmers in the east had a more secure stake in fertile land, rural areas were less populated, the rate of emigration was higher and the birth rate was lower than in the west. The west was already at a considerable disadvantage in climatic terms because average annual rainfall was higher than in the east. In transportation terms, farmers in the east were more fortunate too; they had more trains and, because they were closer to markets, transit costs were lower.

MacLaughlin argues that Marx's fatalistic prediction of Irish people being banished from Ireland, and the country becoming an English sheepwalk and cattle pasture had largely come true by 1890 but this rationale can hardly be applied to the west.[39] Cousens highlights that in spite of the famine there was considerable resistance to emigration, especially in the west.[40] The decline in population was also facilitated by changes in Irish family patterns from the pre-famine trend of early marriage and large families to high celibacy rates, later marriage, and smaller families. But this shift only becomes evident in the west from the 1881 census.[41] Guinnane argues that there was dramatic cohort depletion in the 20–24 and 25–29 age groups from 1880 to 1920 but that in the west the more dramatic effects of emigration was later than MacLaughlin suggests. Guinnane also highlights how 70 per cent of the 5–14 cohort resident in the west in 1881 had left by 1911.[42] In the congested districts people did not retreat from farming as a core source of income nor was there a relative decrease in the number of holdings in the west. In fact, families did all they could to earn the rent for their plots, as is clear from the numbers migrating for the harvest season. While average rents were low in the congests, the baseline reports show a strong correlation between areas of higher rents and areas of high rates of migration. Several witnesses to the Bessborough Commission noted smallholdings, consisting partly of bog and unreclaimed land, earning high rents of £1 sterling per acre in parts of Mayo and Donegal; both counties represented areas of high seasonal migration.[43] The baseline reports show that the opposite was true in areas with low rent – in other words, a strong link between low rents, levels of local initiative, low rates of seasonal migration and cottage industry.

---

38 Jones, *Graziers, land reform*, p. 239.   **39** J. MacLaughlin, *Ireland, the emigrant nursery*, p. 8.   **40** S.H. Cousens, 'Emigration and demographic change in Ireland 1851–1861' (1964), p. 286.   **41** Solow, *The Irish land question*, p. 117.   **42** T. Guinnane, *The vanishing Irish: households, migration and the rural economy in Ireland, 1850–1914* (1997), p. 186.   **43** Ó Gráda, 'Seasonal migration and post-famine adjustment' (1973).

According to the baseline reports, people in exceptionally poor areas (such as Cloghaneely) had a lethargic attitude towards work at home, very few migrated, they were lazy about improving their condition and were resigned to a life of poverty: ' "We do as our fathers did, and our sons will do as we do" seems to be their motto, and it is excessively difficult to get them to move out of the old groove.'[44] In that baseline report, a return is given for families in ordinary circumstances and another for very poor circumstances where cash receipts did not exceed £9 a year. As a result Cloghaneely contained some of the poorest families in the congested districts who were always on the brink of starvation.[45]

Ó Gráda argues that the availability of seasonal employment 'helped to maintain the link between small western tenants and their homesteads. Such employment must have been at least partly responsible for the persistent poverty. Whereas in the rest of the country rural smallholdings decreased in number, cottiers and labourers emigrated in vast numbers in the post-famine decades but this was not so in the west'.[46] Western smallholders were guaranteed work on large British and Scottish farms because they worked for a lower wage than native farm workers. O'Dowd traced the movement of seasonal migrants from 1830 to 1915 and accredits the Connachtmen for the most carefully planned route that maximized both time and wages. 'In 1905 they still found much worthwhile employment at hay, early potatoes, corn harvest and main crop potatoes in a journey which took them from Lancashire to Lincolnshire and Cambridgeshire and on to Warwickshire at the end of the season.'[47] Seasonal migration from Connacht and Donegal was proportionately higher and the tradition lasted longer than in other counties. Surplus children (those other than the inheriting son) migrated seasonally to contribute to the household budget; this maintained their right to live in the family home but did not give them a stake in the holding.[48] Instead, it provided a base while money was saved for either a dowry or for permanent emigration.[49] Although many permanently left the west, at least one family member would stay on the smallholding, rearing calves, pigs and carrying out a small amount of tillage; in short, the number of smallholdings remained the same. Cousens sees this 'clinging to the land' as a social, not an economic phenomenon.[50] Arensberg identified the inherent link between land and peasant ancestry in 1937 and, as Solow states, these sentiments must have been much stronger fifty years earlier.[51] In contrast, the more financially secure ranchers did not consider land an ancestral possession.[52]

---

44 Gaskell, *Gartan*, p. 9. **45** Gahan, *Gweedore*, p. 7. **46** C. Ó Gráda, 'Seasonal migration', p. 71. **47** A. O'Dowd, *Spalpeens*, p. 31. **48** In the post famine era there was one-inheriting son, the rest were regarded as 'surplus children'. **49** For a wider discussion on the Irish stem family see D. Fitzpatrick, 'Irish farming families before the first world war' (1983). **50** Cousens, 'Emigration and demographic change' p. 288. **51** C. Arensberg, *The Irish countryman: an anthropological study* (1937), cited in Solow 'A new look at the Irish land question' p. 311. **52** Jones,

MacLaughlin asserts that the large numbers of young people leaving barred any possibility of social or political revolution, but the level of land agitation in the west between 1850 and 1880 goes against his theory.[53] As Vaughan points out, outrages were more frequent in autumn and winter (slacker periods in the agricultural year) and 'frequent in 1849/52, 1862/70, and 1879/82'.[54] Tenant right groups and nationalist politicians romanticized the sentiment that 'the land of Ireland belongs to the people of Ireland' but the harsh fact was that they encouraged people to hold on to uneconomic holdings.[55] The tenant movement, which received huge support in the west, did have some victories. As a result of the Plan of Campaign, the 1881 land act was overturned and new provisions were incorporated into the 1887 land act which officially afforded tenants more rights by awarding courts the right to revise judicial rents. Incidentally this legislation did not make allowances for the poorer regions, therefore, it made no provisions to help the masses that fuelled the tenant campaign. Geary argues that the main repercussions of the Plan were that smallholders in the west became more politically aware and that landed Protestants became politically and socially isolated.[56] However, the landlord class was reduced considerably by 1880 and the baseline reports indicate that smallholders on uneconomic holdings were less concerned with political affairs than were more affluent or middling farmers.

By 1890 the tenant rights movement had effectively run out of steam and certainly did not inspire the western smallholder. In fact, the Gartan baseline report was the only one to mention surviving effects of land agitation. It noted that a large tract of 600 acres of once cultivated land lay waste and was rapidly returning to its original condition. The land was the property of Mrs Adair of Glenveagh, whose husband had evicted the tenants years before and the land had since remained unoccupied.[57] Major Gaskell, who conducted the baseline report for North Inishowen, suggested that if the provisions of the 1881 land act were extended to include farms valued at £4, more farms would have qualified. Rosmuck was the only congested area where almost all the occupants had purchased under the act. Inspector Henry Doran believed that if the people of Mohill were made peasant proprietors, they would have more self-esteem and would concentrate more on improving their holdings. Grappling with legal implications relating to tenure was an obvious starting point for the board but altering the socio-economic mentality of the residents proved a more arduous task. Generally speaking, the people were not thrifty, their houses and surroundings were in a very dirty condition and they made no systematic attempt

---

Graziers, land reform and conflict, p. 155. **53** MacLaughlin, *Ireland, the emigrant nursery*, p. 6. **54** W.E. Vaughan, *Landlords and tenants in mid-Victorian Ireland* (1994), p. 156. **55** Solow, *The Irish land question*, p. 179. **56** Geary, *The Plan of Campaign*, p. 143. **57** Gaskell, *Gartan*, p. 2. **58** Gahan, *Grange*, p. 12.

to improve their lands because they did not have the motivation or the means. Besides the lack of ambition, begrudgery kept people

> down in the old grooves. This feeling is one ingrained through long years, and one which cannot be all at once eradicated. However, as time goes on and education progresses, no doubt the people will see, each for themselves, what is clearly for their own interests and will act accordingly, without having regard to the gradually decreasing mocking of those who would live themselves on the lowest level and would keep others there if they could.[58]

Condition of agriculture according to the baseline reports

Although average Irish production yields were on the increase by the 1890s, many areas in the west fell into the 'at risk of distress' category in the winter of 1891.[59] Failure of the potato crop, the death of livestock, or sickness in a family could have a devastating impact, putting families into poverty-stricken circumstances from which it usually took a few years to recover.[60] The major fall-out of the changes in agriculture, for the smallholder, was that farming became very fragmented; it was rarely the only source of income in the congested district households. By 1890 smallholders in the west were increasingly concerned with earning cash not only for the purpose of paying rent but to enable them to participate in the widening cash economy. With subsistence farming the smallholder could remain aloof from international market trends, but the pressures to engage in a cash economy made farming hypersensitive to market trends. In evidence to the royal commission on congestion (1906), Fredrick Wrench highlighted how increased international trade on the British market effected what was produced in the west; he stated that:

> It must be borne in mind that, except in the smaller agricultural industries of poultry, pigs, and dairying, and in the raising of young stock, the tendency of the age is against the small farmer of indifferent land, who cannot produce either corn or cattle of the first quality, that will readily sell in the open market. Nothing has been more marked in recent years, since the growth of foreign importations, than the difficulty sometimes of selling bad cattle almost at any price. Good cattle will generally sell, as the buyers of stores, who produce the finished article, must have a good foundation to start on, while the inferior article, at the same time, is almost unsaleable; and though the system of small cultivation may be vastly improved, and enable the class of very smallholder to live a better life, it would, in my opinion, be almost criminal to encourage them in the hope, even when they become proprietors under the Land Purchase

---

59 Agricultural Statistics, Ireland, [C6517], HC 1892, lxxxvii, p. 4. **60** Doran, *Drumreilly*, p. 5.

Acts, that they can never compete with the experts all the world over in the production of the finished article. [61]

With respect to the baseline evidence it can be argued that tillage was more significant for daily survival than animal husbandry, which provided for large cash outlays such as rent and settling the shopkeeper account. The national trend was to engage more in cattle rearing and less in tillage but the west did not come into alignment – firstly because of farm size, secondly because the lands had been rendered practically infertile through years of bad farming, and thirdly because the people did not know how to improve their lot. The baseline example of North Inishowen, Co. Donegal, gives an account of a relatively more progressive and varied farm compared with other congests. Average holdings of seven acres valued at £4, were cultivated by planting three acres with oats and barley, and one and a half with potatoes; one and a half was used as meadow, while turnips and cabbage were grown on the remaining acre. The soil was described as stoney clay or a light sandy loam and was fertilised with a mixture of peat mould (a mixture of peat soil and compost), seaweed and artificial manure; turnips were left in the ground and pulled as needed. Here the methods of cultivation were relatively advanced as wooden ploughs were replaced by iron ones that could be purchased for £4 5*s.* each, repayable over two years. Most tenants had a horse, cart, plough, harrow, and horse-hoe, and some farmers owned small horsepower threshing machine and hand winnowers. Every farmer produced milk and butter, but production within a four-mile diameter was insufficient to support a co-operative creamery.[62] Oats were usually more extensively grown in the Donegal districts and played a big part in the diet. In Clonmany, the average farm was from 4.5 to 5.75 acres and was planted chiefly with oats, but contained no meadow; meaning that animals had no hay for winter fodder and were fed with nutritionally inferior oaten straw instead. There were no restrictions on tenants in relation to land reclamation, but this tiresome work could only be conducted in winter during shorter daylight hours often meant smallholders had to hire help to fulfil the labour requirements; this was relatively costly. In contrast, during the summer months the *meitheal* system of co-operative help was widespread during cultivation and harvest. In Grange, the meitheal system worked all year round, people did not have to pay for labour, a system was in operation whereby if a man had a horse he would borrow a plough and would lend his horse in return, and so on.

61 RCCI, Appendix to Third Report, Evidence of Fredrick Wrench, [Cd. 3414] HC, 1906, Q14689. p. 77.   **62** Gaskell, *North Inishowen*, pp 2–3. The peninsula was very exposed; the wind tunnelled through the hills, stripping the valleys of both soil and crop; so Gaskell suggested shelter planting to shield the only arable land. He also advised extensive drainage because the rivers flowing through the valleys flooded often and damaged crops during the summer.

Although cattle and beef production was the main Irish niche in the international market, pig production was more important in the congests. Estimates based on tables 4.1 and 4.2 show that in monetary terms cattle rearing was as significant as the pig industry; however, all the reports indicate that in terms of reliable income pigs were more valued. Kiltyclogher, Co. Leitrim, was the only report that noted money from the sale of calves, rather than pigs, paying the rent.[63] Calf prices were relatively lower than pig prices; consequently pigs received preferential treatment to other animals and were the best-bred beasts in the west. Piglets or bonhams were bought early in the summer kept until November or December, and then sold when they weighed between 1 and 1.5 cwt live weight.[64] Indeed, pig markets, such as the Pontoon fair, were big social events, and allowances are made in the family expenditure returns for a drink on fair days (traditionally a custom to seal a bargain). Pigs required about 4 lb of a balanced cereal ration to produce 1 lb of pig (live weight) and, as Staehle points out, they competed directly with humans in dietary terms (some Irish pigs were fed buttermilk).[65] Despite the high calorific intake, it was generally a 'much greater sign of poverty to be without a pig than it is to be without a cow'.[66] Most congests relied heavily on the sale of pigs, the only major exceptions being South Connemara, which was the only area that had no pigs, but there were 2,350 sheep, 1,850 cattle and 143 horses. On Tory Island, where most animals were poor and scraggy, pigs grew to a great size of 4cwt but dealers were slow to buy them because the flesh was coarse and flavourless.[67] Tory Islanders often used a man on the mainland to sell the pigs as his own, but this was not always successful. In most districts there was an appreciation of pedigree, and efforts were made to improve existing breeds. A young migrant from Clonmany brought home five piglets or bonhams taken in part payment of wages for seasonal employment in Scotland. When he tried to ship them from Glasgow, he found an order from the privy council in Dublin was necessary to get them home. He went to the trouble of telegraphing for the order, which was granted on the condition that he obtained a veterinary certificate, costing 10s. but the migrant knew the money was retrievable in the sale of the finished beast.[68]

Outside of the pig industry, the baseline inspectors were shocked by the high degree of inadvertent cruelty to animals in the congests. In Carna, the cattle and sheep were small, stunted and difficult to fatten. On Gorumna and Lettermore (the islands in the South Connemara district), and Crumpaun, the narrow peninsula leading out to them, animals died of starvation every spring, especially sheep, which came last in the order of feeding priority. Also in mar-

---

63 Gaskell, *Kiltyclogher,* p. 2.   **64** Gaskell, *Pontoon,* p. 3.   **65** Professor Johnson, 'Raw materials for Irish animal husbandry' (1950), p. 362. Staehle, 'Statistical notes', pp 452–4.   **66** Gahan, *Cloghaneely,* p. 2.   **67** Gahan, *Tory Island,* p. 2.   **68** Gaskell, *Clonmany,* p. 4.

itime areas, where fishing was remunerative, people were even more feckless about animal welfare. In general, sheep were badly bred and very poorly valued in all districts; there is no mention of mutton or lamb consumption in the reports. As sheep were cheaper, and relatively less bothersome to rear than cattle, they were plentiful but generally left to their own devices. The land was too wet for them and hundreds died every winter due to liver fluke. On the poorer farms of South Connemara, that could not afford to keep pigs, sheep were housed at night and well cared for.

Horses were badly treated and over worked in the congested districts; for example, they were used to transport turf long distances, and each family required about fifty loads a year. North Inishowen is one of the few districts where the people appreciated their value and while horses were of coarse breed money was spent on improving pedigrees. Only one of the eighty-four reports gives a blacksmith's bill as expenditure, but this craft was in steady decline. Itinerant smiths were probably operating in the congests, and these were likely to have been paid in kind.[69] In Clonmany, even the poorest tenants kept horses for carrying turf, seaweed and manure. They were big animals, coarsely bred from Clydesdale sires, they were fed oaten straw even during the spring when they should have been on grass, and the result was light bodies on heavy inactive limbs.[70] In counties where horses were scarce, such as Leitrim; donkeys were numerous, they were rare in Donegal, with the exception of the Fanad area.[71] Goats were an uncommon feature in the congested districts but were kept by nearly all households in the congests of Leitrim. Goats' milk was used in tea, much to the detriment of the kids, which were half starved as a result. In this region dairy farming was more prominent and cows' milk was reserved for butter.[72]

Cattle were also badly bred and inferior to those reared in more prosperous areas of Ireland, they were hand fed in winter, which meant they got a daily ration, and as a rule they were kept in at night. Inferior breeds continued to deteriorate over time because the farmers did not buy their own bulls and were stingy when it came to insemination: 'One hears on all sides that the small farmers and even some of the better class will not pay 2*s*. 6*d*. for the service of a good animal when they can obtain a bad one for 1*s*.'.[73] When the board introduced a better breed of Kerry cattle to Desertegney, they took three times as long as the existing breed of Shorthorn to mature. Nearly all of them perished as calves at seven months because they were fed oats in the sheaf immediately after being weaned and this feeding was too coarse. On the islands of the South Connemara

---

69 N. Ó Ciosáin, 'Boccoughs and God's poor: deserving and undeserving poor in Irish popular culture' (1998). For a comparative analysis of nomadic people see D. Mayall, *Gypsy-Travellers in nineteenth-century society* (1988). See also J.P. Liegeois, *Gypsies and Travellers: socio-cultural data* (1987). **70** Gaskell, *Clonmany*, p. 3. **71** Gaskell, *Fanad*, p. 3. **72** Gaskell, *Kiltyclogher*, p. 3. **73** Gaskell, *North Inishowen*, p. 2.

district, animals were badly treated through the ignorance of the people, and many perished from 'pine' and 'cripple', pine being starvation arising from nutrient deficient grass, and cripple being rheumatism from over-exposure to damp conditions in badly constructed byres. The islanders believed that 'if a calf born on the islands were to get more milk than it could drink, it would not live a year unless changed to the mainland, and the sooner the better, once it is six months old'.[74] It was more profitable to sell cattle young, because it cost about 30s. to send an animal away to fatten for the season, which lasted for five months and the money spent was not recovered when the animal was sold.

Cattle ownership was not as common in the Donegal districts as cattle herding. In Fanad, a barter system existed where cows 'on milk' were sent to graze on mountain farms. The farmer looked after the cow and the milk was bartered for the grass, 'being a convenience on both sides and not having any monetary basis for the transaction'.[75] Traders abused this system when they noticed a poor man in arrears; to save themselves from loss, they would extract the value of what was owed by buying a cow that was going dry (in the period before calving) and send it to graze upon the debtor's farm. The debtor had to feed and herd the cows in exchange for its manure and milk, which was very little at this point. When the cow was nearer calving, she was taken away and a couple of others were sent up. On rare occasions, cows were left after the calving, in which case the farmer had use of the milk but had to rear the calf as well as the mother. Shopkeepers also sent dry cattle on what was termed the 'grazing system' where a heifer or bullock was sent up to graze on the land and the farmer only had the benefit of the manure. Aside from shopkeepers settling accounts in this way, people also took grazing cattle at so much per head; one dealer in Glenswilly owned several hundred cattle that were put out for grazing. Prices varied according to the size of the beast, from 8s. to 12s. for the year. Because the 'on milk' and 'grazing' systems reduced the tenant to the position of a herdsman, needless to add the board wanted to abolish both systems.[76] While Jones accounts for the existence of herdsmen as an occupation ranking higher than a landless labourer, there is no reference to the above types of abuses. This highlights the clandestine nature of the system and shows the magnitude of shopocracy power in the congests.[77]

Invariably both humans and animals occupied the one dwelling, and visitors to the west found it difficult to distinguish between the animal outhouses and human dwellings. Arthur Bennett compared the houses in Connemara to pigsties: 'I might be accused of indulging in language of the hyperbole but when I say that I have seen scores of stables that are palaces by comparison, I am stat-

---

[74] Gaskell, *South Connemara*, p. 14, Appendix D. [75] Gaskell, *Fanad*, p. 10. [76] Gahan, *Brockagh*, p. 4. [77] Jones, *Graziers, land reform and conflict*.

ing the simple truth. A large proportion of them are unfit for human habitation.'[78] Micks observed in his report on The Rosses that 'cattle in many instances are housed at night at one end of the day room, and the poultry often perched overhead'.[79] The following baseline account of family life was commonplace:

> The owner's cattle share the living room. I have seen a half-naked child of four to five years lying asleep before the turf fire, with his head on a rough block of wood, while the cow stood over him as if watching and guarding the child. After dark the family and their friends sit round the fire, and the cow, heifer, calf, and pig, get as near it as they can. The poultry are also under the roof, wherever they can perch. The customs of daily life are simple and natural; and the sense and manner of the dwellers in these rude homes are such that one can never enter or quit one of them without paying a mental tribute of respect to its owner. The pig's lair in a one-roomed house is often 'under the bed', especially when the pig is the mother of a litter. This I have also seen.[80]

In general, animals in the west were not particularly hardy, and they would have perished outside. The residents believed that there were many advantages to keeping them in the house: the animal contributed a considerable amount of heat and the farmer could observe its health, especially if it was in calf. In the Ballyshannon district the cows were kept inside specifically for the sake of the manure, which was mixed with large quantities of turf-mould, sand or straw. It was customary to have a cesspool in front of the houses, where 'bog-mould is put to sour, and any manure ... collected is placed therein'.[81] Surprisingly, this appalling practice did not contribute to ill health; in fact, the Kiltimagh report mentions that where turf-mould or black mud was used in cesspools, fever epidemics did not occur as frequently, possibly because the pH[82] content of bog soil killed the harmful bacteria.[83] Turf mould (very wet peat moss) was rendered acidic by rain water and alkaline by fresh spring water, both of which acted as a disinfectant; rain water gave it a pH of 3.5 to 4.2 and, according to Foss and O'Connell, when fresh water springs feed into bogs, the soil is alkaline, reflected in a pH range of between 7 and 8.[84] Manure heaps were kept outside the family dwelling and the liquid manure (the most beneficial) was allowed to drain and waste away. In most instances, a way was made to let the liquid to overflow; 'none of them have any idea of making a compost heap, and they would laugh at you if you told them that the manure heap would be better if it

---

[78] Bennett, *John Bull*, p. 56. [79] Micks, *Rosses*, p. 7. The baseline reports do not account for sheep occupying the family dwelling. [80] Gaskell, *South Connemara*, p. 7. [81] Doran, *Ballyhaunis*, p. 4. [82] pH=potential of Hydrogen; used as a measure on a scale from 0 to 14 of the acidity or alkalinity of a solution, where 7 is neutral and greater than 7 is alkaline and less than 7 is acidic. [83] Doran, *Kiltimagh*, p. 4. [84] P. Foss and C. O Connell, 'Bogland: study and utilization' (1997), p. 184.

was under cover, and until these and many other prejudices are removed, it will be extremely difficult to improve their methods of farm culture'.[85] Instead of making compost, the people bought and used artificial manure 'to an extent that is injurious to the land'.[86] Gaskell argued that over-use of guano actually impoverished the land, but the tenants were convinced that they could not grow a crop without it.[87]

To radically alter living standards in inland districts the board realised that animals had to be removed from the family dwelling. Sanitation laws were commonly ignored in the congests. Rural dwellers had a major advantage over urban dwellers because they had readily available building materials (houses were made out of wood, stones and rushes for the roof) and could escape infringement of sanitation laws, which were enforced more stringently in the urban districts. All the reports refer to disregard for personal and general hygiene, stating that the people and their environments were filthy. Only the district of Moore reported measures taken against those who broke sanitation laws. There the baseline inspector met the medical officer and the relieving officer on their way to enforce sanitary law on a tenant who persisted in keeping a sow and a litter of pigs in his house (they were acting on a complaint made by a relative who shared the house).[88] Baseline inspectors complained of the general disregard for cleanliness; they noticed how lime, which was used for making whitewash, a form of paint, was recognized as an important disinfectant, but it was unavailable in many areas. Houses were usually whitewashed outside and, as a rule they were not whitewashed inside, except when local authorities gave free lime in times of 'rampant fever'.[89]

The reports show that animal breeding and welfare required serious attention but they also showed that (in line with national trends) animal husbandry was in a much better state than tillage. In the congested districts, basic reaping and sowing was practised, but crops were not rotated and people made many false economies. The most commonly grown crops in the west were potatoes, turnips, wheat, barley and oats. Flax was still grown in some northern districts, and it exhausted the soil so much that farmers believed that land could not be tilled profitably for about nine years after a flax crop.[90] Along the coast of Fanad, barley was sown with oats because it was believed that it would yield a better crop. There was no scientific basis for this custom, known locally as *pracas*.[91] This cultivation system was also practised in Rosguill, people thought that seaweed (a natural fertilizer) was bad for potatoes, and no weeding or hoeing of any sort was carried out. Gaskell remarked that 'as a general rule there are quite

---

[85] Gahan, *Lough Eask*, p. 3. [86] Doran, *Ballyhaunis*, p. 2. [87] Gaskell, *Levally*, p. 2. People in Levally bought guano instead of using compost. [88] Gaskell, *Moore*, p. 4. [89] Gahan, *Teelin*, p. 15. [90] Gahan, *Brockagh*, p. 1. [91] Gaskell, *Fanad*, p. 2; from Gaelic, literally means a mixture.

as many weeds as potato plants' in the Rosguill district.[92] On small farms, potato seeds were pressed (kibbed or dibbled) into the ground and covered with a bare handful of manure, which was insufficient. There was limited knowledge of the properties of lime as a soil acidity regulator but the good effects were negated by kibbing. Green crops were not grown in Glencolumkille because the farmers had no fences to keep stray sheep from eating them. On Clare Island, the tillage plots were unfenced, and family members took turns in guarding the crop from trespassing animals.[93] Fencing was a very fundamental way of protecting a crop, lowering the risk of disease (such as foot and month or bovine TB) and basically marking out boundaries; this was an issue that later received careful consideration from the board.[94] In Rath Hill, Co. Mayo, the people burned or pared the land to get rid of gorse and weeds and they believed this also fertilised the land. Land was dressed with sea-sand and gravel and set alight. This practice was, according to the baseline inspector, the curse of the district.[95] Subdivided holdings had invariably poorer land, rotations were a see-saw between oats and potatoes, people persisted with the futile practice of over-filling the ridge, leaving seeds less than 6 inches apart. This custom left very little room for the crop to grow, it impoverished the yield and wasted the seed.[96] When paring and burning concurred with short rotations, land was ruined.[97]

CDB agricultural improvement policy

Agriculture was narrowly defined as the science of land cultivation, and the land committee of the CDB dealt with it under the following categories: forestry, improvement of livestock and poultry, seed supply, amalgamation of holdings, migration and emigration. Some of the agricultural improvement work had to be done in conjunction with the agricultural branch of the Land Commission (because the Land Commission continued to carry out all surveys and it facilitated the sale of holdings, which incorporated valuations and inspections). The commission also helped the board in the areas of sample holdings, forestry, livestock improvement and beekeeping. Due to financial and legal constraints, the board could do little at first in relation to farm size. Instead, it endeavoured to keep the resident population busy at home and concentrated on teaching the people how to cultivate and maximize the output of their holdings. Working on the recommendations of the baseline inspectors, the CDB spent the first seven years (1891–8) concentrating on basic agricultural development.

---

92 Gaskell, *Rosguill*, p. 3. **93** CDB, Fifth annual report, 1896, p. 12. **94** Gahan, *Glencolumkille*, p. 1. **95** Ruttledge-Fair, *Rath Hill*, p. 2. **96** Gahan, *Teelin*, p. 3. **97** Bell and Watson, *Irish farming*, p. 235.

From their knowledge of the residents, the baseline inspectors believed that the only way to change agricultural methods was to physically show the people – which would entail their living among them. In 1893 baseline inspectors Butler, Roche and Ruttledge-Fair completed their contracts, but Gahan, Doran and Gaskell continued to work for the CDB as agricultural inspectors.[98] The board was established in August 1891, which was late in the agricultural year, but it made immediate efforts where possible to initiate better farming practice. In 1890 the Irish Government had bought 820 acres of rough mountain and bog near Carna in Connemara and began a forestry experiment there, to relieve distress. As the area was in the congested county of Galway, the CDB took over the project in 1891 and employed a full-time forester to teach his craft to the residents of Knockboy. Size-wise, sheep were probably the most suitable animal for the western terrain, so the board endeavoured to improve the breeds of sheep and people's respect for the animal; 151 pedigree, black-faced Scotch rams were sent to Donegal in 1892. After the first winter 31 died, these heavy losses being attributed to a mixture of severe weather conditions and bad pasture. The experiment proved costly, but it showed the people the value of good breeding, as the lambs bred from CDB rams fetched higher prices than the local breeds.[99] The following year the surviving rams were moved to Galway and Mayo where conditions were marginally better. In 1893, the duties of the forester at Knockboy were extended to manage other pedigree animals. A house was provided for him, and a range of stone sheds with slate roofs were built close to the house to accommodate the CDB pedigree stallions, horses, bulls, cows, pigs, and poultry.[1]

In 1893, in tandem with efforts to improve livestock, the board organized 'example plots' in centrally located areas and employed instructors to teach new methods, following the example set by the Royal Dublin Society (which had employed an instructor in Swinford since 1889 to work an example plot). It took at least a year for the plots to mature, but the board was confident that the policy would work and would create a domino effect – that well cultivated grass would lead to improved hay, better food for the stock and so on – but the people were slow to grasp any new idea and were still suspicious of this new movement.[2] Prior to the foundation of the board, the government made paltry efforts to develop agriculture through technical instruction. The schemes were carried out by the Commissioners of National Education in the Albert Institution in Glasnevin, and the Munster Institution in Cork, and in national school gardens. Bell and Watson argue that the reputation of these institutions was 'marred'

---

[98] CDB, Second annual report, 1893, p. 30. [99] Ibid., p. 13. [1] Ibid., p. 9. During the same year, the board built stables on a stud farm near Dublin to winter horses that were stationed in the congested districts. [2] Gahan, *Cloghaneely*, 1892, p. 7.

because tenants believed their purpose was to encourage improvements in order to raise rents.[3] The baseline inspectors noted that none of the congested population had attended the Albert Institution nor had anyone availed of local classes run by the itinerant instructors employed by the National Board of Education. Comparative experiments were conducted in Skull and Crookhaven to show the benefits of using good quality seed potato. The board purchased and distributed Sharpe's Victor seed and compared the resulting crop with the ordinary crops of the district; the people witnessed a higher return, adopted the new methods and steps were taken to start market gardening as an industry there.

In the summer of 1895 the board started to give demonstrations of potato spraying and £1,371 was spent on spraying materials (supplied either free or at three quarters of the cost price to farmers). Lee claims that spraying was widespread before the board, but the CDB reports suggest its absence.[4] Bell and Watson, referring to a DATI report in 1907, maintain that spraying became more widespread in Connacht, Ulster and Munster than in Leinster, thanks to the efforts of the board. Had it already been a widespread practice, the board would not have met with the problems it did when implementing the new scheme in the west.[5] In parts of Donegal and Kerry, the owners of potato plots refused to have their potato plants sprayed, due to fodder shortage (cattle were fed on grass and weeds growing on the headlands – and it was believed that herbage sprayed with copper sulphate and lime was dangerous food for animals).[6] Furthermore, Ó Gráda argues that the people were slow to undertake the responsibility for the spraying machines in case they broke down. Although the board practically gave the machines away, no allowances were made for aftercare and they were expensive to service. He notes that the people did eventually adopt new modes of cultivation but improvised so as not to incur the expense of machinery, and he cites Synge's account of an old lady 'spraying her patch with an old broom dipped in bluestone solution'.[7]

The board found similar opposition to better practice in animal care when it introduced the new practice of sheep dipping in 1895 at Doon near Clifden. Prior to this, dipping was not used as a preventative measure; it was only used when the animals were badly infested with scab or ticks.[8] Moreover, people poured the liquid over the animals because they did not have containers bigger than petrol barrels to use as a bath; this was a futile, slow and wasteful process. Two itinerant instructors were appointed (one for the Cork and Kerry region and the other to deal with areas of Donegal that had no previous instructors). A portable sheep dipping apparatus was first used in 1900 and 25,000 sheep were

---

3 J. Bell and M. Watson, *Irish farming, 1750–1900* (1986), p. 12.   **4** Lee, *Modernisation*, p. 124.
5 Bell and Watson, *Irish farming*, p. 133.   **6** CDB, Fifth annual report, 1896, p. 8.   **7** Ó Gráda, *Ireland before and after the famine*, p. 143.   **8** CDB, Eleventh annual report, 1902, p. 11.

treated. An inspector was employed to supervise the work of instructors and, by 1908, over £22,000 was spent on this scheme.

Beekeeping also fell under the charge of the agriculture committee, and in 1892 the board initiated a beekeeping venture on the advice of the Irish Beekeepers Association (IBA), hesitantly lending £50 to start an experimental beekeeping scheme. Turlough O'Byren, of the IBA, conducted preliminary investigations in Swinford and selected ten people with whom he supplied with ten swarms of bees, hives and managerial instructions. Five of the ten hives were supplied to schools, to raise children's interest in the hope that it would result in hives being established at their homes.[9] Women and children would have figured prominently in this activity because the beekeeping season concurred with the migratory labour season, which left only women and children at home to mind the hives.[10] In 1893 a further grant of £160 was made available by the CDB for more experiments to encourage beekeeping among smallholders. O'Bryen distributed the money to other counties using a system approved by the best authorities on bee-keeping.[11] The Revd A.H. Delap assisted in the bee-keeping industry in Fanad. In his first year the output of honey doubled, and one man paid his rent out of the sale of honey. 'In Fanad, and presumably at many other places, it is considered that each hive makes a nett annual profit of £1, so that farmers can readily estimate how many hives are of equal value to a pig'.[12] The Board provided special boxes and set up depots to buy, store and market honey on behalf of the hive owners; it did not profit from the honey industry. For example, in 1897 the board bought 431 lb of honey from beekeepers at a cost of £96 and sold it for £109 to the Thomas Lipton company, but it still cost the board £30 for freight and crates.[13]

The board continued to support the industry and in 1896/7 one hundred and four hives were supplied to beekeepers in congested districts. They were sold to smallholders at reduced rates on a system of payment by instalments.[14] Production rose in 1898 to 22,925 lb or an average of 54.5 lb per hive.[15] The following summer was unusually long and dry and hives produced an average of 66.5 lb each. The total quantity of honey sold by the CDB was 59,936 lb, but this represents about one third of all honey produced as suppliers found new markets.[16] The industry grew rapidly until a highly contagious bee disease called 'foul brood' was detected. However, this could be treated by disinfecting the hives with formaline. CDB hives were re-designed and fitted with a large hole

---

9 CDB, Second annual report, 1893, p. 15.   **10** Smith, 'I thought I was landed', p. 220.   **11** CDB, Third annual report, 1894, p. 6.   **12** CDB, Sixth annual report, 1897, p. 11.   **13** CDB, Seventh annual report, 1898, p. 13.   **14** CDB, Sixth annual report, 1897, p. 11.   **15** CDB, Ninth annual report, 1900, p. 12.   **16** CDB, Eleventh annual report, 1902, p. 13. Many districts used heather and mountain herbs in the making of honey, which was of a superior quality and could have been sold for a higher price than at the depot.

covered with perforated zinc and a sliding shutter, so that a cloth or sponge saturated with a 10 per cent solution of formaline could be retained in the hole; these hives were manufactured by C.N. Abott in Dublin and remained in use for many years.[17] The honey business earned a cash income; moreover it kept people busy at home. A fruit and market gardening expert, Mr Peter Brock, was appointed to complement the honey trade and create an alternative industry. In his first year of service, over 5,700 fruit trees were planted and 200 copies of a book entitled *Profitable Fruit Growing* were sold.[18] Local agricultural inspectors helped Brock to encourage people to grow fruit trees. It was a successful venture, and by 1903 the custom of planting trees was common. A total of 6,680 apple trees, 534 pear, plum and cherry trees and 3,360 currant, gooseberry and raspberry bushes were sold through the board that year. Beekeeping and fruit tree growing took off in certain areas; these were entirely new industries; they were cheap to organize and were generally self-supporting from an early stage.

In 1895 instructors managed a mere twenty example plots, and some were abandoned during the course of the year because it appeared that the people were 'either unwilling or unable to give the requisite attention to the cultivation of the plots'.[19] The example holdings were reduced to eleven during 1896 and a new system was put in place. Instead of operating one big centre, the board put smaller example plots on smallholdings on an experimental basis. Smallholders were supplied with free seed and artificial manure on the condition that the plot was worked under the direction of the board's local instructor. Each plot demonstrated the advantages of using good seed and artificial manures in conjunction with improved systems of tillage and cultivation. The experiment flourished and before long the board managed 59 plots – 36 in Co. Donegal and 23 in Co. Galway. This new measure started a healthy rivalry, with the smallholders vying to have example plots on their land, and it encouraged small farmers to carry out improvements. Drainage, reclamation and fencing work had to reach a satisfactory level before candidates could qualify for an example plot on their holding. In turn this raised general awareness about good cultivation and helped the smallholders to detect trader misconduct in other areas, particularly in relation to seed quality. Research conducted by the agricultural inspectors into the calibre of fertilizers sold within the districts showed that traders selling artificial manures rarely complied with the provisions of the existing legislation. To rectify this, the board supplied traders and farmers with information on fertilizers, indicating the advised guaranteed minimum percentage of nitrogen, of soluble and insoluble phosphates, or of potash contained in the fertilizers sold.[20]

---

[17] CDB, Eleventh annual report, 1902, p. 13. I am grateful to Michael Hurley for further information on CDB hives. [18] Ibid., p. 10. [19] CDB, Fourth annual report, 1895, p. 5. [20] CDB, Fifth annual report, 1896, pp 5–7.

Challenges and administrative change

The CDB functioned well as a centrally controlled agency until 1896, and in the first five years it implemented many elementary but formative agricultural changes in the west. However, it had to be as fluid as possible in its operations to incorporate agricultural advances, external pressures and the regional variation of problems. By 1897 the fishing and poultry industries had reached maximum potential with regard to numbers engaged. At this point the poultry industry was under the control of the IAOS, but fisheries remained under the auspices of the board. Henry Doran, a former baseline inspector, who was re-employed as a resident agriculture inspector in Donegal realized that the issue of basic living conditions required more direct attention but did not fall neatly under the responsibility of existing CDB divisions (except when the board built new houses on reorganized holdings). He also discovered that where livelihoods were dependent on cleanliness, such as the shirt-sewing districts of Donegal, the houses were better kept; while they were not necessarily of a completely different design they were brighter and better aired. Doran also noted that in areas where there was an absence of medical officers, landlords were very influential in raising living standards. A notable example was Lord Palmerstown who took an active interest in his tenants in Grange, Co. Sligo. Gahan the baseline inspector noted,

> On entering the district from the northeast side one is struck with the cleanliness and comfort of almost all the cottages, they are well built and have large good windows, a marked contrast to the tiny light holes one is accustomed to see in County Donegal. The reason for this is that Lord Palmerstown, who took a very deep interest in his tenantry, used to give prizes for the best built and best kept houses, gardens etc.; he also supplied windows to all his tenants.[21]

In contrast, in the townlands outside Lord Palmerstown's estate very poor houses were found. Gahan also noted where literacy levels were low educated people (especially priests) were revered by the peasant classes. While some argue that this gave this group a 'disproportionate moral and political influence over Irish rural and working class communities'; Doran saw it as a modem for promoting cleanliness and self-help.[22] For example, he noted in Gweedore, where the notorious Fr McFadden was parish priest, that the houses were cleaner and were whitewashed both inside and out.[23]

---

21 Gahan, Grange, p. 10. **22** Mac Laughlin, *Ireland the emigrant nursery*, p. 10. **23** Fr MacFadden was a strict disciplinarian and moral guardian to his parishioners for further information on his notoriety see B. MacSuibhne, 'Saggart aroon and gombeen-priest: Canon James MacFadden, 1842–1917' (1998), p. 155.

Doran proposed that the board should harness these existing control mechanisms to promote basic development and he devised a parish committee scheme with the basic aim of removing cattle from the family dwelling. Under existing rules he had to get a board member to bring his idea to the attention of the board; Fr Denis O'Hara, parish priest in Kiltimagh, Co. Mayo, readily obliged. The proposed committee was to act as an intermediary body between the people and the board, thus alleviating pressure on the central offices. When CDB income was increased in 1896, the surplus money gave the board an opportunity to delegate responsibility. Doran's parish committee scheme was approved, and in October 1897 the experiment began in the inland district of Swinford, Co. Mayo. This was identified as the poorest and most densely populated inland district; holdings were tiny; men migrated for three to nine months of the year, and during the winter months they were idle. Local rates were not collected in under-resourced regions and therefore minimal outdoor relief works were carried out. Initially, parish committees were ex-officio; local clergy, landlords or any state employee could apply to be members, but had to be residents of the area in question. Temporary members were also elected and were usually ratepayers in the district, and salaried members had no voting power. Inspectors highlighted in the baseline reports that it was the shopkeepers and their credit system that kept the people poor. While this was not true of all shopkeepers, the board was fearful that unscrupulous shopkeepers, if they had positions on the committees, would use them to either embezzle funds, to show favouritism to loyal customers or to influence decisions on customers for personal gain. To counteract this possibility, shopkeepers were strictly prohibited from becoming committee members or to hold paid positions of supervisor or secretary.

The parish scheme began with an experimental budget of £1,520, which was given in grant aid to twelve parishes in the densely populated districts of east Mayo (the printed instructions for the guidance of parish committees were first issued in 1897 and revised in 1899). Each parish scheme received between £50 and £120 annually, meaning that the committees had to use small cash incentives to encourage improvements; money was administered in prizes, grants (non-repayable) and loans repaid on borrower-friendly terms. The board could not possibly afford to fund entire projects and payment was only given when work was complete but the money provided an incentive, for example, approximately £2 was given to encourage holders to build outhouses costing £12.[24] To achieve basic objectives, the parish committees initially provided grants to move cesspools a set minimum distance from dwelling places and prizes were allocated for the most successful ventures. The removal of a manure pit and the conversion of the site into a yard or garden earned a prize of money, seeds or small trees. Further

---

24 RCCI, First Report, 1906, Evidence of the Revd Denis O'Hara, pp 180–5.

prizes of 5s. were given for neat houses with well-kept dairies. Daughters of landholders could enter flower plot competitions, which awarded 10s. There was an over-all competition, which gave the grand total of 20s. to the cleanest house with the neatest surrounds. Applicants could only enter one competition a year and prize winners could not re-apply to the winning category. Inspectors observed the strong contrast between the industrious nature of the migrants abroad and their idleness during the winter months at home, and they found it difficult to understand how the small incentives provided through the parish committee schemes brought about such dramatic changes.[25] Once local committees proved successful in Mayo, the parish schemes were extended very gradually to the other congested counties, leaving the board more time to concentrate on the broader issues of land purchase and fisheries.

Parish committees also sold seed at cost price to farmers and lent or sold implements such as ploughs, harrows and rollers. Poorer smallholders required more instruction and guidance in planning and carrying out improvement works to this end more supervision was provided in their districts (temporary supervisors were put in charge of two or three parishes, being paid £1 per week and were employed for about six months of the year).[26] This close level of supervision ensured that jobs were completed to the highest standards. Each committee had a secretary that was paid out of the committee budget, but it could not exceed £6 per annum.[27] Aside from the ordinary allocation for parish committee grants, an extra £100 had to be allocated in 1899 to two of the poorest districts in Co. Donegal, a local committee was established in each area to distribute the grants of £2 for the purpose of building small extensions on to cottages for use as a dairy to store milk and butter. The chief land inspector prepared specifications for the new buildings and the estimated cost varied from £2 6s. for a thatched building to £6 for a slated one (this excluded payment for skilled labour). Money was saved through this grant system, as frequent inspections were unnecessary usually, one visit from CDB staff sufficed to ensure that the set plans were used.[28] Under the 1899 Department of Agriculture and Technical Instruction Act, the board received an additional £25,000, which was earmarked specifically for administration (including inspection), estate improvement, resettlement and technical instruction for rural industry. On the strength of this money, the board was able to employ seven more agricultural instructors for Donegal, Mayo and Galway, to advise smallholder on management and improvement of their land and stock, to lend farm implements and to inspect animals bought under the various schemes. The inspectors also took charge of the agricultural schemes that included 31 example holdings, and about 500 experimental and example plots by 1899.[29]

25 CDB, Ninth annual report, 1900, p. 43. **26** CDB, Tenth annual report, 1901, p. 47. **27** CDB, Thirteenth annual report, 1904, pp 104–5. **28** CDB, Ninth annual report, 1900, p. 16. **29** Ibid., p.

In 1900 the cost of supervision of various projects rose to £666 and the amount allocated by the board for parish committee works was £3,186.[30] The improvement of dwellings and surrounds under the authority of the parish committees produced excellent results and ensured that money was strictly controlled. Once the initial parish committee objective of removing cesspools was achieved, the grants were expanded to incorporate structural and other sanitary improvements. Because the parish committee scheme was successful in its endeavours, and the efforts of members were voluntary, in 1902 the board extended committee duties to the improvement of holdings. Parish committees received grants based on performance. Following the Wyndham land act, the 102 committees in Connacht and Munster received grants amounting to £8,427, an average of nearly £83 each, while the 34 parishes in Co. Donegal received £1,924 in 1904. The board did not monitor the transactions of the Donegal committees as closely because less money was at stake.[31]

As time progressed the committees moved into a second phase of grant aid – for building outhouses. Applications for these grants were entertained only on the strict condition that cattle were not in the dwelling-house and that manure-heaps or cesspools were removed the prescribed distance of twenty yards from the kitchen doors.[32] To get a grant for agricultural improvement, people applied directly to the local committee. A supervisor conducted the assessment to ensure that work started prior to CDB approval was disregarded and that official board specifications were used at all stages (he was paid a small fee per case). If approved by the supervisor he estimated the cost using a schedule of prices issued to him by the board. The case was then brought before the committee, which decided the cases worthy of grant aid. On completion, a board inspector examined the holdings and was subsequently answerable to the chief land inspector. All the approved work had to be finished and the account closed before the end of March. Any money uncollected or remaining had to be returned, with the exception of areas with high numbers of seasonal migrants. By the end of March 1904, £20,224 5*s.* 6*d.* had been given out in grants.[33] Later, the board estimated that 'the value of the work in several of the parishes represents from eight to twelve times the amount of the grant'.[34] Parish committee schemes were discontinued after 31 March 1908, partially because the basic aim of removing cesspools was achieved. Funds were reallocated to CDB estate development. When the board began purchasing estates, it held ownership for a while to conduct improvements and during the course of estate improvement new dwellings were built on previously unoccupied holdings. For example, when the CDB bought the Great Blasket Island from the earl of Cork in 1907,

---

10. **30** CDB, Tenth annual report, 1901, p. 47. **31** CDB, Fourteenth annual report, 1905, p. 40. **32** Ibid., 1905, pp 38–9. **33** Ibid., 1905, p. 96. **34** CDB, Sixteenth annual report, 1907, p. 32.

it spent ten years reorganizing the land and building roads and houses. The board built eight four-roomed houses at a cost of approximately £150 each and three were two-storey.[35] All houses built by the board had slate roofs, which meant one outlay of cash and relatively no maintenance costs. Between March 1897 and 31 March 1909, when all returns were final, a sum of £224,728 was spent on schemes to improve houses structurally.[36]

---

35 J. and R. Stagles, *The Blasket Islands, next parish America* (1998), pp 70–7. Peig, one of the Blasket writers, acquired one of these houses because her husband helped to build them. The board also provided funds for marine works to service the Islands. Robin Flower and Thomás Ó Criomthain became lifelong friends after working together on the Island road. For further information see Mac Congail, *The Blasket Islands* (1987), pp 127–237. **36** CDB, Eighteenth annual report, 1909, p. 11.

5

Amalgamation and land purchase

Once the board had dealt with the fundamental issue of bad farming practice, it could concentrate on land purchase. In legal terms this was the most complex issue of CDB work and consequently absorbed a lot of energy. In theory the board was to act as an intermediary between landlords and tenants but moreover to ensure lands were in good condition prior to their transfer. Under the terms of the 1891 act, the board was restricted to buying untenanted land situated in the scheduled congested counties. There was very little such land, and the board found that existing tenants were very slow to sell their rights (which represented the value of the work conducted by tenants and the board needed to acquire the rights so it could resell). Indeed, Jones goes so far as to argue that it was tenants not landlords who controlled the supply of land on the market.[1] This limitation was exacerbated by another clause, which stipulated that it could not purchase a landlord's interest; meaning the board could only become a tenant. When George Fottrell was appointed board solicitor in charge of land purchase in April 1893, he realized that the Land Commission could buy or hold lands on behalf of the board, or, in effect act as landlord to the board. However, using the Land Commission to buy land created more bureaucracy for both bodies as Fredrick Wrench, land commissioner and member of CDB, and another board member, Charles Kennedy, had to be appointed trustees to oversee transactions. Fottrell was commissioned to draft the next CDB amendment bill in 1893; it incorporated a clause allowing the board to act as landlords, and was passed without opposition.

In a typical case where the board bought untenanted land, or the interest of a large tenant, it subdivided the land into larger holdings of at least 15 acres but over £10 valuation. In order to amalgamate, improve and re-allocate holdings the board had to have land in its possession for a period of time (the amount of time depended on the condition of the lands prior to CDB acquisition). To this end, arterial drainage schemes were necessary, but the board had no power to conduct these schemes alone. Instead, it was necessary to form district drainage

---

[1] Jones, *Graziers, land reform and conflict*, pp 164–5.

boards involving a few local government departments and this generated more paperwork.[2] As soon as drainage was complete, the large tract was then divided and fenced; then the difficult process of migration began. Basically this meant moving families from small to larger holdings within the scheduled congested districts. The only alternative to migration was state-assisted emigration, a measure that Tuke favoured, but to which nationalists remained vehemently opposed. Nationalists blamed English misrule and rancherism for high levels of emigration, but policies that encouraged peasant masses to 'keep a firm grip on your homestead' were unrealistic, did little to improve the economy and in many respects discouraged people from availing of CDB migration schemes. As a result, the board found the migration process very challenging and the cost incurred in moving a tenant to a new holding on vacant land was very high. Plunkett felt that the board was not cautious enough when redistributing land, and he identified ill-equipped candidates taking up lands as the greatest flaw in the land redistribution schemes. He suggested that a stringent rating system be adopted with strict regard to how much the people were taking advantage of educational and other means provided for them. But, legally, lands could only be given to tenants whose rent did not exceed £7, and the order of merit was that the smallest tenants got the largest new holdings. Invariably it was small farmers with very poor holdings who were most willing to migrate, most unlikely to acquire the capital under existing mechanisms – and most likely to fail in the long run. Tenants of larger holdings were more feasible candidates for the CDB migration schemes because they left holdings in a reasonably good condition, they had good means but they refused to move.[3]

Smallholders were granted new holdings on the condition that they gave the board possession of their former ones. For cost efficiency, removal from a congested area had to be beneficial to remaining occupiers. If the CDB was lucky and strategic in its planning, vacated land could be used to enlarge adjacent smallholdings. Another way the board enlarged farms was by giving tenants a portion of untenanted land not immediately adjoining their own farms, but connected by an accommodation road that was built to serve a few tenants.[4] When migrants entered into possession of a new holding, they had to pay a fine to the previous occupier to clear tenant rights. This agreement had nothing to do with the board and was a reasonable price arranged between the buyer and the tenant.[5] When a new holding was given to a person with no land to surrender, the board required an outrageous cash payment – the difference between

---

2 CDB, Second annual report, 1893, p. 30. In 1893 the board made its first efforts in relation to large scale drainage but to participate it had to appoint a solicitor, Mr J.M. Ross, who also had the duty of administering the fishery loan funds. **3** CDB, Eleventh annual report, 1902, p. 23. **4** CDB, Second annual report, 1893, p. 16. **5** CDB, Tenth annual report, 1901, p. 29.

the capital sum, represented by an annuity equal to fair rent, and the actual cost of the new holding.[6] This was to dissuade the landless from buying land; for breakdown of migration costs see table 5.2 (see p. 147), in this case the tenant would have to come up with over £400). Sometimes when tenants on the estates of other landlords migrated to CDB lands, difficulties arose in sorting out finances. To avert conflict with existing tenants when redistributing lands, the board gave preference to tenants already on CDB estates.

The Ffrench estate, near Mount Bellew in Co. Galway, was the first estate to become available in the congests; it cost £7,600 but because CDB funds were low payment was staggered over two years. Before the CDB purchased the Ffrench estate, 75 agricultural tenants occupied 862 acres at £400 9s. rental, one grazing tenant rented 350 acres at £182 10s., and 208 acres were either bog or under forest. At this point the Land Commission was operating as the board's landlord, and on 20 May 1893 the board obtained possession of the 350-acre grazier portion, but legally, it could not alter the other holdings without the consent of the tenants and many had migrated for the summer months. As a result, it found itself supporting the grazier system as it had to lease the 350 acres for cattle grazing while legal rights were being sorted.[7]

Table 5.1. The Ffrench estate

Expenditure	£ s. d.	Receipts	£ s. d.
Paid for estate	7,600 0 0	Sale of 75 holdings	9,260 0 0
Building and repairing houses	474 0 0	Value of two holdings unsold	140 0 0
Roads fences	528 11 7	Payments of 3 tenant purchasers	150 0 0
Drains	219 2 3	Arrears of rent	425 3 4
Redemption of charges	350 3 10	Grazing and sale of hay	232 2 7
Legal expenses	490 2 4	Incidentals	2 17 6
Incidentals	167 6 7		
Total	£9,829 6 7	Total	£10,210 3 5

Source: CDB, Third annual report (Dublin, 1894), p. 10.

Once the board acquired tenant consent, it concentrated on land redistribution. When the estate was transferred to the board, tenants owed £1,200 6d. in arrears of rent (equal to three years' rental). The board decided that future tenants would be assessed by their credit rating; tenants in severe arrears did not

---

6 CDB, Thirteenth annual report, 1904, p. 16. 7 Ibid., p. 16. The remaining land was used for meadow and that summer both sources earned a sum of £232 2s. and 7d.

qualify for an increase of land but were forgiven at least two years' rent, and those who did not owe more than two years' rent and wished to enlarge had to pay some arrears. George Fottrell and Henry Doran, a civil engineer who had won an agricultural gold medal for drainage on his own farm, had the job of surveying and rearranging the new holdings. The board purchased rights to as many smallholdings surrounding the estate as possible and used the main farm of the Ffrench estate to increase the size of these. Sixty of the agricultural tenants obtained enlarged holdings of arable land, all of which contained strips of turbary and cut-away bog.[8] Tenants then entered into a new contract and the redistributed holdings were sold through the Land Commission under the terms of the land purchase acts. Those hoping to avail themselves of the CDB migration schemes had to have some kind of collateral and the notable absence of working capital posed a big problem for many. Money was available to tenants under the terms of the land acts, repayable on an annual basis to the Land Commission on favourable interest terms – but for long and somewhat daunting periods of time. Under the 1885 Ashbourne act, land purchase increased nationally and in the first six years 16,788 tenants bought their holdings, compared with a mere 877 tenants under the 1870 act.[9] Rents had already dropped to such levels in the congests that even the more favourable terms of the Ashbourne act were unattractive to tenants that had bad, or no, previous credit rating. If a tenant wanted to become an owner-occupier, he acquired the deposit from one of two sources – the joint stock banks or the gombeenman.[10] The Bank of Ireland had many branches in the congests but 'the small farmer and farm labourer were not in a position to satisfy the banks requirements'.[11] A tenant usually had to spend all of his money acquiring the land and faced the new venture with no working capital to buy stock; he usually got another loan.

A contemporary critic estimated that a day spent dealing with the bank for a loan of £5 could cost the farmer 8*s.* 2*d.*, between 'standing a drink' to guarantors and the cost of his own day's work. At the end of the day he received only £4 17*s.* 6*d.* of a £5 loan because some of the interest was paid upfront. The smallholder was always at a disadvantage as he remained under obligation to his guarantors and the repercussions of failing to make repayments were severe.[12] It is important to distinguish between the two usual types of creditors operating in the congests – shopkeepers and moneylenders; the latter were not necessarily from the locality. Transactions with moneylenders, who advertized themselves in national newspapers in a semi-philanthropic light, were discreet and only resorted to in family emergencies such as meeting dowry, emigration and funeral

---

8 CDB, Third annual report, 1894, pp 8–10. **9** Solow, *The Irish land question*, pp 186–8. **10** P.J. Hannon, 'Agricultural banks in Ireland' (1898). **11** Hall, *The Bank of Ireland*, p. 305. **12** Ibid. **13** Articles in the *Irish Homestead* referred to them as the '60 per cent philanthropists'.

costs (the extent to which they were used to aid land purchase up to 1890 was negligible).[13] Bolger notes the existence of moneylenders as separate entities from gombeenmen; 'in contrast to the 'straight' moneylender, the gombeenman was a combination of shopkeeper/ produce-buyer/ usurer, common to an impoverished rural economy in every country ... one of the main reasons why country people fell into the hands of money-lenders (including gombeenmen) was because they alone provided the countryman with a source of credit'.[14] Hannon adds that credit bound the farmer 'hand and foot to the shopkeeper. And any attempt on the part of the farmer to avail himself of more favourable terms of purchase brings upon him the weight of all the instruments of debt recovery which the law of the land places at the disposal of creditors.'[15] Ordinary shopkeeper credit for groceries was in many respects an expensive loan but was not as severe as the interest charged on late repayments to a moneylender.

Plunkett would have preferred a more aggressive CDB approach to the agrarian-based poverty, which would have meant taking direct measures to curb the gombeenman hegemony. His friend and colleague R.A. Anderson commented: 'I gathered that he was not always happy on that Board, which was too paternal for his robust ideas, and too timid in dealing with problems which might possibly infringe on the rights of the class, self-styled legitimate traders.'[16] Irritated by the fact that his co-operative notions were not applicable to the congested counties (where butter production was too low to support a creamery) Plunkett acted independently. He founded the Irish Agricultural Organizational Society in 1894 to act as a central body for the new and developing co-operative creameries. Being particularly concerned with the availability of cash, it aimed to finance farmers and market creamery produce a system. It was designed to end (or, as some would argue to replace) the reign of the gombeenman. This 'swop system' was common, O'Halpin argues that the 1898 Local Government Act (which extended the franchise but did little to serve smallholders) was essentially a system where grand juries previously controlled by larger landowners were replaced with councils, controlled by larger tenant farmers but remaining extremely corrupt.[17]

Hannon notes that in Bavaria and Wurtemberg the peasantry had fallen prey to unscrupulous money-lenders and to ameliorate circumstances Fredrich W.

---

14 Bolger, *The Irish co-operative movement* (1977), pp 158–63. **15** Hannon, 'Agricultural banks', p. 5. **16** Anderson, *With Plunkett in Ireland* (1935), p. 62. This comment insinuates that the board tiptoed around shopkeepers/ gombeenmen in the congests, but it is important to note that in fact the opposite occurred, as the CDB blatantly discriminated against them. Shopkeepers were not permitted to act on parish committees or have anything whatsoever to do with administering CDB relief. However, the social status of a shopkeeper in each community was high. He ranked as important as the priest and his support was necessary in implementing policy. **17** O'Halpin, *The decline of the Union*, p. 16.

Raiffeissen founded the concept of co-operative credit in 1849. Co-operative credit or Raiffeissen banks joined the assets of a number of small farmers, thereby creating a down payment. On the strength of this guarantee, farmers were able to borrow large sums of money at a low rate of interest. Ten years after this system was introduced in an area, the people were free from the clutches of moneylenders.[18] The Prussian model was viewed as a good parallel for Ireland because in the mid-nineteenth century peasant farmers in regions of Prussia were immersed in a similar economic cycle; the IAOS adopted the Raffeissen concept and operated it in the west. An elected committee managed the bank loans that were issued to trusted members who were obliged to produce one or two sureties.[19] At first, only credit associations had 'unlimited liability' and were allowed to take deposits from members only. Initial funds were obtained from joint stock banks and local depositors, but in poorer districts the board lent amounts varying from £30 to £200 to individual societies to start up, for which the bank paid an interest rate of between 2.5 and 3.5 per cent.[20]

Migration and enlargement of holdings cost the CDB a lot of money and if the new tenant failed it had no way of recouping losses. Failure was a major possibility for smallholders because the temptation to earn cash away from their own holdings (through labouring) was high and their personal financial outlook did not stretch further than the settlement of the next instalment of credit. It was this myopic attitude towards money that, in Inspector Gaskell's experience, made it difficult to start any kind of co-operation in the congests. The board was more than willing to let the IAOS found co-operative credit associations so that small farmers with poor credit ratings could borrow money to help them get out of shopkeeper debt at reasonable and fixed interest rates. In 1894 it allocated a sum of £250 (under Gaskell's management) to the society to teach and promote the objects of co-operation in the townlands of Bohola and Killasser, Co. Mayo.[21] Of course, Plunkett's position as president of the society had a bearing on the issue but in giving this money the board officially affiliated itself with the society but both entities encouraged self-help so the board could rationalize its financial aid. The existence of the co-operative banks complemented the CDB's policies of relocation and land reorganization and the IAOS helped to finance willing tenants. The Societies Borrowing Powers Act passed in 1898 extended the power of institutions to borrow and accept unlimited deposits, thereby enabling banks in poorer districts to expand and become more independent.[22] Between 1898 and 1910 the board gave loans amounting to £7,345 to 80 agricultural co-operative banks for initial capital.[23]

18 Hannon, 'Agricultural banks' p. 6. **19** RCCI, Final Report, 1908, p. 33. **20** Ibid., p. 773. **21** CDB, Third annual report, 1894, p. 6. **22** CDB, Twenty-eight annual report, 1921, p. 14. The board recalled these loans but the repayment account was not closed until 1920. **23** CDB, Twenty-

As time progressed, the board discovered more legal limitations in relation to land purchase especially when it continued to purchase and amalgamate holdings. Up until the 1896 CDB amendment act, the board was very limited in the amount of land it could purchase; it was also restricted to selling holdings valued over £10. Rateable valuation could be altered if buildings were upgraded, so the board continued to improve holdings, especially on untenanted or vacant holdings, by building new dwelling houses and outhouses. For example, when it purchased Clare Island in Clew Bay for £5,000 in 1895, the estate had only 68 legal tenancies according to the landlord register but it was subdivided among 98 agricultural tenants. Existing tenants were in arrears of rent, but the archbishop of Tuam and William O' Brien MP acted as guarantors for the Land Commission. Henry Doran was placed in charge of rearranging the lands, but this time the board sold Clare Island directly to the tenants; because the rearranged holdings were valued at less than £10. Legally the board was not supposed to sell these holdings but it managed to get away with it because Doran arranged a separate loan system for the islanders (whereby tenants repaid loans to the board at 3.5 per cent interest over 68 years). This loan system included the smallest occupiers and worked well on Clare Island; it was adopted in the 1903 Wyndham act.[24]

On conducting the background research to Raffeissen banks Plunkett noted the significant agricultural progress of other European countries and was concerned about Irish producers losing their stake in the British market entirely. He formed a committee of MPs from all political parties to confer about Irish economic issues; because this committee could only meet when parliament was not in session, it came to be known as the Recess Committee. This committee conducted extensive research into the condition of agriculture at home and abroad. Plunkett, at his own expense, sent T.P. Gill to Denmark and France, and Michael Mulhall to Prussia and Switzerland to investigate agricultural advances. The results were condensed into a report in August 1896 and forwarded to Gerard Balfour, the chief secretary, who incorporated the report into a bill to start a department for agricultural affairs in Ireland. The bill met with major opposition, as the findings in the Recess report highlighted the negligence of successive governments in relation to Irish agriculture. The report, together with Plunkett's relentless letters and newspaper articles, eventually resulted in the Agricultural and Technical Instruction bill being passed in October 1899. Under this act a Department of Agriculture and Technical Instruction (DATI) was created; it had its own minister along with a board of agriculture and a board of technical instruction to manage its activities.[25] Like the board, it operated inde-

---

eight annual report, 1921, p. 14. **24** CDB, Tenth annual report, 1901, p. 27. **25** O'Halpin, *The decline of the Union*, p. 14.

pendently of Dublin Castle and centralized the power to improve and develop agriculture and fisheries; according to T.A. Finlay, this constitution closely resembled the corresponding institution in the kingdom of Wurttemberg.[26] The 1899 act stipulated that the DATI's agricultural endowment of £100,000 was earmarked for the non-congested portions of Ireland; moreover, it could not apply funds to area unless it raised sufficient rates.[27] In essence, the department had the same power as the CDB – but on a national scale and with a larger budget; but some confusion arose as to whether or not the CDB would still fund agricultural schemes in the congests.[28] Under the department act, the rural district of a county was the responsibility of the department whereas the unit of congestion was the electoral division, which fell into the rural district of local government. To temporarily overcome administrative difficulties the board contributed toward the county rate, proportionate to the scheduled congested area within the county on condition that the department gave the same amount for non-congested areas.[29]

Following the 1899 act, the function of the board altered dramatically; it became more like a land commission for disadvantaged areas. Unscheduled lands remained outside of the board's jurisdiction, meaning that it was still not allowed to migrate tenants to non-congested areas; this was a major setback, particularly in cases of overpopulated districts bordering non-congested areas. Consolidation of holdings was the only way to rid the country of uneconomic holdings but large tracts of land coupled with large-scale arterial drainage schemes (to reclaim land) were necessary to achieve this. As arterial drainage was costly and difficult to organize the easier option was to buy up all available property. CDB income was increased from almost £52,000 to £74,600, and it was relieved of a considerable burden of responsibilities but had to ensure that spending on any given drainage scheme was reduced to £5,000 a year by 1904–5. In turn, this curtailed progress on drainage schemes necessary for land reclamation. Section 4 of the act also placed the CDB on a par with other landlords with regard to selling holdings of less than a £10 valuation; it also altered section 43 of the 1896 act, which gave the Treasury power to temporarily extend the limit of stock issued (stock was used as collateral for purchases). As each county had made a proportionate contribution to a central stock fund the board was entitled to borrow twenty-five times the amount of the initial contribution to fund land purchase in each county. This was vital and designed to provide enough collateral to purchase the Dillon estate, which spanned three counties.[30]

26 T.A. Finlay, 'Our Department of Technical Instruction' (1900). See Hoctor, *The department's story*, pp 40–1. 27 RCCI, Fourth Report, 1907, Appendix iv, p. 201, evidence of Professor J.R. Campbell. 28 Bolger, *The Irish co-operative movement*, pp 77–9. In 1899 the work of the agricultural branch of the board was partially transferred to the newly formed DATI and they liaised carefully about expenditure in the west. 29 CDB, Tenth annual report, 1901, p. 17. 30 CDB,

On 11 May 1899 the board purchased the Dillon estate for £290,000 but with the sale the board inherited arrears of rent amounting to £27,000. Encompassing 87,669 acres in Mayo, 5,652 acres in Roscommon and 136 in Westmeath, this was the biggest estate the board had handled to date, having 4,200 tenants, most of whom paid less than £4 rent. Gross annual rental for the entire estate was £20,370, but payments of almost £3,000 went on county cess, poor rates, drainage charges, tithe and quit rents. Redistribution of the Dillon estate took a long time, and particularly strong allegations were made against the board that it was trying to create 'model farms' before transferring them to the new tenants.[31] Generally speaking, the board could easily justify such delays. In the first instance, lands bought up for redistribution were usually in terrible condition, particularly if they had been vacant or grossly subdivided. Secondly, the board started new cultivation patterns (a process that was time-consuming) in the hope that the tenants would continue them. Finally, it had limited resources, and legal constraints such as clearing tenant rights caused further delays. By March 1902, the board's work had reached a stalemate. Aside from the process of redistribution via amalgamation, it had bought only 43 estates. This estate reallocation work translated into the provision of a mere 132 new migrants' holdings; but each had a slated cottage, outhouses and boundary fences. The holdings varied from 14 to 50 acres and the rents from £7 to £23, but most were from 20 to 30 acres at rents of £10 to £15.

During the first five years the board's work was in keeping with government expectations; it raised living conditions above the 'at risk of distress' level and as a result its income was raised under the 1896 land law act. Section 43 of the 1896 act advanced limited use of guaranteed land stock, the 1898 land act increased the power of the CDB in relation to land purchase and amalgamation but agricultural work was on an even kilter until 1899 when the DATI was founded. In the first nine years the agricultural branch of the board managed to alter the existing structure of farming in the west. In the opinion of William Micks, the provisions of the 1893 act altered the role of the board, making land purchase its primary function. At that point, all other functions (livestock improvement, poultry, fisheries and industry) were pushed into a secondary position. In fact, all these responsibilities were gradually delegated to the IAOS in 1894, to parish committees in 1897 and to the department of agriculture in 1899. Central board administration became progressively more concerned with land purchase and redistribution. Without the participation of the CDB and financing from IAOS banks, the farms would not have changed ownership, as in monetary terms potential tenants could not have afforded the new

---

Ninth annual report, 1900, p. 3. **31** RCCI, Appendix to fourth report, 1907, Q. 21481, Lord Dudley, p. 131.

plots or afford to build houses on previously vacant lands. However, the CDB needed wider powers and more money to transform the western landscape into a profitable farming industry.

Ambiguities in relation to the DATI and board duties continued to pose problems. Horace Plunkett made a personal plea to the chief secretary in October 1903 to clarify the powers of both bodies because section 18 of the DATI act, which did not state how to deal with over-lapping areas. He suggested that, to liberate time and resources, the board should deal with land purchase and the relief of congestion, and the department should take over the agricultural schemes in the scheduled congested districts. This letter led to the repeal of section 18 thereby making it possible for the department to finance schemes in the congested districts as elsewhere, but its income was not increased (although the originally allocated sum was for non-congested Ireland).[32] The 1903 land purchase act gave additional powers to the board in relation to land purchase and a further £20,000 per annum, and allowed the board to use cash advances instead of stock (the value of which fluctuated). Jones argues that the United Irish League also influenced the decision to widen CDB powers and put the board into direct conflict with grazier interests, especially because increased powers enabled the board to acquire more untenanted lands (that was previously used as 'eleven month' pasture).[33] The board was also permitted to advance money to the value of 60 times the guarantee fund in each county. Turbary rights were broadened and simpler procedures were enforced for land purchase; the tenant lodged a map of the intended purchase area and rental accounts with the board; if accepted, the board lodged the land request at the Estates Commissioners, who investigated the title. Once it was cleared, the commissioners obtained an advance from the National Debt Commissioners, the Estate Commissioners released the purchase money and then vested the estate in the board.[34]

On the advice of Fottrell and Doran, the terms of the Land Act of 1903 were more favourable to the smaller tenant farmer. For example, an annuity of £15, at the rate of 3.25 per cent, covered a capital sum of £461, or, according to the estimates in table 5.2 provided enough to purchase a standard holding (over 15 acres), leaving no loss to the board in the transaction.

---

32 RCCI, First report, 1906, Appendix ii, p. 270, memorandum attached to evidence of Sir Horace Plunkett.   **33** Jones, *Graziers, land reform*, p. 196. The UIL advocated boycotting methods on shopkeeper-graziers and land grabbers at the time and this was causing a stir. The UIL distrusted landlords, especially in land sale negotiations, and under the 1891 and 1896 acts tenants had to deal directly with the landlord. This opinion was voiced at UIL meetings and public rallies and as a result the Wyndham land act widened the powers of the board and the estates commission to enable them to purchase estates on behalf of tenants. See also M.D. Higgins and J.P. Gibbons 'Shopkeeper-graziers and land agitation in Ireland, 1895–1900' (1982).   **34** CDB, Thirteenth annual report, 1904, p. 5.

Table 5.2. Cost incurred to CDB in creating a new holding (1903)

	£	s.	d.
Price of land	337	10	0
Cost of new house	100	0	0
Fencing	20	0	0
Total	457	10	0

Source: CDB, Thirteenth annual report, p. 16.

To clear up ambiguities re jurisdiction, when the 1903 act came into operation it was agreed between the board, the department and the government that all rates should be equally divided at county level.[35] Central authorities assisted schemes in non-congested districts by paying 25s. to 30s. for every £1 raised by the rate.[36] The CDB promised an annual contribution of £3,002 5s. 2d., for congested areas (divided as shown in table 5.3).

Table 5.3. Money raised in respect of rates (1903)

	£	s.	d.
Cork	248	11	3
Donegal	528	13	11
Galway	351	17	6
Kerry	524	7	6
Leitrim	246	0	0
Mayo	690	11	3
Roscommon	212	15	0
Sligo	199	8	9
Total	£3,002	5	2

Source: CDB, Twelfth annual report (Dublin, 1903), p. 15.

Despite Plunkett's plea for clearer lines of demarcation concerning responsibilities, the work of the board and the department was further intertwined by the 1903 act. For example, the DATI could only use its endowment fund to operate agricultural schemes in the congested districts at the request of the board. When DATI county committees prepared schemes for livestock improvement or for agricultural or technical instruction, the schemes were confined to the

[35] CDB, Twelfth annual report, 1903, p. 15. [36] RCCI, Final report, 1908, p. 763.

non-congested portions of counties, unless the board approved the schemes and provided a grant equal to that made by the department for the non-congested area.[37] Indeed the board continued some technical instruction and could supplement the work of the department in areas of exceptional distress. This overlapping created more bureaucracy for all concerned; sometimes more energy went into writing about schemes than into conducting them. Some overlapping was alleviated when, shortly after the 1903 act was passed, it was agreed, between the Irish government, the board and the department that the work of agricultural development should be transferred from the board to the department. Chief Secretary George Wyndham's minute of 13 October 1903 indicates that the transfer was made so that the board could concentrate fully on land purchase and resettlement. The board had been spending £11,000 a year on agricultural works so it was decided by statute that it should make a set annual contribution of £2,000 to the department.[38]

In the lead-up to the 1903 land act, Wyndham, and Sir Anthony MacDonnell, under-secretary, increased their involvement in CDB affairs. Micks felt that both men wrongly saw the board as solely for land purchase, and that this influenced subsequent legislation. Neither of them appreciated its independent status, and they often summoned board members to attend meetings in Dublin Castle. As a matter of principle Dr Patrick O'Donnell, Catholic bishop of Raphoe and long-standing member of the CDB, never attended these impromptu meetings. On 18 August 1902 an additional £10,000 per annum was granted to the board, making its total income £85,208. One of the conditions for this extra income was that it appoint another solicitor to the staff (a position incidentally filled by a friend of the under-secretary, R.H. Tighe).[39] Apart from this blatant act of nepotism, which McDowell argues was commonplace in the Irish administration, the CDB secretary was constantly going to and from the Castle.[40] Micks was not the CDB secretary at the time and commented that his successor was not confident enough to set the chief secretary's office straight on the status of the board. He believed that MacDonnell only fully realized the status of the board at the Dudley Commission four years later, when Micks recited Balfour's memorandum that outlined why the board should be independent. MacDonnell's tenure of office ended in July 1908 and his membership of the board ended accordingly. Micks noted how his period in office between 1902 and 1908 was the only time that the board resembled a government department.[41]

Although the DATI was also independent of Dublin Castle and it dealt extensively with the CDB, the ordinary people did not see it in the same light

---

[37] CDB, Twelfth annual report, 1903, p. 6. [38] RCCI, Final report, 1908, p. 765. [39] The money was derived from the 'Civil Contingencies Fund'. [40] MacDowell, *The Irish administration*, p. 37. [41] Micks, *An account of the history*, pp 110–15.

as the paternalistic CDB. For example, John Dillon, the nationalist leader, should have been, by definition, opposed to the board because it was as a measure that could kill home rule. He had served a jail sentence during the period of coercion 1887–92, and his political stronghold was in the poorest congested districts of East Mayo. Bolger argues that nationalist politicians were unwilling to associate themselves with any of the three groups (CDB, DATI and IAOS) and he cites how Plunkett failed in his attempts to involve John Dillon in the co-operative movement or the board.[42] Lyons argues that the British policy of amelioration put nationalist politicians in a difficult position as it had 'the declared object of stifling the demand for Home Rule, they could not be accepted uncritically in case they did precisely that. Dillon was well aware of the danger and … became almost obsessed by it'. Initially Dillon did not display unequivocal support for the board (at that time he personally disliked Plunkett) but he could not remain aloof from CDB developments. He did not protest against the conciliatory operations of Constructive Unionism, namely the work of the board, in his constituency. By 1897 he was campaigning in the House of Commons for compulsory land purchase powers to be granted to the board.[43] He also helped and liaised frequently with William Micks, the board's secretary, and Mother Morrough Bernard of Foxford Woollen Mills.[44] While the board was viewed as apolitical, both the IAOS and the DATI were more associated with strong Unionist connections; Plunkett was vice-president of the former, a member of the latter and a Unionist MP from 1892 to 1900. He personally paid the society's administration costs or else they were met by funds channelled through him. His reputation for radicalism preceded him, but the publication of his book *Ireland in the New Century* caused a commotion. In it he argued that the industrial character of the nation was weakened because Roman Catholicism was non-economic in its tendencies, and he pointed to excessive and extravagant church-building as having a pauperizing effect on poor communities. He also claimed that the ethos of the church repressed individuality among 'people whose lack of education unfits them for resisting the influence of what may present itself to such minds as a kind of fatalism with resignation as its paramount virtue'.[45] The Catholic clergy and the *Freeman's Journal* launched an attack on the book; public outcry ensued and reduced the co-operative movement to the 'atheistic' status it originally experienced in Britain.[46]

---

42 Bolger, *The Irish co-operative movement*, p. 71.   **43** F.S.L. Lyons, *John Dillon: a biography* (1968), pp 169–75.   **44** Dillon was encouraged by Plunkett to get directly involved in the operations of the board but he declined. For correspondence with Micks and Mother Bernard see Dillon papers, TCD 6800–6801/129–155.   **45** Horace Plunkett, *Ireland in the new century* (1903), pp 101–2.   **46** Letter to John Dillon from P Mulhall, Dillon papers (TCD) 6835/5, letter dated 14 November 1906. Criticizes Plunkett for 'having foolishly identified himself with this aggressive body [IAOS] and weakly yielded to their clamour for a grant of Government and also because of

Relations between the society, the department and the board specifically intersected in relation to the Raffeissen banks. While the agricultural banks usurped the role of the local usurer/gombeemen, they never became self-sufficient and some 'village banks' began to fail when the society 'lost its government subsidy following a political wrangle in 1907'.[47] The board and the department had gradually invested money in the IAOS banks and in 1907 nearly two hundred branches were in operation (the department had invested a sum of nearly £13,000 and the CDB had invested almost £6,000, at 3 per cent interest).[48] Thomas Russell, who had succeeded Plunkett as president of the DATI, particularly despised the society, and he used his position to weaken the IAOS by reducing the funds allocated to it by the department.[49] The aid was due to be gradually reduced to £3,000 in 1908, £2,000 in 1909, £1,000 in 1910, but it was axed completely in 1908 in part because of a letter written by T.W. Rolleston, a prominent DATI member, to John Redmond in America. The letter, which was published in the *Freeman's Journal*, denounced John Dillon and was interpreted as an admission that Plunkett's co-operative efforts had ulterior motives all along.[50] This gave Russell the perfect opportunity to cut off funds immediately.

In spite of the CDB, DATI and IAOS efforts, by 1906, the stark reality was that the problem of congestion was no nearer resolution; the prospect of losing an animal still spelled dire straits for the smallholder. The only way to counteract this was a system of livestock insurance, but the board could only insure animals on CDB lands (this was a temporary arrangement as lands held by the board were pending resale).[51] Although the 1903 act gave the board wider powers, it was still restricted in its policy of enlarging and amalgamating holdings and subdivision could still occur. For the Land Commission the process of joining rents of an existing holding with rents of the added portions was not easy (until notices had been served on the owners and mortgagees of the particular estate).[52] Without consolidating the rents, both portions of land constituted separate tenancies – making it impossible to prevent sub-division; furthermore the 1891 act still prohibited the board from bringing holdings over £20 valuation.[53] These issues

---

his notorious book, which was the emanation of vanity, and forfeited the confidence and respect of a large and influential sect of the people'. **47** Ó Gráda, *Ireland*, p. 269. **48** Ibid., p. 169. **49** Bolger, *The Irish co-operative movement*, p. 99. Russell 'saw the IAOS as a conspiracy of conniving landlords, gentry, clergy and industrialists ... led by Plunkett, they were using the country people for their own ends in an effort to preserve something of the old order'. **50** Bolger, *The Irish co-operative movement*, pp 100–1. See also Hoctor, *The department's story*, p. 56. **51** CDB, Seventeenth annual report, 1908, p. 14. Farmers who had insured were paid two-thirds of the value of stock that died. The board declined to take uninsured animals to graze on their lands in 1908. The small premium charged covered all the losses, even though the board did not charge farmers for the grazing if stock died. The board could not extend the scheme outside of its own lands but the scheme started a good habit that encouraged people to exercise caution in case of unforeseen circumstances. **52** CDB, Fifteenth annual report, 1906, p. 17. **53** CDB, Twelfth annual report,

needed to be addressed, and the board was also hoping to amend section 75 of the 1903 act (which limited the extent to which the board could relieve neighbouring poor but officially non-congested areas). The board petitioned government to amend the CDB acts to free up the laws pertaining to land purchase. It requested an increase in income, permission to borrow money from the Board of Works to purchase tenant rights, and the removal of legal difficulties in relation to clearing the title of holdings. Apart from needing more powers, it also needed more salaried and experienced staff to radically alter life in the west.

The response to its requests came in the form of an official inquiry – the Royal Commission on Congestion for Ireland (RCCI) appointed on 20 July 1906 to examine the effectiveness of the board in dealing with congestion (the issue of increasing funds was postponed until the commission was over). It was not, as Micks implies it should have been, designed to assess the capability of the board to deal with the whole country. In fact dissolution was a more likely prospect for the board. The commission coincided with a significant lull in CDB activities; beside this other odds were stacked against the board. Arthur Balfour inopportunely resigned his honorary membership of the board in 1907. His imperial duties had kept him from attending meetings, but his membership symbolized continuity and had contributed to the prestige of the board. Charles Kennedy, one of the original members, died in 1908; also in 1907 the CDB salaried staff were engaged in a wage dispute with the Treasury. The salaried staff of the CDB wanted parity with other civil servants and took their superannuation case to the high court where they lost; they appealed to the House of Lords, which found in their favour.[54] The board's work reached a standstill in 1907; it had about one million pounds at its disposal for land purchase but had exploited practically all the available untenanted land in the scheduled congests and had to turn to migration schemes, to which there was still major opposition.[55] There was also a squeeze on spending, with the impending and highly controversial 'People's Budget'.[56] It is worth noting that a Scottish Congested Districts Board was founded in 1897 to deal with what was perceived as similar problems of congestion in the Highlands. Apart from McCleery's unpublished PhD thesis, no comprehensive study exists on the Scottish CDB, but it is generally accepted that it was a failure because its creation of new holdings was not in keeping with crofter expectations (it was wound up in 1912).[57]

1903, p. 19. **54** McDowell, *The Irish administration*, pp 101–3. **55** CDB, Sixteenth annual report, 1907, p. 12. **56** For further information on the budget see H.V. Emy, 'The impact of financial policy on English party politics before 1914' (1972) and B. Murray, 'The politics of the "People's Budget"' (1973). **57** A.M. McCleery, 'The role of the Highland Development Agency: with particular reference to the work of the CDB, 1897–1912' (1984); D. MacKay, 'The Congested Districts Boards of Ireland and Scotland' (1996).

Devine argues that the Scottish board 'was hampered by inadequate funding' but it started off with an annual income of £35,000 for 56 districts in contrast to the Irish board, which had 84 districts to cater for and a start-off income of just over £41,000.[58] The income of the Scottish board did not reach the same heights as that of the Irish board. It appears from Devine's and Cameron's deductions that the Scottish board was unsuccessful because 'it failed to secure the cooperation from both crofters and proprietors which it required to operate efficiently'.[59]

The royal commission was very thorough and lasted for three years; Lord Dudley presided (hence it is also known as the Dudley Commission). Evidence was taken in London and Dublin from board officials, land commissioners and DATI staff. The commission also took evidence in each of the congested counties with the purpose of assessing and how the board functioned, how it interacted with the department, the land commission and the Local Government Board. The commission then moved to Dublin where local witnesses from each of the congests were called in to help the commission determine the current conditions and needs of poorer areas. The actual inquiry focussed on three main things; it addressed the request of wider powers, determined the extent of progress the board had made in solving congestion and scrutinized the manner in which the board had resettled estates.[60] Witnesses made extensive use of annual reports in their testimony; this was weighed against material contained in the baseline reports and provided a clear indication of the extent of CDB works in each district. The evidence emphasized the important work of parish committees and the extent to which the board was necessary to facilitate rural development in the west. As most of the witnesses were directly involved in CDB activities, they were in a position to suggest other possible solutions to congestion; in this respect the evidence of Horace Plunkett was the most unorthodox. At this point, the board was trying to defend its position as an agricultural development agency but being realistic in his approach to the west and conscious of how congestion was perpetuated, Plunkett suggested the revival of industries as an alternative to miserable plots.[61] During the Dudley inquiry, a number of witnesses bore testimony to the remarkable improvements made thanks to grants administered through the parish committees. Jones highlights the significance of the fact that seventy-five Catholic clergymen gave evidence to the royal commission (many more than in any previous inquiry). Arguing that priests used the commission as a forum to voice their opposition to the

---

58 T.M. Devine, *The Scottish nation, 1700–2000* (1999), pp 444–5. **59** E. A. Cameron, 'The Highland issue, 1860 to the 1920s' (1993), pp 60–79. **60** RCCI Final Report, 1908. **61** He suggested the board take over and reopen the disused quarries at Liscannor, Co. Clare; a project which did not materialise RCCI Appendix to the third report, 1907. Evidence of Sir Horace Plunkett, p. 233.

ranching system, he notes the clergy's affinity with agrarian protest during the land war but fails to acknowledge the active role that local clergy played in CDB parish committees.[62] Support from local clergy was invaluable to the board, some provided rooms free of charge for technical instruction classes and often worked voluntarily on behalf of the board. Both the United Irish League (UIL) and the National League had representatives giving evidence at the Dudley commission; Jones argues that both were there specifically to address the ranching question, which pressed for compulsory powers to be given to the board and the Estates Commission with respect to the purchase of estates and untenanted land.[63] Jones probably over-emphasizes the influence of the National League, which, as Geary argues, had lost its hegemony by the late 1880s.[64] But the UIL may have had an effect on the CDB portion of the 1909 land act in relation to untenanted land, or indirectly, the ranching issue.[65]

Although the Dudley Commission took three years to complete its work it only sat for a total of 134 days; it finished gathering evidence on 4 October 1907 and reported in May 1908. MacDonnell was still under-secretary and, ex-officio, a commissioner on congestion; and he used this position to grill the board members. Of the eight members of the Dudley Commission, four had reservations with the recommendations; three of these were relatively unimportant but the harshest criticism was voiced in MacDonnell's dissent, appended to the final report of the Dudley commission. He had personal grievances with the independent status of the CDB and wanted to terminate its existence.[66] His strongest objection to the board was that it duplicated the work of other bodies, such as the DATI and that of the Estates Commission (the latter could buy and sell land in both congested and non-congested counties). In his 'Minutes of Dissent' (appended to the final report of the Dudley commission) he objected to 16 of the 52 proposals and recommendations, suggesting that £40,000 be transferred to the DATI for its work in agriculture and that the CDB duties in relation to fisheries be suspended and given to the department as well.[67] He alleged that the board's administrative shortcomings was his main reason for dissolution (that it only met once a month sitting for three days at most), but he failed to note that the members worked on a voluntary basis.

Still, despite dissent, the findings of the commission favoured the continuance of the board because of its separate status from ordinary government agencies, and it concluded that:

---

62 Jones, *Graziers, land reform,* p. 203. **63** Ibid., pp 195–6. **64** Geary, *Plan of Campaign,* p. 108. **65** For further discussion on the role played by the UIL in orchestrating terms of land acts see Philip Bull, 'The significance of the Nationalist response to the Irish Land Act of 1903' (1993), pp 283–305. **66** McDowell, *The Irish administration,* pp 27–9. McDowell notes MacDonnell's dissatisfaction with Irish administration in general, but with the CDB and the local government board in particular. **67** RCCI, Final Report, 1908, pp 172–4.

Table 5.4. Scheduled congested districts, 1909

	Original congested districts 1891	Added in 1909	Total in 1910	Rest of Ireland	Ratio between congested districts and rest of Ireland
Area in statute acres	3,608,569	4,049,545	7,658,114	13,174,631	1 to 2
Population in 1901	505,723	616,718	1,122,441	3,336,334	1 to 3
Rateable valuation	£577,043	£1,794,871	£2,371,914	£13,164,854	1 to 6

Source: CDB, Nineteenth annual report (1911), p. 6.

> great is the difficulty that will beset any body in the work of relieving congestion (involving as it does the shattering the hopes of those who have so long cast their eyes upon the promised land), unless that body is supported by public opinion; and this is one of the chief causes which has led us to think that a semi-independent Irish body, with a large elective element, such as the new Board is more likely to be successful in relieving congestion than an ordinary Government department.[68]

The paternalistic image of the board that Horace Plunkett abhorred so much was eventually its saving grace. In 1909 the Dudley commission concluded that the powers and finances of the board should be extended, and these provisions were incorporated into the Birrell land act, which also reconstituted the board with more staff on increased salaries due to increased responsibilities. Board membership was increased to fourteen; corporate status was granted, allowing the board exclusive rights to buy, hold and sell lands within the congested counties; but the Estates Commission held the power to fix prices for untenanted lands. The chief secretary, the under-secretary and the vice-president of the DATI continued to be ex-officio members of the board the last mentioned being charged to ensure good relations between the board and the department. As many commission witnesses had requested, the three temporary members were removed and replaced with representatives elected from each of the nine county councils. It was anticipated that the inclusion of elected local candidates would help to strengthen the argument for migration.

The commission made several recommendations to remove obstacles that restricted progress, beginning with the definition of congestion. The system of using the ratio between population and valuation was ammended; instead, whole counties were scheduled as 'congested' to simplify administration and help ease tenants' aversion towards migration.[69] Under the provisions of the 1909 act, the

68 Ibid., p. 788. **69** Ibid., p. 776.

area of congestion was enlarged to include the whole counties of Donegal, Leitrim, Roscommon, Mayo, Galway, Kerry and the six districts in West Cork as per 1891. Six new districts in Clare (Ballyvaughan, Ennistymon, Kilrush, Scariff, Tulla and Kildysert) were also included (see table 5.4).

To simplify the legal status of the board, the ten acts that previously dealt with congestion were repealed and replaced by the 1909 act. Income was increased to £250,000 a year, of which £19,000 was given to the DATI for its work of technical instruction in the congests, but the CDB was empowered to nominate two members to the agricultural board (the DATI was divided into an agricultural and technical instruction). The CDB used this power to insist that the department locate agricultural instructors in the vicinity of poorer migrant colonies. It argued that migrants coming from poorer holdings, who were accustomed to working manually, were not suitable for the new holdings unless an instructor was living among them to give instruction and advice in approved methods of farming and machinery.[70] Responsibilities for seed provision, agricultural instruction, forestry and animal breeding were also transferred to the DATI. The CDB was still limited to redistributing lands held in its possession and was not permitted to exceed £500,000 annually for land purchase. Although this new limitation was inconvenient, the 1909 act granted the CDB compulsory purchase powers in the congests, and granted parallel powers to the Estates Commission in non-congested areas.[71] The power of 'compulsory purchase' was a crucial element in overcoming the difficulty of acquiring lands, it discouraged landlords from taking advantage of the board by looking for exorbitant prices for land and to a lesser extent it was to ease friction caused between CDB tenants and tenants on neighbouring non-congested estates (as had happened between the Dillon/ CDB estate and the adjoining De Freyne estate between 1899 and 1902).

Following the Dudley Commission, the primary function of the board was to create as many economic holdings in the congests as possible. The commission defined an economic holding as a farm big enough to support the family independently and one that could be worked without outside assistance. In 1909 the congested districts contained 84,954 agricultural holdings, 73,413 of which did not exceed £10 valuation. Average valuation of holdings was only £3 17s., so in order to make these holdings economic the board needed to acquire lands to the value of £741,242.[72] In relation to redistribution, the commission set out definite guidelines for what class of occupier would be entitled to redistributed lands. The commission also argued that the farm should have only one inheriting son or daughter and the other children should find alternative livelihoods elsewhere. In implementing the Dudley commission recommendations the CDB encountered

---

70 CDB, Nineteenth annual report, 1911, p. 25. 71 Jones, *Graziers, land reform*, p. 211. 72 RCCI, Final report, 1908, p. 40.

strong resistance in relation to migration policies specifically to the introduction of migrants from sons of tenants and landless men resident in the area.[73] While selling lands to occupiers of inadequate holdings was considered 'destructive', the commission deduced that giving lands to smallholders was a lesser risk than giving it to the landless; it further stated that granting that land to the landless merely stalled the prospect of emigration for one generation. Children of smallholders, occupying labourers' allotments, ranked higher on the eligibility scale than the landless – but only just about. A 'labourer's allotment' was defined as a vegetable patch allocated to non-inheriting sons in exchange for seasonal labour, in contrast an 'economic holding', which varied between six and ten acres, was valued at a minimum of £10. The board's actions in relation to the landless had always been partially discriminatory but they were consistently pragmatic and realistic. For example, when the Labourers act of 1906 was passed, rural district councils petitioned the CDB for lands to build cottages. The board objected as it did not want to accept responsibility for labourers, which would effectively mean bringing paupers with no work prospects into congested areas.[74] It also objected on the grounds that resettled migrants would have no need for hired help but said it was prepared to consider providing sites near to towns or large villages for labourers' cottages. From the outset, the board's basic purpose was to get the population out of the 'at risk of distress' category and to relieve congestion therefore the introduction of landless would have reversed the process. It adhered to the demands of the commission and did not occupy new farms with the landless.

Jones argues that the UIL tried to use the Dudley Commission to further the ranch war but it did not influence the recommendations of the commission. The commission acknowledged that there was a need to establish a minimum holding size, and although the aim of the CDB in relation to agriculture post-1909 was to bring average valuation up to £10, it was not 'desirable to scale down every other holding to that standard'.[75] The Dudley Commission feared that downsizing would be potentially detrimental to the cattle trade, so the Commission recommended that, aside from breaking up grasslands, land reclamation could also enlarge holdings. However, the board still could not conduct large-scale arterial drainage schemes alone. It was still inhibited and had to co-ordinate with other bodies. The Development Commissioners lent the money necessary for carrying out projects and the Board of Works formed a local drainage board to control it.[76] In the six years between 1909 and 1915, when land purchase schemes were suspended by parliament due to the outbreak of war in Europe, the board purchased nearly three times the total amount of land bought in its first nineteen years.

---

[73] Ibid., p. 787. [74] CDB, Seventeenth annual report, 1908, p. 16. [75] RCCI, Final report, 1908, p. 787. [76] CDB, Twenty-second annual report, 1915, p. 8. The money was made available under the 1909 Development Fund Act: see Hoctor, *The department's story*, pp 80–2.

AMALGAMATION AND LAND PURCHASE

Compulsory purchase powers proved invaluable in cases where landlords and the board could not negotiate a sale. The board had powers to submit a final offer, which had to be cash, and if this was rejected it was 'authorised to send a requisition to the Estates Commissioners calling on them to acquire the lands compulsorily'.[77] This power was used against the marquis of Clanricarde who refused final offers concerning seven estates and who applied to the High Court for an injunction against the board and its compulsory purchase powers. The marquis was granted the injunction on the grounds that the CDB offer of £228,075 for 49,741 acres did not comply with the meaning and requirements of the 1909 land act. The case dragged on and eventually rights of compulsory purchase for the Clanricarde estate were awarded in December of 1914 on the condition that the board increase the price by £10,000; it conceded, but this was a once-off deviation from normal procedure designed to combat negative media coverage.[78] The board had also been subject to negative media coverage on 5 May 1913, when a letter from the chairman of the Lettermore district council was published in a Dublin newspaper highlighting an outbreak of typhus and typhoid fevers. He argued that the council, because of its limited means, was unable to cope with the situation; but he went on to document the near starvation of the people, their 'farm rockeries ..., shivering sheep ..., an emaciated caricature of a cow ... and a pinched, wizened little pig to pay the rent'. The editor set up a public subscription and £1,870 was collected. This infuriated the board members who believed that their work was providing long-term relief as opposed to the temporary effects of public subscriptions.[79]

When the parish committee grant schemes ended in 1908, people did not continue to maintain dwellings and improvement schemes were restarted in 1910. The CDB set aside a budget of £35,000 for home improvements and the building of outhouses. An allocation of £20,000 was made for grant money, but grants were available only to owners of agricultural holdings whose property was valued at less than £7. This time a closer eye was kept on spending, and local committees that were careless or cavalier about the rules of the board had money deducted (this was done on an annual basis and equal to the amount badly spent in the previous year).[80] Under this scheme smallholders could apply for grant aid to build a new house or repair an existing one. The maximum amount allocable as a grant was £7 10s. for the purposes of building a three-roomed slated house. Grants were paid only on completion of the building. The remaining £15,000 of the £35,000 was administered through a loan system to tenant purchasers to build dwellings. In this case, applicants could borrow a minimum of £10, and the maximum amount allowed per household was £50.

---

77 CDB, Twentieth annual report, 1912, p. 10. **78** Ibid., p. 15. **79** Ibid., p. 12. **80** CDB, Twenty-first annual report, 1913, p. 16.

All the buildings had to comply with specifications laid out by the board; expenses for labour and materials were borne by the borrower, with the exception of materials required for a slated roof. This clause was inserted to discourage the use of alternative roofs such as corrugated iron, and to phase out the use of thatch. Local government boards partially permitted the use of thatch in the construction of rural labourers' cottages but forbade the use of corrugated iron. The scheme continued for five years and was abandoned during the war.[81]

The only organized attempt for home improvement after the war was a special scheme for the Connemara district, where housing was particularly inferior. In 1920 loans were given for home improvement on a sporadic basis to individual tenant purchasers with a well-pleaded case. In 1919–20, 2,950 windows were distributed free of charge, but the scheme pertained to Connemara only.[82] While parish committees were no longer used, various schemes were adopted by central administration for giving assistance in building, enlarging or repairing houses, and any aid offered was generally availed of. The board substituted fixed windows with movable double-sash windows; concrete floors were put in kitchens; boarded floors were put in bedrooms; and manure pits were moved a safe distance from the house. Through these schemes thousands of houses previously unfit for human habitation were made sanitary and comfortable. In total, a sum of £1,030,665 was spent on home improvements between 1897 and 1922.[83] The board spent £1,556,565 on estate improvements between 1893 and 1919, and a total of 23,807 holdings were dealt with. While it did not manage to build new houses on a greater number of holdings, it facilitated the sale and enlargement of many others.

On the declaration of war in 1914 many of the large-scale drainage works were suspended, and large numbers of workmen were dismissed. Other land improvement operations were slowed down or stopped. The men found alternative employment, and when the board was in a position to re-employ it could not get the numbers of workmen necessary because many had enlisted.[84] During the war, because of the necessity for higher yields within the UK and in compliance with the Defence of the Realm Acts (DORA), the government requested the board to invest efforts in food production. The board had to arrange maximum cultivation of as much land as possible, especially that under its control. It was accused of keeping its best land when it offered tillage lettings for the crop season but it did not have full control of lands in the west. Every owner and occupier of land was given liberty under the regulations to choose the one-tenth section of his land, which he cultivated himself or offered for cropping.

---

81 CDB, Twenty-third annual report, 1915, pp 12–13. **82** CDB, Twenty-eight annual report, 1920, p. 10. **83** Micks, *An account of the history*, pp 152–3. **84** CDB, Twenty-third annual report, 1916, p. 10.

The lack of tractors, manures, seeds and labour made it impossible to till large tracts of land in the congests so instead plots were cordoned off near highly populated areas.[85] In fact, as a result of the tillage schemes during the war the board suffered great losses; it was not compensated.[86] Following the war, the board reverted back to estate purchase and improvement, but wage expectancy had increased nearly threefold for estate improvement work.[87]

From 1909 to 1922 the board opened up land-owning prospects for the disadvantaged and helped to create 'modest farmers' (holdings over 10 but under 40 acres) out of smallholders. There was a shift in holding size as can be seen in the following table, with the notable upward shift in farms ranging from 15 to 100 acres and consequently a decrease in the number of farms over 100 acres. The number of allotments, or holdings under one acre, increased but this was not attributable to the work of the board.

Table 5.5. Total number of holdings in Co. Mayo

	Under 1 acre	1–5	5–15	15–30	30–50	50–100	100–200	100–500	Above 500	Total
1881	1,958	4,349	15,473	9,172	2,432	1,224	695	443	219	35,965
1891	1,702	3,276	14,690	9,305	2,852	1,496	685	421	227	34,654
1917	2,125	2,654	13,345	10,878	3,414	1,655	597	408	187	35,263

Source: Agricultural Statistics, Ireland[88]

As shown in table 5.5, instead of reducing the number of households dependent on the land between 1891 and 1917, the total number of holdings in Co. Mayo, which contained the poorest land, increased. This innate, 'clinging to the land' (as Cousens calls it) became even more apparent in the first twenty years of the Saorstát. Household continuity was the norm in the west and the board did not manage to break that trend.[89]

What did the board achieve as a development agency?

When the CDB was founded, the west was in a general state of poverty despite the fact that in proportion with other areas in the British Isles it reaped more

---

85 CDB, Twenty-fifth annual report, 1917, pp 9–11. **86** CDB, Twenty-eighth annual report, 1921, p. 11. **87** Ibid., p. 10. **88** Agricultural Statistics, Ireland, 1881 [C.3332], lxxiv. 1890 [C.6518] xci. 1920–21[Cmd.1316] xli. **89** D. Birdwell-Pheasant, 'Irish households in the twentieth century: culture, class, and historical contingency' (1993), pp 19–38.

Treasury benefits. It was significantly poorer because it endured the regressive rigours of indirect taxation and exorbitant interest at the hands of local traders. McCann estimates, that two million of the Irish peasantry paid £1 to £1 5s per head per annum indirectly to the exchequer for their consumption of tea, sugar, tobacco, porter and whiskey, while local taxation (amount raised by local government in various rates) only amounted to between 10s. and 12s. 6d. per head.[90] Consumer abuse thrived in the congested district where local merchants added further costs of 'interest'. Baseline inspectors identified the economic patronage of the gombeenman as a primary factor in rural poverty and shopkeeper debts as one of the biggest obstacles to rural development. The costs levied by shopkeepers was not unique to the west, but in the rural context it was exacerbated by the prevalence of the truck system, the system of barter or payment in kind that shopkeepers used to exchange goods.[91] Due to lack of competition and limited cashflow, the gombeenman's influence was intensely intertwined in the daily lives of the people and it took the board a long time to reduce dependency on shopkeeper credit

Gombeenman control started with cash loans but extended to incorporate a bonded labour market where s/he could also profit through insisting that farm produce be bartered.[92] Rapacious interest rates were charged on credit, so people were unaware of the full value of their produce. The baseline inspectors noted that shopkeepers were even more dishonest when dealing with women, the group most likely to trade goods on a regular basis, and that tea was the most abused commodity in the west. Exchange payment for eggs and butter was widespread and to a lesser, but significant, extent for textile outwork. Clarkson and Crawford mentions instances where shopkeepers mixed chicory with coffee, cocoa shell with cocoa powder, and where toxins such as iron oxide were added to tea to enhance colour, and they also note that fresh tea was mixed with recycled tea leaves.[93] Evidence of adulteration with toxins or other vegetable matter is not borne out in the baseline reports, but the inspectors testify that inferior teas were mixed with finer blends at a high price, and that if tea

90 J. McCann, *Irish taxation and Irish transit: two speeches delivered in the House of Commons on the overtaxation of Ireland* (1901), p. 20. **91** R. Millward and S. Sheard, 'The urban fiscal problem, 1870–1914: government expenditure and finance in England and Wales' (1995). They argue that central government was not willing to address the inequalities of indirect taxation, the onus being on local government to deal with the issue. The lack of a consistent directive from central government led to variations in expenditure policy for each local authority that led to variations in transportation costs, which provided traders with an excuse to raise prices. **92** I am grateful to Dr Margaret Ó hÓgartaigh for highlighting the existence of a gombeenwomen in Donegal. See McFeely, *Lady inspectors*, pp 76–7, 79, 83. **93** Clarkson and Crawford, *Feast and famine*, p. 266. Kennedy and Johnson argues that higher duties on tea, tobacco and sugar should have promoted an illicit trade but there is no evidence of this in the congests because merchants were fewer. See Kennedy and Johnson 'The Union of Ireland and Britain' (1996), pp 34–71.

was purchased on credit the interest charged was higher than on any other goods. Dishonest merchants operated unquestioned because adulteration was difficult to detect and customers were afraid to put their credit rating at risk by complaining. Shopkeepers in Irish urban centres were not as exploitative as those in congested areas, probably because they received payments on a more regular basis. To rectify the issue of shopkeeper abuse the board encouraged improvements in poultry and in dairy produce (the most commonly bartered goods) and gave producers access to alternative markets. The truck act, implemented in 1896, endeavoured to eliminate the illegal system of fines in factories (in the textile industry fining and payment in kind was more common than other industries), and inspectors were appointed to enforce this law.[94] Whatever about the act's effectiveness in the urban factories, the incidence of abuse in rural areas was higher because the outwork system was more difficult to police and people were slow to testify against the gombeenman.[95] Gibbon and Higgins do not acknowledge the efforts made by the CDB in ending the truck system of payment for textiles; instead they imply that 'large-scale frauds' were characteristic of the CDB era.[96] But without the board the truck system of payment would probably have continued for a lot longer.

While some historians argue that the board contributed nothing to the development of agriculture in the west, Turner and Vaughan prove through their separate, but conflicting, studies that the opposite is true.[97] Practically all agricultural output is measured by multiplying acreage and livestock numbers by price indexes and the estimates show noteworthy increases in agricultural output for Ireland in general between 1891 and 1920. At a basic level, the board improved agricultural practice, then holdings were enlarged to facilitate a higher output, thereby the west had a more secure share in the Irish agricultural market. A comparison of receipts in 1891 and 1919 shows that, even adjusting for inflation, agricultural output at least doubled for some items, receipts for pigs trebled and butter money increased tenfold even in the poorest areas (see table 6.1). While these estimates show a substantial increase in cash income they are an incomplete indicator of total cash income as they do not include earnings

---

[94] M. Cohen, *Linen, family and community in Tullylish* (1997) pp 243, 183–4. Economic problems varied in accordance with the nature of industry; for example, in Donegal there was a thriving shirt-making industry with a particularly unfair system of fines, while other areas relied on home-knits and lace, both of which had unstable markets. Cohen notes how it did not totally eliminate the fines because there was a loophole; if part of the salary payment was designated a bonus, deductions could be made if a worker was late and some factory owners would lock the workers out to ensure tardiness. [95] McFeely, *Lady inspectors,* pp 78–86. [96] P. Gibbon and M.D. Higgins, 'Patronage, tradition and modernisation: the case of the Irish gombeenman' (1974), pp 27–44. [97] M. Turner, 'Output and productivity in Irish agriculture from the Famine to the Great War' (1990). W.E. Vaughan, 'Potatoes and agricultural output' (1990).

from Old Age Pensions, introduced in 1909. Fitzpatrick indicates in his study of the family unit that parents were likely to remain in the family dwelling even after the inheriting son married, but no allowance is made in the returns for the cash contribution of pensions to the household budget.[98]

Table 5.6. Income, 1891–1919
Average household receipts in Swinford union and similar districts in Mayo, Galway, Roscommon and Sligo

	1891 £ s. d.	1919 £ s. d.
Pigs	6 0 0	20 0 0
Cattle	6 0 0	15 0 0
Butter	3 10 0	35 0 0
Eggs and poultry	3 4 0	2 0 0
Oats	3 10 0	4 0 0
Straw and hay	0 10 0	1 0 0
Potatoes	2 0 0	2 0 0
Migratory earnings	8 0 0	40 0 0
Total	32 14 0	119 0 0

Source: Twenty-seventh annual report, 1920 p. 11

The value of general household consumption is a very significant indicator of rising income levels, and strictly speaking it should be tabulated as expenditure but it is very difficult to ascertain (because it does not feature in the returns of agricultural statistics). While the sample budgets returned in the penultimate annual report show the changes in expenditure patterns, no allowance is made for 'on farm consumption' – so these figures are incomplete. The value of turf is also omitted. This is a particular grievance of Ó Gráda's, who argues that the value of turf (in terms of turf sales and its cost for those who had no access) must have been relatively high. An inconsistent number of baseline reports mention the expenditure on fuel, it was not usually bought; rather it was bartered so the real value is hard to calculate. However, the board was very conscious of fuel costs and was careful to include a strip of turbary in reorganized holdings.[99] From 1891 to 1919 nearly £500,000 was spent on road building, reducing transportation costs which in turn reduced fuel expenditure.[1] During the

---

98 Fitzpatrick, 'Irish farming families before the first world war' (1978), pp 126–43.   **99** This discrepancy is mentioned in C. Ó Gráda, *Ireland* (1994); see also his *Ireland before and after the famine: explorations in economic history, 1800–1925* (1988).   **1** CDB, Twenty-seventh annual

lifespan of the board the use of oil lamps (which would have been considered a luxury item), became more widespread, even in the poorest inland districts.[2] The money spent on flour and meal doubled. But the expenditure on clothes is more interesting, rising from 14 per cent of expenditure in 1891 to almost 16 per cent in 1919. As clothing was considered luxury expenditure, it became the first economy made in times of want, so increased expenditure in this area is indicative of a general rise in cash income. It is also interesting to note rising church and school dues, which reflects an increase in literacy levels and the effects of modernization on traditional societies.[3]

Table 5.7. Average expenditure per household in the South Connemara islands

	1891 £ s. d.	1919 £ s. d.
Flour, meal, tea, sugar, lamp-oil	15 10 0	38 0 0
Clothes and boots	4 0 0	11 0 0
Tobacco	1 5 0	5 0 0
Rent and taxes	4 0 0	2 10 0
Church and school dues	1 0 0	1 5 0
Repairs of boat and gear	3 0 0	5 10 0
Total	28 15 0	63 5 0

Source: CDB, Twenty-seventh annual report (1920), p. 9.

Social problems associated with modernization

The CDB facilitated a rise in cash incomes, and this created a new problem – secondary poverty, a condition where cash income levels increased but money was spent unwisely. Rowntree, in his study of York, identified male expenditure on drink and tobacco as the primary cause of secondary poverty.[4] Reflecting the low levels of cash in circulation in 1891, secondary poverty was minimal in the west when the board was formed, and, as O'Neill argues, poverty certainly prevented excessive drinking in the congested districts. Whiskey was bought on fair days to seal a bargain, and on other occasions such as weddings and wakes the host provided the alcohol.[5] Nearly all the baseline reports con-

report, 1919, p. 27. **2** Nolan, *Within the Mullet*, p. 204. **3** D.G. Boyce, *Nationalism in Ireland* (1982), pp 376–7. **4** B.S. Rowntree, *Poverty: a study of town life* (1902), pp 141–3. **5** T.P.

firm that it was men who consumed alcohol and tobacco; Lane-Poole, an independent observer, commented that there was a notable physical difference between the health of women, who scarcely ever drank, and that of the men.[6] Smoking went hand in hand with the traditional Irish wake customs, where both sexes smoked clay pipes, but daily tobacco consumption was more associated with the male custom of 'botháintíocht,' where men went from house to house discussing the news and drinking tea or poitín.[7]

In its work the CDB alleviated relative and absolute poverty, which existed throughout the congested districts, but when cash income levels rose, secondary poverty became a bigger issue due to spendthrift habits. This problem is especially evident when the role of rural women is considered, but its emergence can be used as a sensitive barometer of CDB progress. All the baseline reports indicate that in the congested districts women held the purse strings. Mary Cullen states that this was a post-famine trend – that in pre-famine, rural Ireland men were in control of family income.[8] The baseline reports also show that pocket money was given to the husbands for a drink on fair days but only if the family income was above a certain threshold.[9] The Claddagh fishing region in Galway bay was an exception (it was not a congested district until 1909 when then the whole county was categorized as congested). It was noted in 1888 that the wives of the Claddagh fishermen maintained control over all spending, although the men were the breadwinners.[10] Cohen's study of Tullylish is an invaluable insight into the role of women in an urban setting and provides a useful parallel; there men worked for wages continuously and women intermittently, so men usually had control of the cash while the amount wives received depended on how much husbands smoked and drank.[11] In stark contrast, Modell's study of Irish behavioural patterns of consumption in America showed that Irish-born emigrants were careful with money, but does not specify who was in charge of the budget.[12] Unfortunately there are no reliable returns

---

O'Neill, 'Rural life' (1957), pp 47–9. Butler, *Caherciveen Report*, p. 8, *Kilorglin*, p. 6. Butler noted that both men and women of Sneem drank a lot on fair days, a day when cash was earned. He advised that a coffee stall be opened in Caherciveen where there were sixty public houses. He blamed the concoctions sold as whiskey for the high numbers in the lunatic asylum in Killarney and recommended that shops selling groceries should be prohibited from selling whiskey. **6** S. Lane-Poole, *North-West and by north; Irish hills and English dales* (1902), p. 34. **7** G. Ó Crualaíoch, 'The merry wake' (1990). **8** M. Cullen, 'Breadwinners and providers: women in the household economy of labouring families 1835–6' (1990), pp 90–1. **9** Contemporary sociologists considered the pocket money given to husbands to spend on smoking and drinking as wilful waste: see Cohen, *Linen, family and community*, p. 238. **10** *IB*, 1 January 1888, p. 14. **11** Cohen, *Linen, family and community*, p. 235. See also James McCann, *Irish taxation and Irish transit*, p. 20. 'I believe that the use of stimulants amongst the Irish peasantry and poor is very much the result of a low standard of living and their coarse and insufficient food and clothing; and in a measure to climatic influences and the uncertainty of their material existence.' **12** J. Modell,

pertaining to alcohol consumption in the congests, probably due to the illicit nature of the trade, but expenditure on tobacco is accounted for in 1891; it amounted to 4.34 per cent of family income, increasing to 7.9 per cent in 1919 (table 6.2).[13] This implies that women had lost, or were losing, control over the family budget.

In 1891 the west was stuck in what Mary Daly calls a pre-famine economic structure where women contributed to the family income through craftwork; and in many northern districts this work was intrinsic to the basic survival of the family unit.[14] The board noted in 1919 that female earnings were still central to the survival of the family unit but where female earnings continued to play an important role in the post-war period, family incomes were notably lower.[15] The penultimate annual report noted that female incomes were regarded as 'household earnings' and spent more wisely than male earnings, being used to buy cattle, sheep, and pigs if a household poor. However, the general rise in family incomes over this period correlates with a remarkable downward trend in recognizable female earnings between 1890 and 1923 as the sale of eggs decreased from £3 4*s*. to £2 (see table 6.1). As a result of increased agricultural output, family incomes had risen to a level which made it unnecessary for women to engage in paid employment; this resulted in women having less spending power. Bourke contends that women were forced back into the homesteads by the home industries associations but she does not place enough emphasis on the changing role of Irish men. Advancements made in agriculture meant a decline in the demand for male Irish labour during the British harvest, so Irish men resumed farming at home on a full-time basis on enlarged holdings and, outside of feeding poultry or calves, women were only needed to work during the harvest when the whole family helped. Mayo was the only exception, as male migration levels remained high until the 1920s, which intimates that women remained working the fields for longer.

In 1925 the commission investigating the Gaeltacht reported that average household incomes in Donegal, on a holding of 9.16 acres, amounted to £216 10*s*. per annum.[16] Of this, earnings through poultry and butter production came to £56 10*s*.[17] It is unfortunate that these two latter items are combined but, assuming the difference stated in the CDB twenty-seventh annual report to be

---

'Patterns of consumption' (1978), p. 206. **13** For a comprehensive account of illicit distillation see K.H. Connell, *Irish peasant society* (1968), pp 1–50. **14** Daly, 'Women in the Irish workforce from pre-industrial to modern times', p. 74. **15** CDB, Twenty-seventh annual report, 1920, pp 6–7. **16** These Irish-speaking regions were very poor according to the Report of Coimissiún na Gaeltachta (1925) p. 41. 'Even in poor districts, it will be generally found that the persons on the poorest holdings are the Irish speakers. The outstanding fact is that the Irish speaking population is insecurely rooted in the land – the only stable basis of livelihood possessed by this population.' **17** Ibid., p. 24.

correct, it is almost certain that most of this income was derived from butter or buttermilk. The high figure also shows that the butter was not hand churned, a task traditionally performed by women. Instead, the milk was now sent to a creamery where 'it was separated by centrifugal separators, and the skim milk given back to the supplier'.[18] Co-operative creameries predominantly paid the landholder, usually the male head of household. As men traditionally conducted the sale of animals and cash crops, they also received these proceeds. Consequently in dealing with this new institution there was a shift in control of family budgets from female to male hands.[19] Surplus daughters were particularly hard hit on enlarged farms, because they were expected to conduct unpaid farm chores, were less likely to have a personal poultry industry and would ultimately be ousted by the inheriting son's wife as there was only room for one female in the household.[20] Although David Fitzpatrick does not emphasize the value of egg money in his study of female occupations, he highlights the importance of general female earnings to the individual: 'savings so accumulated and services rendered were crucial in determining a girl's ability to afford either emigration or marriage'.[21] When other agricultural activities became more profitable, the importance of the egg money was displaced in the household income. In some areas, when general family incomes reached a certain threshold, the poultry industry declined, but this does not conform to Bourke's Victorian tastes hypothesis; rather, it reflects that women were engaged in other, unpaid farm work. On enlarged farms where women continued with the industry, the money became personal money; this had wider social implications. Trends in marriage patterns – to a later age – combined with the shift in inheritance patterns meant that egg money became either a dowry or an emigration fund. By the 1920s young rural women faced one of three options: marriage arranged by parents, spinsterhood or emigration. Congested district girls were not likely candidates for convents as nuns were predominantly drawn from wealthier and better-educated classes.[22]

18 Bourke, *Husbandry to housewifery,* p. 85.   **19** R.E. Kennedy, Jr. *The Irish: emigration, marriage, and fertility* (1973), pp 53–5.   **20** R. Rhodes, *Women and the family in post-famine Ireland: status and opportunity in a patriarchal society* (1992), pp 228–9. Arensberg and Kimball observed that in the 1930s the role of the rural female was reduced to a slave-like status; she would wait until the men and children had eaten and would then eat the leftovers   **21** Fitzpatrick, 'The modernisation of the Irish female', p. 169.   **22** For analysis of social backgrounds of female clergy see C. Clear, *Nuns in nineteenth century Ireland* (1987). Girls stayed in school longer than boys if the family could do without the child earnings. Also non-inheriting daughters had higher emigration potential and learning English was vital component for migrants: E. Delaney 'Gender and 20th century Irish migration, 1921–1971' (2001) p. 215. This choice was further limited under the Free State and particularly in de Valera's Ireland. While no measures were taken to prohibit females, Delaney observes how a clear distinction was made between male and female migration, the latter being highlighted as an area of particular concern.

The CDB has been accused of following the trend of other Victorian reformers that placed female labour in the household, but it was probably not as premeditated as Bourke asserts in her husbandry to housewifery thesis.[23] The propensity of women to find work was clearly linked to family income levels, and Bourke's theory is more applicable to the west in the 1930s and 1940s, that is, later than the earlier period she suggests. Rather, the west in the 1920s continued to conform to Cullen's pre-famine model of women still being breadwinners, even if they had lost control of family budgets.[24] Bourke's thesis as portrayed in *Husbandry to Housewifery* corresponds more to the wider process of modernization, not just the impact of, exclusive reforming groups, such as the board, the IAOS and later the department. Bourke acknowledges how the clergy became more vocal about its opposition to female employment in the early 1900s, but her argument that in late Victorian times female idleness was a status symbol for fathers and husbands is not applicable to the congested districts (the only possible exceptions would be daughters of shopkeepers).[25] While the board contributed to the process of change, it is important to note that from the outset it identified women as the more 'economic gender'; using pre-existing mechanisms it strove to enhance the role of women as breadwinners and ensured that women were paid fairly and directly for their labour.[26] In the first twenty years of the Saorstát more changes occurred but in many respects the rigours of modernization combined with methods of enumerating agricultural labour obscures the extent of work undertaken by the rural Irish female.[27]

Lee suggests that if 'capital invested in uneconomic projects in the west' had been invested in the east it could have transformed emigration into internal migration; Ó Gráda agrees that slow migration from the 'small economy' of the west to the east hindered the process of economic convergence.[28] Had the money been invested in the east, it would probably have ensured convergence with the rest of the UK in general economic terms, but if that rationale been applied the west would have continued to lag significantly behind the east. Also permanent internal migration was not customary. When internal migration occurred, it was seasonal and generally concerned children; for example

---

[23] Cohen, *Linen, family and community*, pp 164–5. Cohen subscribes to Bourke's argument and purports that in the urban setting factory owners acted as surrogate father figures to young female employees in contrast married women were discriminated against and could not get work on the factory floor. However, these paternalistic employers had no problem with married women conducting out-work in their own homes [24] M. Cullen, 'Breadwinners and providers', pp 90–1. [25] The clergy had wielded a particular hold over the Irish psyche in many respects. For further discussion see T. Garvin, 'Priests and patriots: Irish separatism and fear of the modern 1890–1914' (1986). [26] Daly, 'Women in the Irish workforce,' pp 74–184. [27] C. Clear, *Women of the house: women's household work in Ireland, 1921–1961* (2000), p. 13. [28] Lee, *Modernisation*, pp 124–5. Ó Gráda, *Ireland*, p. 272.

girls from Kerry who migrated to Limerick, and Donegal children who went to the Lagan. The east could not absorb unskilled paupers permanently and the trend for adults was to go into exile rather than to permanently relocate to other Irish urban or rural centres.[29] The Malthusian solution to congestion was to relieve the land of surplus population. Balfour favoured this, and indeed both Tuke and Plunkett made strong petitions for emigration schemes, but nationalist opposition viewed these policies as legal deportation. Statistically speaking, the only way to raise the valuation of holdings to £10 in parts of Erris and Connemara was the removal of 80 of the 100 families (except through building improvement). Lee does not acknowledge that, from 1891 to 1909, the board was not legally entitled to remove people permanently unless it was relocating congested district residents to scheduled CDB lands. After the Dudley Commission, the board still faced serious opposition to migration policies. The board was also aware that unless there was a radical change in public opinion that it could not relieve congestion by means of migration to land east of the Shannon (the proposed eastward migration was to be conducted in conjunction with the Estates Commission).

High levels of emigration were characteristic of Gaeltacht areas (literally, the Irish-speaking districts, and in geographical terms all the western Gaeltachts were in the congested districts) but people tended to emigrate singly, leaving the household and the tenure undisturbed.[30] The CDB contributed greatly to the modernization process, but seasonal migratory earnings and remittances had a significant effect on the survival of uneconomic holdings.[31] General trends in seasonal migratory statistics show a decrease in numbers migrating, but in the west the tradition continued for longer. Agricultural statistics show a steady decrease in migration from 22,900 in 1880 to 14,081 in 1890. The figures rose again in 1900 to 19,022 and fell to 10,225 in 1910. The demand for Irish labour was high in 1918. Scottish potato merchants applied to the Ministry of Agriculture for special permits for workers from Achill; some 2,500 such workers travelled annually with approximately 91 gaffers.[32] Migratory earnings still stood at 25 per cent of family cash income in parts of Galway, Mayo, Sligo and Roscommon in 1919 (see table 6.1). CDB schemes were not intended to complement the process of emigration, but they provided a cash income at home, especially for women. The function of the board was to keep people busy at home, but wages provided by the board paid for departure and relieved congestion by thinning population, albeit unintentionally. The CDB's main prob-

---

[29] For further discussion on involuntary departure see K.A. Miller, *Emigrants and exiles: Ireland and the Irish exodus to North America* (1985), pp 345–53. [30] Saorstát Éireann, *Report of Coimisiún na Gaeltachta*, p. 41. [31] D. Fitzpatrick, 'Irish emigration in the later nineteenth century' (1980) p. 126. [32] J.E. Hanley, *The Irish in modern Scotland, 1798–1845* (1947), pp 168–72.

lem (especially in the textile sector) was that workers it trained emigrated as soon as they acquired marketable skills. In fact, the board was resigned to the fact that it could not break the trend, and its last few annual reports show a minor expenditure of about £9 per annum on a female migration fund. Remittances from family members also contributed to the survival of uneconomic holdings, Modell notes that in 1874, in spite of considerable spending power, the Irish spent 25 per cent less than native Americans on rent and 35 per cent less on clothing, and argues that the Irish 'denied themselves all avoidable expenditures, even the comforts of religion'. He suggests that these deviations from the norm could be explained by poverty, ignorance or by deviant tastes, which emanated from hungry times at home.[33] But the pressure to save money in order to send remittances home was probably more significant; remittances did aid chain migration, but they were primarily used to pay rents. Ironically, the work of the board facilitated the extension of posts and telegraphs that subsequently aided the prompt return of remittances.[34] In turn this soft money, or remittances from surplus sons and daughters, continued to sustain the small farmers and in some respects reversed the self-help ethos the board tried to instil.[35]

---

[33] J. Modell, 'Patterns of consumption', p. 206. [34] Although the figures for remittances do not feature to a great extent in the baseline or the annual reports it can be assumed that they were high considering that the Tuke report accounted for a £12,000 aggregate sum sent to Clifden in the 1880s. [35] D.G. Symes, 'Farm household and farm performance: a study of twentieth century changes in Ballyferrter, Southwest Ireland' (1972), p. 26.

Conclusion

Historians have judged the Congested Districts Board very harshly because it has been viewed as part of the legacy of Constructive Unionism, which failed to 'kill home rule'. The main aim of the board was to create a certain degree of self-sufficiency and to protect the congested districts from the threat of famine. To provide a fair assessment of the board, it must be separated from the policy of Constructive Unionism and be assessed for what it was, a development agency. O'Halpin considers the board irrelevant as a development agency, but he is clearly viewing the board in terms of general Irish policy. The establishment of the CDB was a response to the regionally specific 'distress' and it excelled in its performance, especially when compared with its Scottish counterpart and later Free State action (or, as it transpired, inaction).[1] From the outset, Balfour placed the CDB on an independent footing from Dublin Castle because its establishment was more of a humane gesture than a strategic political measure. Because the board had a unique independent status from the Castle, the people of the west accepted help from the Irish board more readily than the IAOS, or the DATI.[2] It is also evident that once the board was established, contemporary nationalist politicians, such as John Dillon, did not perceive it as a threat; and it was treated in effect as an apolitical entity. Its members were mainly Irish, they worked on a voluntary basis and managed to overcome the increasing sectarian divide, a factor that inhibited the growth of the IAOS.

Taken as a whole, the success of Arthur Balfour's constructive unionist policies helped to pacify agrarian unrest and provided his brother Gerald Balfour, chief secretary 1895–1900, with a basis for a progressive Irish policy. When the Local Government act was extended to Ireland in 1898 it enfranchised rural men in the local elections; from then urban, rural and county councils assumed all the fiscal duties formerly exercised by the grand juries and the poor law guardians.[3] Gerald

---

[1] O'Halpin, *The decline of the Union*, p. 14. [2] McDowell, *The Irish administration*, p. 221. [3] Shannon, 'The Ulster liberal unionists and local government reform', pp 407–23. Shannon argues that Gerald Balfour was determined to improve Irish economic, social and political life but local government was to be the limit of political concessions to Irish nationalists. The first elections saw a landslide nationalist victory of 551 seats compared with 125 unionist seats, 86 of which were in Ulster.

Balfour then introduced the DATI act but his adoption of constructive unionist policies cannot simply be viewed as a continuation of his brother's strategies.[4] Arthur Balfour did not intend to prime rural Ireland for any form of self-government as he had no confidence in Irish political ability and firmly believed that Ireland was not economically ready for any form of independence. He maintained his anti-Home Rule stance for many years. Using the aid given by the Treasury to finance the eradication the foot and mouth outbreak in 1912 as an example, he argued that Irish agriculture would buckle without British support. He also contended that the small farmer in the west of Ireland depended too much on the English markets, and that an executive in Ireland separate from Westminster would not serve the smallholder interests.[5] Ironically, his policy of amelioration heightened political awareness in Ireland and in some ways prepared the way for self-government.[6]

Gailey contends that controversial moderates, such as Plunkett, were central to the failure of Constructive Unionism because of their infighting and disunity, and he claims that 'the term implies a collective unity that is flattering but historically false'.[7] Constructive Unionism as a weak policy has been over-stressed rather it could not compete with the surge of nationalism, which was a very pivotal factor in its failure. He asserts that the CDB, coupled with land legislation, sustained the rural economy, and 'institutionalised and strengthened existing power and patronage structures, and was quickly absorbed into the local political culture where the adherence to home rule was a basic assumption'.[8] According to the baseline reports, the patronage structure in rural communities was under the control of local traders and subsequently the position of this class was weakened because of the board's activities. At the turn of the century, Irish society was consumed with nationalism in all its manifestations, culturally, physically and politically, but less so in the west than in the east. Irish was *teanga na mbocht* (the language of the poor) and was also the language of the congested districts. Although the Gaelic League identified the west as a linguistic model, the tenant class in the west was concerned that their children would have a proficiency in English that would prepare them for eventual emigration.[9] Cultural nationalism

---

4 A. Gailey, 'Unionist rhetoric and Irish local government reform, 1895–9' (1984), p. 55.   **5** A.J. Balfour, *Aspects of home rule* (1912), pp 64–5. For a more detailed opinion on home rule, see A.J. Balfour, *Nationality and home rule* (1913).   **6** Hansard, 3, cccxxv, 503, cited in C.B. Shannon, 'The Ulster Liberal Unionists' p. 413.   **7** A. Gailey, *Ireland and the death of kindness: the experience of Constructive Unionism, 1890–1905* (1987), p. 131.   **8** Gailey, *Ireland and the death of kindness,* p. 314. In the first regard, the board acquired all the powers and duties of the Board of Works (which dealt with arterial drainage and land improvement), the National Board of Education (which was responsible for agricultural instruction) and the Science and Art Department (then in charge of technical instruction) and the Fisheries Board or the Board of Works. By promoting organization at community level with parish committees the board broke down pre-existing hegemonies, which in some respects ripened conditions for the successful running of local government.   **9** Rhodes, *Women and the family in post-famine Ireland,* p. 269.

was gaining some momentum in rural societies (particularly in relation to the Irish language as a component of nationalism and identity) but as Ó Cúiv notes from census returns, the success of the Gaelic revival was more evident in non-Gaeltacht areas or non-congested Ireland.[10] Perhaps the most enduring effect that the board had on Irish nationalism was its contribution to the shift in land ownership: many smallholders became owner-occupiers, and this deepened the sense of national identity. Gailey also implies that the CDB 'determined a fiercely parochial and conservative society which would have little interest in social revolution, as the years after 1916 demonstrated. Moreover this ethos was in turn maintained by the Free State in the form of the Land Commission and the Gaeltacht policies' but the Gaeltacht did not receive exclusive attention in Saorstát Éireann. When the CDB was wound up in 1923 it had very few liquid assets (only £55,393 18*s*. 4*d*.) but it held just over £138,862 in securities (British govt. Stocks) and it was owed £35,365 in outstanding loans.[11] Its fixed assets (improved lands, valued at nearly £800,000) had been purchased for cash (out of CDB funds, not through the land acts) and the value of these lands had been enhanced by improvement schemes.[12] In economic terms, there was no continuity as Gailey implies what happened to the CDB assets is unclear; indeed Frank Fahy questioned what happened this money in 1928: 'As far as I could discover – and if I am wrong I would like to see it proved where I am wrong – the C.D. Board handed over £800,000 when it was taken over. I do not know what has happened that £800,000.'[13] The most likely reason for its disappearance is that it was subsumed into general land purchase and reallocation schemes; there is no evidence to suggest that it was spent specifically on Gaeltacht areas.

Following the 1922 Anglo-Irish treaty and the establishment of Irish government departments, the CDB was allowed to continue in existence for over a year. Even if nationalists aspired to removing all remnants of the British administration, the board had amicable relations with the new Department of Agriculture of the Free State. On 12 September 1922 the minutes of proceedings were headed 'Bord na gCeanntar gCumhang i n-Éirinn' for the first time, in keeping with the language policy of Saorstát Éireann.[14] Patrick Hogan, the newly appointed Minister for Agriculture, assigned to a commission (the Drew Commission) the task of examining the condition of agriculture in 1922. When that commission reported in 1923, the problem of congestion was still far from resolution, the board had reorganized 29,200 holdings and about 30,000 were still in process of improvement when the board was dissolved. The board, well aware that its work was unfinished, wrote to the department of agriculture to convince it to continue

---

10 B. Ó Cúiv, 'Irish language and literature, 1845–1921' (1996), p. 389. **11** CDB, *Receipts and expenditure of the Congested Districts Board in each year from 1891 to 1923* (1927), p. 10. **12** Saorstát Éireann, *Report of Coimisiún na Gaeltachta* (1925), p. 39. **13** DÉ, vol. 23, 2 May 1928, Gaeltacht Commission Report. **14** CDB, Minutes of Proceedings, 12 December 1922, p. 5.

separate policies for the west.[15] The Drew Commission took the recommendation into consideration but the new department did not make provision for a separate body to deal with congestion.[16] In fact, the considerable debate that occurred in the Dáil throughout 1922 related to the CDB staff.[17] The net result of this debate was that its employees were re-instated as either advisors or employees of the Irish Free State, but they were not necessarily employed in the same kind of capacity as before. Not only did the Saorstát acquire the staff and its finances; at the last CDB meeting held on 29 May 1923, it was decided that all CDB property would be presented as gifts to the respective communities. In other words, the board bequeathed a system and the requisite operational materials to each community, but the Saorstát did not use the funds to take advantage of this relatively well-oiled mechanism and in the absence of allocated staff to follow up on outstanding loans this money was not recovered.[18]

Although Minister of Agriculture Hogan was verging on the excessive in his praise of the board, and although he appeared to have a full understanding of its functions, he was quite adamant about the re-centralization of power (see appendix E). He was more concerned about the general issue of the outstanding loan of about 130 million to the British exchequer, which was forwarded for land purchase. Using the recommendations of the Drew Commission, it was decided that the Land Mortgage Bank be given powers to lend money, similar to those previously held by the CDB, the Board of Works and the DATI. Under a Transfer of Functions Order, the office of Commissioner of the Irish Land Commission ceased to exist and a new Land Commission was founded. The new body had the responsibility of land purchase and it absorbed the land purchase functions of the former Land Commission and of the CDB. When the Land Act was passed into law in May 1923, the CDB was dissolved.[19]

It was clear that it was general policies that contributed to and perpetuated the problem of congestion in the first place despite this Saorstát Éireann regressed to a general policy in which the congested districts did not receive priority; as Boyce argues, the Gaeltacht withered away in independent Ireland.[20] The CDB managed to raise living standards significantly, as is clear if one compares sample family budgets compiled in 1891 and with those of 1919. Data compiled by the 1923 Drew Commission showed that an institution like the CDB was highly

---

15 Ibid., 10 May 1923. **16** Dáil Éireann vol. 1, 17 Nov 1922, Committee on the Estimates, CDB. **17** G. Mitchell, *Deeds not words: the life and works of Muriel Gahan* (1997), pp 19–55. For example, Henry Gahan, a civil engineer, had worked first with the Cavan and Leitrim light Railway Company. He worked for the Congested Districts Board as a baseline inspector and was kept on as an agriculture inspector until the board's dissolution in 1923. He was then transferred to the Land Commission, from which he retired in 1926. His expertise was held in such high esteem that he was called upon in his retirement to conduct valuation work for the ESB for the Poulaphouca hydro-electric scheme. **18** CDB, Minutes of Proceedings, 29 May 1923 **19** Ibid., 29 May 1923 **20** Boyce, *Nationalism in Ireland*, p. 355.

necessary to ensure sustained and further growth in the west. However, no Saorstát measure was put in place and, by the time Comisiúin na Gaeltachta reported in 1926, conditions in these areas had deteriorated. That commission also advised that the west should receive separate attention. Indeed, its recommendations took all CDB policies into consideration, emphasizing extensive migration as the best possible solution for congestion.[21] The recommendations of both Saorstát commissions were a dead letter until James Dillon, Minister for Agriculture, tried to implement a Land Reclamation Project in 1949, which was an attempt to revive initiatives akin to the CDB to aid the west.[22] It was not until post World War II that the government was in a position to assist development in the west but this money, derived from external sources through Marshall Aid, was not allocated as carefully as the CDB had used funds in its time.[23] In fact, the Irish government did not make separate allowances for the depressed regions of the west until the Department of the Gaeltacht was established in 1956.

The Congested Districts Board was a development agency of singular importance and it has been unjustly categorized solely as a tool of Constructive Unionism. By its own standards and according to its initial stated aim of raising the west out of the 'at risk of distress' category, the board had already succeeded by the turn of the century. In the early twentieth century its schemes began to bear fruit. For example, from 1880 to 1891 (years of particular distress) over half a million pounds was spent by the exchequer on objectless relief works. Distress was not as evident from 1908 to 1919 when CDB schemes effectively replaced short-term relief works and during this time 'no money was voted by Parliament for relief of distress in Ireland'.[24] If it had not delegated powers to parish committees, the board would probably not have been as successful on a micro level. On a macro level, its powers were, from the outset, insufficient to solve the problem of congestion: they were too narrowly focussed, and when they were extended it was too little too late. While the CDB was a good model for dealing with congestion and was relatively successful, it highlighted the harsh reality that the problem was not a shortage of cash. The population dependent on the land needed thinning out, farms needed enlargement, and farming methods needed modernization. CDB evidence showed that the west needed an injection of alternative industries, and that the development of fishing required a fall-back agency. If the board had had the power to relieve congestion by removing surplus population through assisted emigration or internal migration the economic problem of congestion in the west would have been solved at a faster rate.

---

21 Saostát Éireann, *Report of Coimmisiún na Gaeltachta*, p. 37. The commission reported on 'Irish Speaking and Partly Irish Speaking Districts now defined in this report are very largely co-terminous with the original Congested Districts'. **22** See B. Whelan, *Ireland and the Marshall Plan, 1947–1957* (2000), pp 265–86; F.S.L. Lyons, *Ireland since the Famine*, p. 564. **23** J.J. Lee, *Ireland, 1912–1985* (1989), pp 303–6. **24** CDB, Twenty-seventh annual report, 1919, pp 28–9.

APPENDIX A

List of congested districts

The counties considered congested under the 1891 Land Purchase (Ireland) Act were; Donegal, Sligo, Mayo, Galway, Leitrim, Roscommon, Kerry and the west riding of Cork, which was divided into two separate counties for electoral purposes.

1. North Inishowen	29. Knockadaff	59. Glenamaddy
2. Clonmany	30. Belmullet	60. Woodford
3. Desertegney	31. Rathhill	61. Boyle
4. Fanad	32. Bangor Erris	62. Tumna
5. Rosguill	33. Ballycroy	63. Castlerea
6. Gartan	34. Achill	64. Roosky
7. Brockagh	35. Newport	65. Moore
8. Dunfanaghy	37. Islandeady	66. Listowel
9. Cloghaneely	38. Clare Island	67. Causeway
10. Tory Island	39. Louisburgh	68. Brosna
11. Gweedore	40. Aghagower	69. Coom
12. The Rosses	41. Partry	70. Castlegregory
13. Aranmore	42. Foxford	71. Brandon
14. Glenties	43. Swinford	72. Dingle
15. Glencolumbkille	44. Kiltamagh	73. Killorglin
16. Teelin	45. Ballyhaunis	74. Caherciveen
17. Killybegs	49. Claremorris	75. Valencia
20. Ballyshannon	50. Carna	76. Waterville
21. Kiltyclogher	51. South Connemara	77. Sneem
22. Kiltubbrid	52. Rosmuck	78. Kenmare
23. Drumreilly	53. Spiddal	79. Castletownbeare
24. Mohill	54. Aran Islands	80. Bealanageary
25. Grange	55. Oughterard	81. Sheepshead
26. Ardmaree	56. Annaghdoon	82. Skull
27. Tobercurry	57. Levally	83. Baltimore
28. Ballaghadereen	58. Dunmore	84. Courtmacsherry

APPENDIX B

List of baseline headings of inquiry

1 Whether inland or maritime.
2 Average quantity of land cultivated on holdings at and under £4 valuation, under (a) oats, (b) potatoes (c) meadow, (d) green crops.
3 Extent of mountain or moor grazing, and rights possessed by tenant, whether in common or otherwise.
4 Extent and description of land, if any, which could be profitably reclaimed and added to existing adjoining holdings.
5 Particulars as to any suitable land in the district, which could be obtained, and to which families, could be migrated with a reasonable prospect of success.
6 Method of cultivation, manures, rotation of crops, etc., etc.,
7 General information with regard to stock, and suggestions as to improvement of breeds of – (a) cattle, (b) sheep, (c) horses and donkeys, (d) pigs, (e) poultry, etc., etc.,
8 Markets and fairs for cattle and produce of district; also statement as to where the people obtain food, and other supplies, and with regard to the disposal of butter, eggs, and poultry; top what extent they are sold in the first instance to local shop men, and dealers, and generally speaking how old the eggs are when sold to the first buyer, and about how old when they reach their ultimate destination in Great Britain.
9 Rail, steamer, sailing boat, postal and telegraph facilities.
10 Employment for labourers in district, whether temporary or constant, and rate of wage.
11 Migratory labour, average earnings per head, and where earned.
12 Weaving, spinning, knitting, and sewing, whether used locally or sold, and where.
13 Kelp-burning, and sale of seaweed.
14 Sale of turf, nature and extent of bogs.
15 Lobster fishing, number of men and boats employed.
16 Sea fishing. Facilities for sale of fish, and number of men and boats solely employed in fishing.

17 Number of boats and men employed in fishing, or carrying turf or seaweed. Classification of boats.

18 Fish, whether consumed at home or sold.

19 Extent of fish curing.

20 Piers and Harbours, existing and suggested, and how far those existing are adapted to wants of districts.

21 Extent of salmon and freshwater fisheries – number of men earning their livelihood there from.

22 Banks and Loan Funds.

23 Mineral and other resources.

24 Relative prevalence of cash or credit dealings, length of credit, interest charged, extent of barter, etc., etc.,

25 Estimated cash receipts and expenditure of a family in ordinary circumstances.

26 Estimated value of homegrown food consumed, and period during which it lasts.

27 Dietary of people—number of meals daily, and the kinds of food throughout the year.

28 Clothing—whether homemade or bought, etc., etc.

29 Dwellings—kinds of houses, home life and customs, etc., etc.

30 Character of the people for industry, etc., etc.,

31 Whether any organized effort has been made to develop the resources or improve the condition of the people. – If so, by what means.

32 Suggestions as to any possible method for improving the condition of the people in future. One to seven concerned the land, livestock and possible improvements of it.

APPENDIX C

Course outline for domestic economy classes

Cookery
    Making of tea, coffee and cocoa.
    Breadmaking by yeast, buttermilk, and water and cream of tartar.
    Different methods of cooking meats.
    Different methods of cooking vegetables.
    Plucking, cleaning, trussing and cooking of fowl.
    Making of sauces to be served with meats fish and fowl.
    Making of simple puddings and sauces to go with them.
    Different methods of cooking fish.
    Different methods of cooking eggs.
    Pastry making (for fruit and meat).
    Soups for meat and vegetables.
    Invalid cookery- Beef tea, chicken broth, barley water, gruel, arrowroot, lemonade, custard.
    Ways of using cooked foods.

Laundry
    Washing and drying of flannels.
    Washing starching, ironing, and folding of all white wash clothes, bed linen, and body linen.
    Removal of stains from table linen.
    Washing, starching, ironing, and folding of table linen.
    How to wash, starch, and iron a white shirt.
    How to wash, starch, and iron cuffs and collars.
    How to wash, stiffen, and iron lace and silks.

Domestic economy lessons
    How to dress a bed.
    How to set a breakfast, dinner and tea table.
    How to wait a table.
    How to clean up a sittingroom and bedroom.

Cleaning of silver, brass, and tin ware.
Cleaning of knifes and forks.
Washing of china and glass.
How to blacklead a grate or range.
How to clean and prevent irons rusting.
How to clean windows, boots etc.
The making of poultices, linseed meal, mustard and bread.
Personal and household cleanliness.

Source: CDB, Ninth annual report (Dublin 1900), Appendix xxxvii p. 104.

APPENDIX D

CDB receipts and expenditure, 1892–1923

Year ended 31 March	Receipts (including balance of previous year £ s. d.	Payments £ s. d.
1892 (from 5 August, 1891)	16,590 5 5	3,660 13 1
1893	58,365 1 4	50,265 14 1
1894	70,141 4 2	47,264 4 3
1895	92,133 4 11	74,887 13 4
1896	110,244 1 8	80,962 15 8
1897	106,917 16 7	86,333 5 9
1898	112,062 7 10	98,379 0 10
1899	111,152 16 4	106,165 12 10
1900	444,130 18 0	416,644 18 5
1901	185,435 1 11	168,864 5 1
1902	206,951 15 9	199,626 17 2
1903	232,668 2 9	212,150 5 4
1904	204,938 2 4	197,452 5 11
1905	238,846 5 10	229,064 9 11
1906	400,058 14 2	374,990 10 4
1907	350,499 5 0	341,580 10 5
1908	322,581 0 2	314,462 18 8
1909	269,619 2 9	242,007 2 8
1910	292,679 7 1	248,420 13 3
1911	409,350 0 4	282,160 7 6
1912	532,440 14 3	393,078 6 6
1913	594,442 18 1	419,556 8 3
1914	677,635 0 2	607,484 12 6
1915	721,263 12 4	673,563 2 8
1916	859,736 15 3	623,094 4 4
1917	965,492 15 3	930,655 18 9
1918	1,003,859 15 5	953,458 19 0
1919	891,564 17 5	846,762 13 7

1920	866,447	15	1	814,840	9	8
1921	910,913	17	10	878,057	4	11
1922	895,360	3	5	830,854	5	3
1923	748,622	18	0	673,993	11	11
Period from 1 April to 23 July, 1923	203,349	6	1	147,955	7	9

Source: CDB Return showing the receipts and expenditure of the CDB in each year from 1891 to 1923 (Dublin 1927), p. 3.

APPENDIX E

Letter of gratitude from Saorstát Éireann to CDB

Letter from Patrick Hogan, Minister for Agriculture, dated 7 May, read at CDB meeting, 8 May 1923.

Dear Sir,
On the 31 March last, as a result of the operation of the Transfer of Functions Order, the office of Commissioner of the Irish Land Commission ceased to exist and the government are now under the necessity of constituting a Land Commission. It has been decided that the new body shall administer all services in connection with land purchase, that is to say, that it shall include the land purchase functions of the former Land Commission and of the CDB it is proposed to give effect to this decision in a Land Commission Bill and a Ministries Bill, both of which will be introduced in the Dail in a month.

The passing of these bills will not in any way prejudice the positions of the existing staffs or of officials who have been superannuated. In coming to this decision, the Government had in mind not only the necessity for economy but also the fact that Ministries of Industry and Commerce and Fisheries have been constituted and that, in the normal course, the functions of the CDB in regard to industries and fisheries would be transferred to these Ministries.

The Government fully realize that in the absence of an Irish Parliament it was of the utmost importance that the administration of land purchase and particularly, its most urgent aspect, the relief of congestion, should be in the control of a representative Irish board, and they feel that they are speaking for the whole country in offering to the members of the CDB the Nation's thanks for their unselfish services and for the efficient and lasting work which they have accomplished.

I would be glad if you would bring this letter before your board, and I need only to add that I wish to be identified with the Government in this matter, and in particular to express my thanks to Sir Henry Doran and Mr Micks for their unfailing co-operation last year.

Yours Truly
P. Hogan

The Congested Districts of Ireland 1891

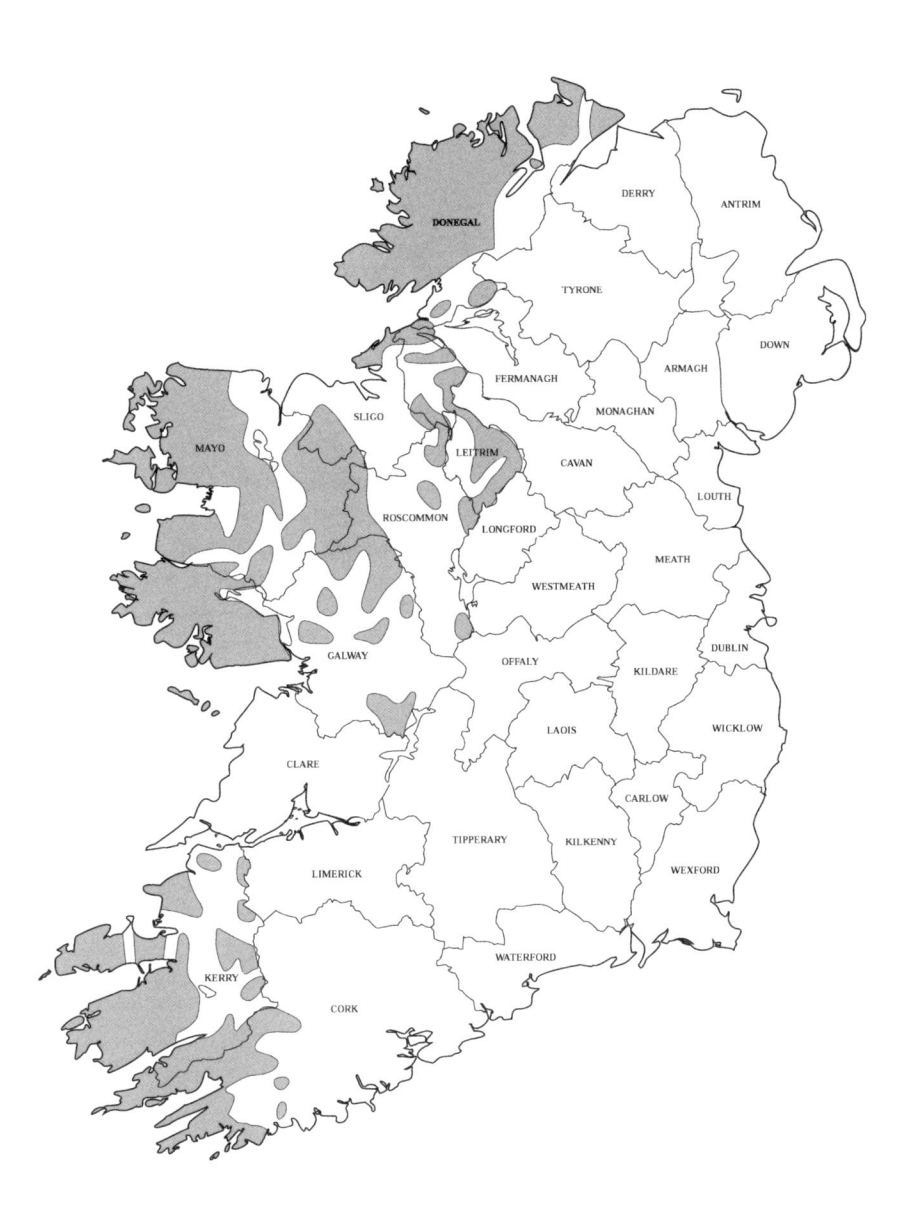

The Congested Districts of Ireland 1909

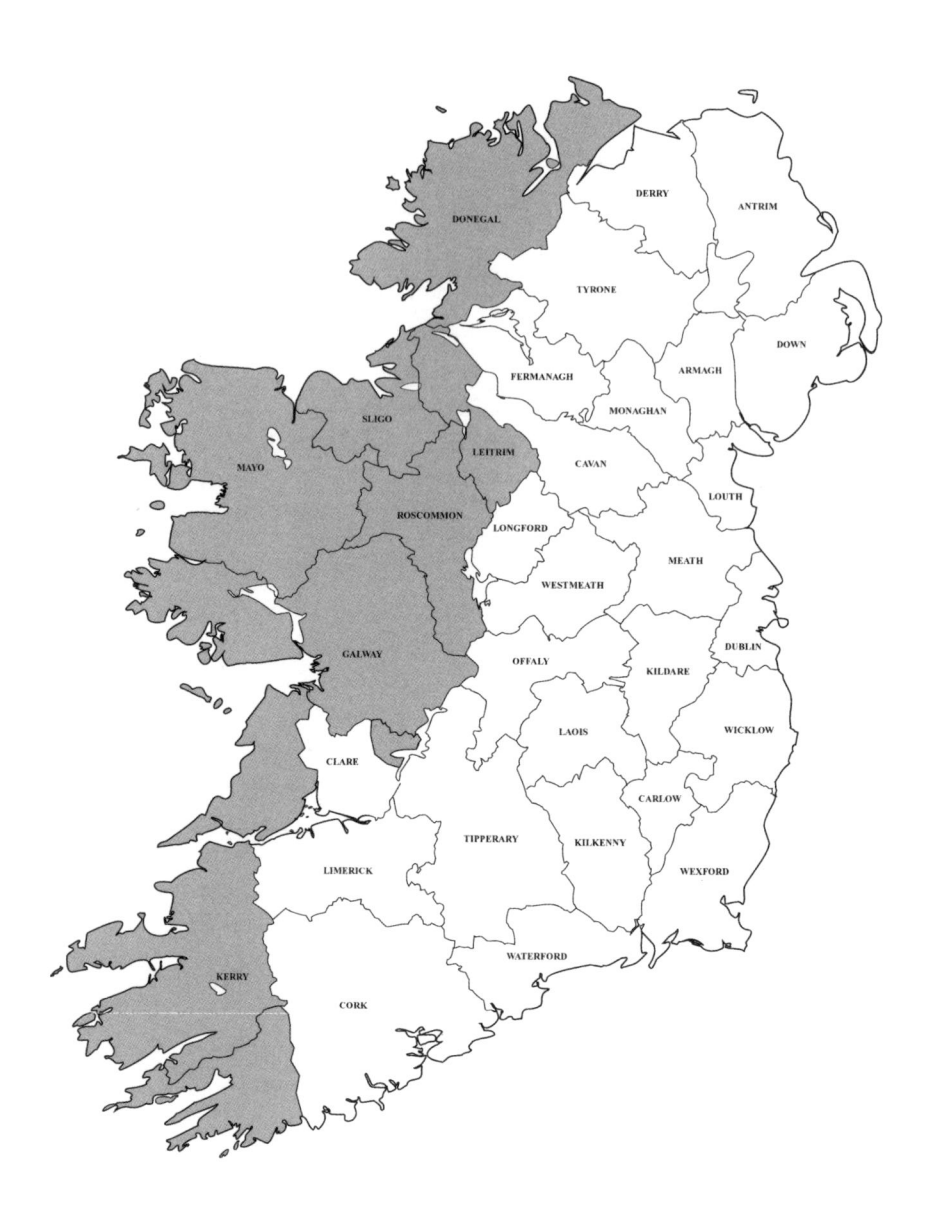

Bibliography

OFFICIAL PUBLICATIONS

Annual Reports
CDB, First to twenty-eight reports, 1893-1921: [C.6908], HC 1893-4, lxxi; [C.7266] HC 1893-4, lxxi; [C.7522] HC 1894-5, lxviii; [C.7791] HC 1895-6, lxxix; [C.8191] HC 1896-7, lxviii; [C.8622] HC 1897-8, lxxii; [C.9003] HC 1898-9, lxxvii; [C.9375] HC 1899-1900, lxxvii; [Cd.239] HC 1900-1901, lxviii; [Cd.681] HC 1900, lx; [Cd.1192] HC 1902, lxxxiii; [Cd.1622] HC 1903, lv; [Cd.2275] HC 1904, lxiii; [Cd. 2757] HC 1906, xcvii; [Cd.3161] HC 1906, xcvii; [Cd.3767] HC 1908, xxiii; [Cd.4340] HC 1908, xxiii; [Cd.4927], HC 1910, xvi; [Cd.5712], HC 1911, xiii; [Cd.6553], HC 1912-13, xvii; [Cd.7312], HC 1914, xvi; [Cd.7865], HC 1914-16, xxiv; [Cd.8076], HC 1914-16, xxiv; [Cd.8356] HC 1916, vi; [Cd.8853] HC 1918, xxvi; [Cd.9139], HC 1918, vii; [Cmd.759] HC 1920, xix; [Cmd.1409], HC 1921, xiv.
CDB, Receipts and expenditure of the Congested Districts Board in each year from 1891 to 1923 (Stationary Office, Dublin, Dublin, 1927).

Royal Commission on Congestion Ireland
RCCI, Appendices to the first to final report, 1906–8: [Cd.3267], HC 1906, xxxii; [Cd.3319], HC 1907, xxxv; [Cd.3414] HC 1907, xxxv; [Cd.3509] HC 1907, xxxvi; [Cd.3630], HC 1907, xxxvi; [Cd.3748], HC 1908, xxxix; [Cd.3785], HC 1908, xl; [Cd.3839], HC 1908, xli; [Cd.3845], HC 1908, xli; [Cd.4007], HC 1908, xlii; [Cd. 4097], HC 1908, xlii.

Agricultural Statistics
Agricultural statistics, Ireland [C.3332], HC 1882, lxxiv; [C.6099], HC 1890, lxxix; [C.6518], HC 1890–91, xci; [C.6777], HC 1892, lxxxxviii; [C.9389], HC 1899, cvi; [Cd.143], HC 1900, ci; [Cd. 5382], HC 1902, cviii; [Cmd.1316], HC 1920–21, xli.

Miscellaneous BPP
Local Government Board for Ireland Report regarding Distress, 25 April 1883, HC 1883, lix.
Royal Commission of Inquiry into the Working of Landlord and Tenant (Ireland) Acts 1881: *Reports, Minutes of evidence, Apps.*, [C.2779] [C.2779–1][C.2779–111] (Bessborough Commission)

Royal Commission on Land Law (Ireland) Act, 1881, and Purchase of Land (Ireland) Act 1885: *Reports, Minutes of Evidence, Apps.* 1887 [C. 4969] [C.4969–1], xxvi, and *Separate report* by Mr T. Knipe 1887 [C.5015] xxvi.1241.

Mr Tuke's Report on Relief of Distress in West of Ireland, 1886 (31 sess. 2), lvii.

Seventeenth report on the poor law in Ireland [C.5769] HC 1889, xxxvi, App D. p 116.

Report on the failure of the potato crop and condition of poorer classes in west of Ireland, 1890–1891 (131) lxii.

Report from Poor Relief Inquiries Commissioners, 1887 [C.5043], HC 1887, xxxviii.

Hansard's Parliamentary Debates, vols. 354–5 (London, 1891).

Irish Government Publications

Saorstát Éireann, *Drew Commission on Agriculture* (Baile Átha Cliath, 1923).
Saorstát Éireann, *Report of Coimisiún na Gaeltachta* (Baile Átha Cliath, 1925).
DÉ, Historical debates, vol. 23, 02 May 1928.

British Library
Add. MSS 49817 ff. 169–255 Arthur Balfour papers.

Archives of the Irish Sisters of Charity, Sandymount, Dublin.

SOURCES

Aalen, F. H.A., 'The rehousing of rural labourers in Ireland under the labourers (Ireland) Acts 1893–1919', *JHG* 12 (1986), 287–306.

Akenson, D.H., *The Irish educational experiment* (London, 1970).

—, 'Pre-university education, 1890–1921', in W.E. Vaughan, and T.W. Moody (eds), *A new history of Ireland: Ireland under the Union, 1870–1921,* vol. vi (Oxford, 1996), 532–3.

Alderson, B., 'Arthur James Balfour: the man and his work' (London, 1903).

Anderson, R.A., *With Plunkett in Ireland: the co-operative organiser's story* (Dublin, reprinted 1983).

Anon. *Thomas Plunkett Cairnes: JP, a memento* (1984).

Arensberg, C. and S.T. Kimball, *Family and community in Ireland* (Cambridge, 1968).

Arensberg, C., *The Irish countryman: an anthropological study* (New York, 1937).

Balfour, A.J., *Aspects of Home Rule* (London, 1912).

—, *Nationality and Home Rule* (London, 1913).

Barrington, T., 'A review of Irish agricultural prices', *JSSISI* 15 (1927), 249–80.

Bell, J., 'Hiring fairs in Ulster', *UF* 25 (1979), 67–77.

— and M. Watson, *Irish farming, 1750–1900* (Edinburgh, 1986).

Bennett, A., *John Bull and his other island* (London, 1889).

Bew, P., *C.S. Parnell* (Dublin, 1980).

—, *Land and the national question in Ireland, 1858–82* (Dublin, 1979).

Birdwell-Pheasant, D., 'Irish households in the twentieth century: culture, class, and historical contingency', *JFH* 18 (1993), 19–38.

Blake, J. A., *The sea fisheries of Ireland* (Waterford, 1868).

BIBLIOGRAPHY

Bloomfield, J.C., *The fisheries of Ireland, international fisheries exhibition* (London, 1883).
Bolger, P., 'The CDB and the co-operatives', in W. Nolan, L. Ronayne, and M. Dunleavy (eds), *Donegal history and society* (Dublin, 1995), 649–75.
—, *The Irish co-operative movement its history and development* (Dublin, 1977).
—, 'Horace Plunkett – the man', in C. Keating (ed.), *Plunkett and co-operatives* (Cork, 1983), 33–8.
Bourke, J., 'Women and poultry in Ireland', *IHS,* 25 (1987), 293–310.
—, *Husbandry to housewifery: women, economic change and housework in Ireland, 1890–1891* (Oxford, 1993).
Boyce, G.D., *Ireland, 1823–1923: from ascendancy to democracy* (Oxford, 1992).
—, *Nationalism in Ireland* (London, 1982).
Brailsford, H.N., *Some Irish problems* (Dublin, 1903).
Breen, R., 'Farm servanthood in Ireland, 1900–40', *EHR* 36 (1983), 87–102.
Browne, C.R., 'The ethnography of Inisboffin and Inishshark', *PRIA* 3 (1893–6), 317–70.
Bull, P., 'The significance of the nationalist response to the Irish Land Act of 1903', *IHS* 27 (1993), 283–305.
—, *Land, politics and nationalism* (Dublin, 1996).
Burke, H. *The people and the poor law in nineteenth century Ireland* (Dublin, 1987).
Burke, J.F., *Outlines of the industrial history of Ireland* (Dublin,1933).
Butler, K., *The Story of Benada* (Sligo, n.d.).
Callan, T. and B. Nolan, *Poverty in the 1990s* (Dublin, 1996).
Cambray, P., *Irish affairs and the Home Rule question* (London, 1911).
Cameron, Ewen, A., 'The Highland issue, 1860 to the 1920s', *SHR* 72 (1993), 60–79.
Campbell, Niamh, 'The CDB and the development of fishing in South-west Donegal, 1890–1923' (unpublished MPhil UCG, 1997).
Clancy, J.J., *A year of 'Unionist' coercion* (London, 1888).
Clark, Samuel, 'The importance of agrarian classes: agrarian class structure and collective action in nineteenth-century Ireland', in P.J. Drudy (ed.), *Ireland: land, politics and people (*Cambridge, 1982), 11–37.
—, *Social origins of the Irish land war* (Princeton, 1979).
Clarkson, L.A., 'The modernisation of the Irish diet', in J. Davis (ed.), *Rural change in Ireland* (Belfast, 1999), 32–45.
— and M.E., Crawford, *Feast and famine, a history of food and nutrition in Ireland, 1500–1920* (Oxford, 2001).
Clear, C., *Nuns in nineteenth century Ireland* (Washington, 1987).
—, *Women of the house: women's household work in Ireland, 1922–1961* (Dublin, 2000).
Clerical and lay members of the Church of Ireland in the diocese of Meath, *Thomas Plunkett Cairnes, JP a memento* (1894).
Cohen, M., *Linen, family and community in Tullylish, County Down, 1690–1914* (Dublin, 1997).
Comerford, R.V., 'Gladstone's first Irish enterprise1864–1870', in W.E. Vaughan, T.W. Moody (eds), *A new history of Ireland: Ireland under the Union, 1801–1870,* vol. v (Oxford, 1989), 431–49.
Connell, K.H., *Irish peasant society: four historical essays* (Oxford, 1968).
Corkery, D., *The hidden Ireland: a study of Gaelic Munster in the eighteenth cenury* (Dublin, 1925).

Cousens, S.H., 'Emigration and demographic change in Ireland 1851–1861', *EHR* 22 (1961), 275–88.
Coyne, W.P. (ed.), *Industrial and agricultural* (Dublin, 1902)
Crawford, M., 'Diet and the labouring classes in the nineteenth century', *Saothar* 15 (1990), 87–95.
—, 'Indian meal and Pellagra in nineteenth-century Ireland', in J. Goldstrom and L.A. Clarkson (eds), *Irish population, economy and society* (Oxford, 1981), 113–33.
Crawford, W.H., *Domestic industry in Ireland: the experience of the linen industry* (Dublin, 1972).
Cronin, M., *A history of Ireland* (New York, 2001).
Crossman, V. *Local government in nineteenth century Ireland* (1994).
Crotty, R.D., *Irish agricultural production: its volume and structure* (Cork UP, 1966).
Cuddy, M. and C. Curtin, 'Commercialisation in west of Ireland agriculture in the 1890s', *EHR* 14 (1983), 173–84.
Cullen, L.M., 'Population growth and diet' (1981).
—, *An economic history of Ireland since 1660* (London, 1972).
Cullen, M., 'Breadwinners and providers: women in the household economy of labouring families 1835–6' (1990). In *Women surviving*, see Luddy, pp 85–116.
Curtis, L.P. Jr., *Coercion and conciliation: a study in Conservative Unionism* (Princeton, 1963).
Daily Express, 'Mr Balfour's tours in Connemara and Donegal' (n.d.)
Daly, M.E., 'Women in the Irish workforce from pre-industrial to modern times', *Saothar* 7 (1981), 74–82.
Daly, Mary E., *Social and economic history of Ireland* (Dublin, 1981).
Davis, Revd C., *Deep Sea Fisheries of Ireland* (Dublin, 1886).
Delaney, E., 'Gender and 20th-century Irish migration, 1921–1971', in P. Sharpe (ed.), *Women, gender and labour migration* (London, 2001), 209–23.
Devine, T.M., *The Scottish nation, 1700–2000* (London, 1999).
Dillon, T.,'Iodine and Potash from Irish Seaweed', *Studies* 19 (1930), 267–78.
Diner, H.R., *Erin's daughters in America: Irish immigrant women in the nineteenth century* (Baltimore, 1983).
Donnelly, J.S., Jr. *The land and the people of nineteenth century Cork* (London, 1975).
Doran, Sir Henry, 'Self help among the western congests: a review of thirty years of official labour', in W.G. Fitzgerald (ed.), *Voice of Ireland* (Dublin, 1924), 330–9.
Drudy, P.J. (ed.), *Ireland: land, politics and people* (Cambridge, 1982).
Dugdale, B.E.C., *Arthur James Balfour* (London, 1936).
Dunleavy, M., *Dress in Ireland* (London, 1989).
Emy, H.V., 'The impact of financial policy on English party politics before 1914' (1972).
Evans, E.E., *Irish heritage: the landscape the people and their work* (Dundalk, 1942).
Fás and Turasóireacht Iorrais Teo, *Report of the Erris survey August 1990–May 1994, part 2* (Belmullet, 1994), 37–46.
Finlay, T.A.,'Our Department of Technical Instruction', *NIR* 13 (1900), 233–8.
Fitzgerald, S., *Mackerel and the making of Baltimore, Co.Cork, 1879–1913* (Dublin, 1999).
Fitzpatrick, David, 'The modernisation of the Irish female in rural Ireland 1600–1900', in P. O' Flanagan, P. Ferguson, and K. Whelan (eds), *Modernisation and change* (Cork, 1987), 162–80.

—, 'Irish farming families before the first world war', *CSSH* 25 (1978), 339–74.
—, 'The disappearance of the Irish agricultural labourer, 1841–1914', *IESH* 7 (1980), 66–92.
—, 'Irish emigration in the later nineteenth century', *IHS* 22 (1980), 126–43.
— 'Women, gender and the writing of Irish History', *IHS* 27 (1991), pp 267–73.
Flanagan, K., 'The Chief Secretary's Office, 1853–1914; a bureaucratic enigma', *IHS* 24 (1984), 197–225.
Foss, P., and C. O'Connell, 'Bogland: study and utilization', in J.W. Foster (ed.), *Nature in Ireland* (Dublin, 1997), 84–199.
Fraser, M., *John Bull's other homes: state housing and British policy in Ireland, 1883–1922* (Liverpool, 1995).
Fry, E., *James Hack Duke Tuke, a memoir* (1899).
Gailey, A., 'Unionist rhetoric and Irish local government, 1895–9' (1984).
Gailey, A., *Ireland and the death of kindness: the experience of Constructive Unionism, 1890–1905* (Cork, 1987).
Garvin, T., 'Priests and patriots: Irish separatism and fear of the modern 1890–1914', *IHS* 25 (1986), 67–81.
Geary, L. M., *The plan of campaign, 1886–91* (Cork, 1986).
—, *Medicine and charity in Ireland 1718–1851* (Dublin, 2004).
Gibbon, P., and M.D. Higgins, 'Patronage, tradition and modernisation: the case of the Irish gombeenman', *ESR* 6 (1974), 27–44.
Gildea, Revd D., *Mother Mary Arsenius of Foxford* (Dublin, 1936).
Gmelch, G. and S.B., 'The emergence of an ethnic group: the Irish Tinkers' (1976).
Green, W.S., 'The sea fisheries of Ireland', in W.P. Coyne (ed.), *Ireland industrial and agricultural* (Dublin, 1902), 369–87.
Gribbon, H.D., 'Economic and social history, 1850–1921', in W.E. Vaughan and T.M. Moody (eds), *A new history of Ireland: Ireland under the Union*, vol. vi (Oxford, 1996), 260–356.
Grimshaw, T.W., *Facts and figures about Ireland. Part two* (Dublin, 1893).
—, 'Irish progress during the past ten years, 1881–1890', *JSSISI* 9 (1891), 571–601.
Guinnane, T., *The vanishing Irish: households, migration, and the rural economy in Ireland, 1850–1914* (Princeton, 1997).
Hall, F.G., *The Bank of Ireland, 1783–1946* (Dublin, 1949)
Hanley, J.E., *The Irish in modern Scotland, 1798–1845* (Cork, 1947).
Hannon, P.J., 'Agricultural banks in Ireland', *NIR* 9 (1898), 1–12.
Hareven, T.K., and M. Vinovskis (eds), *Family and population in nineteenth century America* (Princeton, 1978).
Hargreaves, C., 'Economic and social conditions on Arranmore in the nineteenth century', *DA* 5 (1962), 99–114.
Harvey, B. 'Changing fortunes of the Aran Islands in the 1890s', *IHS* 17 (1991), 231–42.
Hearn, M., 'Life for domestic servants in Dublin' (1990).
Helleiner, J., 'Gypsies, Celts and Tinkers: colonial antecedents of anti-traveller racism in Ireland' (1976).
Higgins, M.D., and Gibbons, J.P., 'Shopkeeper-graziers and land agitation in Ireland, 1895–1900', in P.J. Drudy (ed.), *Ireland: land, politics and people* vol. ii (Cambridge, 1982), 93–119.
Hobsbawm, E.J., *Primitive rebels: studies in archaic forms of social movement in the 19th and 20th centuries* (Manchester, 1978).

Hoctor, D., *The department's story: a history of the Department of Agriculture* (Dublin, 1971).
Holdsworth, E.W.H., *The sea-fisheries of Great Britian and Ireland: an account of the practical working of the various fisheries around the British islands* (London, 1883).
Ireland, J., de Courcy, *Ireland's sea fisheries: a history* (Dublin, 1981).
—, *Ireland and the Irish in maritime history* (Dublin, 1986).
Jackson, J.A., *Irish cottages* (Wicklow, 1985).
Johnson, Professor, 'Raw Materials for Irish Animal Husbandry', *JSSISI* 18 (1950), 392–402.
Jones, D. S., *Graziers, land reform and political conflict in Ireland* (Washington, 1995).
Jones, L., 'Food and meals in a congested district: County Donegal in 1891', in A. Fenton, and T. Owen (eds), *Food in perspective* (Edinburgh, 1981), 157–64.
Kane, Rev. P., 'Aran of the fishermen', *NIR* 9 (1898), 235–46.
Kelly, R.J., 'The congested districts', *JSSISI* 9 (1891), 495–511.
Kennedy, F., *From cottage to crèche, family change in Ireland* (Dublin, 2001).
Kennedy, L., and Johnson, D.S., 'The union of Ireland and Britain, 1801–1921', in D.G. Boyce and A. O Day (eds), *Making of modern Irish history* (London, 1996), 34–71.
Kennedy, L., 'Retail markets in rural Ireland at the end of the nineteenth century', *IESH* 10 (1978), 46–63.
—, 'Traders in the Irish rural economy 1880–1914', *EHR* 32 (1979), 201–10.
Kennedy, R.E. Jr., *The Irish: emigration, marriage, and fertility* (Berkeley, CA, 1973).
Kennedy, T., 'Fifty years of Irish agriculture', *JSSISI* 10 (1899), 398–404.
Kerr, B., 'Irish seasonal migration to Great Britain 1800–1830', *IHS* 3 (1943), 365–80.
Kineally, C., 'Administration of poor law in Mayo, 1838–1898', *JWHS* (1986).
Lane-Poole, S., *North-west and by north: Irish hills and English dales* (Dublin, 1902).
Langan, T., 'The Congested Districts Board', *NMHASJ* 11 (1989/90), 26–33.
Lee, J.J., 'The construction costs of Irish railways', *BH* 9 (1967), 95–109.
—, 'The provision of capital for early Irish railways', *IHS* 16 (1968), 33–63.
—, *Ireland, 1912–1985* (1989)
—, *The modernisation of Irish society, 1848–1918* (Dublin, 1973).
Liegeois, J.P., *Gypsies and Travellers: socio-cultural data, socio-political data* (Strasbourg, 1987).
Luddy, M., and C., Murphy (eds), *Women surviving: studies in Irish women's history in the nineteenth and twentieth centuries* (Dublin, 1990).
Luddy. M., 'Women and work in nineteenth and early twentieth-century Ireland' (2000).
Ludlow, C. G., 'A history of salt in Ireland' (unpublished PhD thesis QUB, 1993).
Lyons, F.S.L., *John Dillon: a biography* (1968).
—, *Ireland since the famine* (London, 1971).
—, *Culture and anarchy in Ireland, 1890–1939* (Oxford, 1979).
Lysaght, Patricia, 'When I makes tea, I makes tea', *UF* 33 (1987), 44–71.
M'Carthy, M.J.F., *Mr Balfour's rule in Ireland* (Dublin, 1891).
Mac Congail, M., *The Blaskets: a Kerry island library* (Dublin, 1987).
MacGowan, M., *The hard road to Klondike* (London, 1964).
MacKay, D., 'The Congested Districts Boards of Ireland and Scotland', *NS* 16 (1996), 35–55.
MacLaughlin, J., *Ireland: the emigrant nursery and the world economy* (Cork, 1994).
—, *Travellers and Ireland: Whose country? Whose history?* (Cork, 1995).

MacSuibhne, B., 'Saggart aroon and gombeen-priest: Canon James McFadden, 1842–1917' (1998).
Maghtochair, *Inishowen, its history, traditions and antiquities* (Donegal, 1935).
Mansergh, N., *The unresolved question: the Anglo-Irish settlement and its undoing, 1912–1972* (Yale UP, 1991).
Mansion House Relief Committee, *The Irish crisis of 1879–1880* (Dublin, 1880).
Mayall, D., *Gypsy – Travellers in nineteenth century society* (1988).
McCann, J., *Irish taxation and Irish transit, two speeches delivered in the House of Commons on the overtaxation of Ireland* (Dublin, 1901).
McCann, M. et al., *Irish Travellers: culture and ethnicity* (1996)
McCleery, A.M., 'The role of the Highland Development Agency: with particular reference to the work of the CDB, 1897–1912' (unpublished PhD, Glasgow, 1984).
Mac Cafraidh, B., 'Bord na gCeanntar gCung', *DA* 3 (1954–1955), 31–41.
McDowell, R.B. (ed.), *Social life in Ireland* (Cork, 1957).
—, *The Irish administration 1801–1914* (London, 1964).
McFeely, M.D., *Lady inspectors: the campaign for a better workplace, 1893–1921* (New York, 1988).
McGill, P.J., 'The Irish woollen industry from earliest times to Donegal homespuns', *JDHS* 1 (1949), 149–80.
Micks, W. L., *An account of the constitution, administration and dissolution of the Congested Districts Board for Ireland from 1891 to 1923* (Dublin, 1925).
Miller, K.A., *Emigrants and exiles: Ireland and the Irish exodus to North America* (New York, 1985).
Millward, R., and Sheard, S., 'The urban fiscal problem, 1870–1914: government expenditure and finance in England and Wales', *EHR* 48 (1995), 501–35.
Mitchell, A., 'An Irish Putumayo: Roger Casement's humanitarian relief campaign among the Connemara Islanders', *IESH* (2004), 67–80.
Mitchell, Geraldine, *Deeds not words: the life and works of Muriel Gahan* (Dublin, 1997).
Modell, J., 'Patterns of consumption, acculturation, and family income strategies in late nineteenth-century America', in T.K. Hareven and M. Vinovskis (eds), *Family and population in nineteenth-century America* (Princeton, 1978).
Moore, J.O., *The possibilities of Irish agriculture and allied industry* (1912).
Moran, G.P., 'Famine and the land war relief and distress in Mayo, 1879–81', *JWHS* (1986), 111–27
—, 'State aided emigration from Ireland to Canada in the 1880s', *CJIS* 20 (1994), 1–19.
—, *Sending out Ireland's poor: assisted emigration to North America in the nineteenth century* (Dublin, 2004).
Murphy, M., 'The Congested Districts Board', *SHS* (1997), 43–57.
Murray, A.E., *A history of the financial relations between England and Ireland from the period of the restoration* (London, 1903).
Ní Eineacháin, S., 'The Congested Districts Board in Erris, Co. Mayo, part 1', *JWHS* 20 (2000), 90–117.
Ní Ghiobúin, M.C., *Dugort, Achill Island, 1831–61: a study of the rise and fall of a missionary community* (Dublin, 2001).
Nolan, R., *Within the Mullet* (Galway, 1998).

Ó Ciosáin, N., 'Boccoughs and God's poor: deserving and undeserving poor in Irish popular culture' in T. Foley, and S. Ryder (eds), *Ideology and Ireland in the nineteenth century* (Dublin, 1998).

Ó Crualaíoch, G., 'The merry wake', in J.S. Donnelly and K.A. Miller (eds) *Irish popular culture, 1650–1850* (Dublin, 1990), 173–200

Ó Cúiv, B., 'Irish language and literature, 1845–1921', in W.E. Vaughan, and T.M. Moody (eds), *New history of Ireland: Ireland under the Union, 1870–1921*, vol. vi (Oxford), 385–97.

Ó Dómhnall, N., *Na Glúinte Róssanacha* (Dublin, 1952).

Ó Gráda, Cormac, 'Seasonal migration and post-famine adjustment', *SH* 13 (1973), pp 49–76.

—, *Ireland: a new economic history, 1780–1939* (Oxford, 1994).

—, *Ireland before and after the famine: explorations in economic history, 1800–1925* (Manchester, 1988).

Ó Sé, M., 'Old Irish cheeses and other milk products', *JCHAS* 53 (1978), 83–6.

O Shaughnessy, R., 'Local taxation in Ireland', in J.W. Probyn (ed.), *Local Government in the United Kingdom* (London, 1882), 319–83.

O'Callaghan, M., *British high politics and nationalist Ireland* (Cork, 1994).

O'Connor, J., *The workhouses of Ireland: the fate of Ireland's poor* (Dublin, 1995)

O'Day, A., *Irish Home Rule, 1867–1921* (Manchester, 1998).

O'Dowd, A., *Spalpeens and tattie hokers: Irish migratory agricultural worker* (Dublin, 1990).

—, *Meitheal, a study of co-operative labour in rural Ireland* (Dublin, 1981).

O'Dowd, A., 'Seasonal migration to the Lagan and Scotland', in W. Nolan, L. Ronayne, and M. Dunleavy (eds), *Donegal: history and society* (Dublin, 1995), 625–47.

O'Halpin, E., *The decline of the Union: British government in Ireland, 1892–1920.* (Syracuse, 1987).

O'Moore, J., 'The possibilities of Irish agriculture and allied industry' (unpublished MA, QUB, 1912).

O'Neill, P., 'A social and cultural study of crofter life on the west Donegal seaboard' (unpublished MA, QUB, 1940).

O'Neill, T.P., 'Rural life', in R.B. McDowell (ed.), *Social life in Ireland* (Cork, 1957), 30–49.

O'Neill, P., *A social and cultural study of crofter life on the West Donegal seaboard* (1940).

Plunkett, H., 'The United Irishwomen', in P. Bolger (ed.), *And see her beauty shining there* (Dublin, 1986).

—, *Ireland in the new century* (Dublin, 1905).

Pollock, V., 'The seafishing industry in Co. Down, 1860–1939' (unpublished PhD, UU, Coleraine, 1988).

—, 'The introduction of engine power in the Co. Down sea fisheries', *UF* 37, 1991, p. 1.

Pomfret, J.E., *The struggle for land in Ireland, 1800–1923* (Princeton, 1930).

Rhodes, R., *Women and the family in post-famine Ireland: status and opportunity in a patriarchal society* (New York, 1992).

Rolleston, T.W., 'The Derry shirt-making industry Ireland', in W.P. Coyne (ed.), *Industrial and agricultural* (Dublin, 1902), 417–19.

Rowntree, S.B., *Poverty: a study of town life* (London, 1902).
Russell, G.W. (A.E.), 'Elections not near. Poultry societies, notice!', *IH* 14 October 1905 in H. Summerfield (ed.), *Selections from the contributions to the Irish Homestead* (Dublin, 1978), p. 64.
—, 'How not to start rural industry', *IH* 4 September 1909 in H. Summerfield (ed.), *Selections from the contributions to the Irish Homestead* (Dublin, 1978), p. 203.
Shannon, C. B., 'The Ulster liberal unionists and local government reform, 1885-98', *IHS* 13 (1973), 407-23.
Shannon, C.B., *Arthur J. Balfour and Ireland, 1874-1922* (Washington, 1988).
Sharpe, P. (ed.), *Women, gender and labour migration* (London, 2001).
Sheridan, F.S., 'The "congested districts" of Ireland and the work of the Congested Districts Board'. Reprinted from the *Monthly Bulletin of Economic and Social Intelligence* (Rome, 1915).
Smith, D.M., ' "I thought I was landed": the Congested Districts Board and the women of western Ireland', *EI* 31 (1996), 209-27.
Smith, R.E.F., and D. Christian, *Bread and salt* (Cambridge, 1984).
Solow, B.L., 'A new look at the Irish land question', *ESR* 12 (1981), 301-14.
—, *The Irish land question and the Irish economy, 1870-1903* (Harvard, 1971).
Staehle, Dr H., 'Statistical notes on the economic history of Irish agriculture, 1847-1913', *JSSISI* 18 (1951), 444-71.
Stagles, J. and R., *The Blasket Islands, next parish America* (Dublin, 1984).
Summerfield, H. (ed), *Selections from the contributions to the Irish Homestead* (Dublin, 1978).
Symes, D.G., 'Farm household and farm performance: a study of twentieth century changes in Ballyferriter, Southwest Ireland', *Ethnology* 11 (1972), 25-38.
Taylor, L.J., 'The priest and the agent: social drama and class consciousness in the west of Ireland', *CSSH* 27 (1985) 696-12.
Thomson, G., *Island Home: the Blasket heritage* (Dingle, 1998).
Townsend, P., *Poverty in the United Kingdom: a summary of household resources and standards of living* (London, 1979).
Trench, George F., *Are the landlords worth preserving or forty years management of an Irish estate?* (Dublin, 1881).
Trustees for Bettering the Condition of the Poor of Ireland, *A summary of the state of the Irish sea coast fisheries* (Dublin, 1872).
Tuke, J.H., *Irish distress and its remedies* (1880).
Turner, M., 'Output and productivity in Irish agriculture from the famine to the Great War', *IESH* 27 (1990), 123-36.
Turner, M.E., *After the famine: Irish agriculture, 1850-1914* (Oxford, 1996).
Vaughan, W.E. and T.W. Moody (eds), *A new history of Ireland: Ireland under the Union I*, vol. v (Oxford, 1995).
—, 'Potatoes and agricultural output', *IESH*, 27 (1990), 79-92.
— and Moody T.W. (eds), *A new history of Ireland: Ireland under the Union II*, vol. vi (Oxford, 1996).
Vaughan, W.E., *Landlords and tenants in mid-Victorian Ireland* (Oxford, 1994).
Went, Arthur E.J., 'Foreign fishing fleets along the Irish coasts', *JCHAS* 54 (1949), 17-24.

West, Trevor, 'The development of Horace Plunkett's thought', in C. Keating (ed.), *Plunkett and co-operatives* (Cork, 1983), 38–45.
Whelan, B. (ed.), *Women and paid work in Ireland, 1500–1930* (Dublin, 2000).
Whelan, B., *Ireland and the Marshall Plan, 1947–1957* (Dublin, 2000).

Baseline reports of the Congested Disticts Board of Ireland
(Dublin, 1892–1898), TCD

There are two copies of the baseline reports in the Early Printed Books Department, Trinity College, Dublin. William L. Micks, secretary of the board, presented the first copy to the library in 1927. This copy contains all eighty-four reports in one bound volume along with a letter, which was a copy of the instructions given to each baseline inspector. Muriel Gahan, a descendant of baseline inspector Henry Gahan, presented the second copy in 1992. Throughout the book the reports are referred to as individual documents and are numbered accordingly.

Index

Achill Island, 42-3, 51-2, 64, 168
Act of Union, 109
alcohol consumption, 163–5, 165n
Aran Islands, 90-1, 93-7, 99-100; Kilronan boatyard on Inishmore, 103; 107-8
Ardara, 56
Arranmore, 48, 51
Arthur J. Balfour, 20; 'Bloody Balfour', 21; foundation of board, 22, 27, 29; liaising with Tuke, 23; trip to west, 24–5; 168, 170–1
assisted emigration, 18, 138

Balfour, Gerard, 143, 170–1
Ballaghadereen, 50, 56-7
Ballyferriter, 43
Ballyshannon, 62, 125
Baltimore, 69, 79, 80, 86, 92, 108
Baseline reports, 35–7, 44, baseline inspectors, 35–7, 129
Beach, Sir Michael Hicks, 19–20
beekeeping, 130–1
Benada, 56-7
Blacksod curing station, 96-8
Blasket Islands, 87, 135, 136n
board of guardians, 33
Board of Works, 11, 151, 173
boat-building, 69, 103
Brockagh, 61
Burdett-Coutts, Lady, 13, 79–80, 92

Carna, 69, 83, 122, 128
cattle rearing, 115–16, 122; herding and grazing, 124
Claddagh, Co. Galway, 92, 106, 106n, 164

Clare areas added in 1909, 155
Clare Island, Clew Bay, Co. Mayo, 42, 143
class awareness, 44
Cloghaneely, 29, 118
Clonmany, 50, 61, 121-3,
Coercion act, 20
compulsory land purchase, 156–7
congested districts, definition, 11; funding, 32–3; original members, 31
cooperages, 69–70, 102
co-operative creameries, 166
county cess, 12
cultural nationalism, 171-2
Currach, 80, 90

DATI, and domestic economy classes, 67; and cured fish markets, 96; loans for motorboats, 104; and agriculture, 143–6, 148–9, 152–6; relations with CDB, 170–5
diet, 37–42; egg consumption, 49; tea consumption, 41–2; fish consumption, 75
Dillon estate, 144–5, 155
Dillon, James, 174
Dillon, John, 20; Plan of Campaign, 24, 149, 170
Dingle, 43, 108
disestablishment of the Church of Ireland, 3
domestic economy classes, 66–7
Donegal carpets, 65
Doran, Henry, 35, 45, 140, 143, 146; and Parish committee schemes, 157; agricultural loan system, 143, 182
Downings Bay, 97, 98n, 102, 105

Drew Commission, 172–3
Dunfanaghy, 42

economic holding, 18
education, 16–17
emigration, 112, 117; female, 166n; 168, 171; remittances, 169, 169n

Fanad, 50, 85, 123-4, 126, 130
Ffrench estate, Co. Galway, 139–40
fishing industry, numbers engaged, 76; Fishery revivals, 77; 1869 fisheries act, 77, 81; condition of fisheries in maritime congests, 88; financing fisheries, 86; repossession of boats, 89, 100–1; steamer services, 87–8; netmending, 90; lighthouses, 90; herring fishery, 91; cured fish, 91; mackerel, 92–94; Baltimore fishery, 79–80, 108; slump in mackerel fishery, 104–5; Norwegian competition, 97; problems associated with fishing industries, 98; co-operative fishing society, 99; Connemara fishermen, 99; lobster fishing, 100; powerboats, 106; impact of World War One on fisheries, 106–7; CDB retreat from fisheries, 102
Fotrell, George, CDB solicitor, 137, 140, 146
Foxford, 45-9, 54, 57
Furniture-making, 45

Gaeltacht Commission, 108, 165–8; Gaeltacht areas, 168
Gladstone, William E., 19, 32
Glenties, 43n, 51, 82, 82n
gombeenmen, 24, 52, 112, 140, 141, 141n, 160, 161, 161n, 124
Griffith's Valuation, 14, 115n

hiring out, 15
Horace Plunkett, 17, 31
horses, 123
housing, 43, 119; poor conditions, 124–5; improvements, 129

IAOS, and poultry industry, 53; and agriculture, 145, 149, 150n, 167, 170
IIDA, 59–60, 64, 71

income and expenditure budgets, 35–40, 45
indirect taxation, 160
indoor relief, 21
industrial schools, 57, 103
industries, 47; CDB funding of, 47; furniture making, 45
industries, in baseline reports, funding for, 47
Irish Loan Reproductive Fund, 87

Killybegs, 69, 103
Kiltimagh, 45, 125, 133
Kiltyclogher, 49, 63, 69n, 122, 123n
Knockadaff, 29, 39, 116n knitwear factory, 63

lace making and crochet classes, 64–8
land acts, 12, 17, 19; Bessborough and Cowper Commissions, 18, 117; 1881 land act, 119; Wyndham land act, 135, 148; Ashbourne land act, 140; limitations of land acts, 145–6, 150–1
Land Commision, 137–40
Land League, 24; 1923 land act, 173; United Irish League, 149, 153
land tenure; subdivision and consolidation, 109–110; eleven-month tenure, 111; ranchers 110–11; graziers/ grazing rights, 110–11, 146; thirty-acre men, 111–12; landless labourers, 44, 111–12, 156; cottiers, 117; tenant right, 119; uneconomic holdings, 119
Levally, 39
Light railways act, 21

MacDonnell, Sir Anthony, 148, 153
male industries, 68–70
Mansion House relief fund, 13
Marlborough relief Committee, 13
McFadden, Fr James, Gweedore, Co. Donegal, 27, 132
medical issues, 41, 43; doctors, 16
Micks, William, 27, 28, 33, 34, 35, 145, 148, 181, 182
money lending, 40

Newport, 53
nomadic workers (Travellers), 112, 123

North Inishowen, 44, 49-50, 61, 87, 119-121, 123

O'Donnell, Dr Patrick, 22–3, 65, 148
O'Hara, Fr Denis, Kiltimagh, Co. Mayo, 135
old age pensions, 162
outdoor relief, 23

Parnell, Charles Stewart, 21, 30
pig rearing, 122
Plan of Campaign, 20-1, 119
Plunkett, Sir Horace, 17, 31, 138, 141, 142, 146, 149, 152, 154, 168, 171
Poor law unions, function, 11
poultry production, 48–52; prior to CDB intervention, 48; value of industry, 51; CDB schemes, 52–3
poverty; causes of, 17; types of, 28–9; pretence of, 43; secondary poverty, 163
Pulathomas, 71

Raiffessen Banks, 142, 150
rail network, 113
RCCI (Dudley Commission), 120, 151–3, 155–6, 168
RDS, 92, 99; RDS vessel *The Fingal*, 92; example plots, 128,
Recess Committee, 143

Salisbury, Lord, 21
Saorstát Éireann, 167
Scotland, 76, 88, Scottish fisheries and kelp, 81-4; relations with Irish fisheries 91-2, 98, 98n, 104; Scottish cattle dealers, 116; seasonal migration to, 122; and farming, 168
Scottish CDB, 151–2, 170
seasonal migration, 15, 16, 118, 130, 134–5, 168
seaweed industry, 80; iodine, 81; kelp-making, 81–5, 100
sheep rearing, 122–3; improvements in, 128–9
shirtmaking, 59–62
shopkeepers, relationship with people, 14
Sisters of Charity, Foxford and Ballaghdereen, 45–9, 149
Skull, 53, 129
Sneem, 67

technical instruction classes, 56,
Teelin, 50, 70, 88, 97, 102, 108, 126n
tillage 126–7; decline in, 112, 121; potato spraying, 129
Tuke, James Hack, 21–2, 27, 35, 138, 168
turf industry, 100, 162
turf, 42–3

Valentia Island, 79, 86

Walker, J.W.D., 59, 80
women, and work, 47; and money, 48; work in fish curing, 105
woollen industry, 62
workhouse system, 12